Israel and the Holocaust

PERSPECTIVES ON THE HOLOCAUST

A series of books designed to help students further their understanding of key topics within the field of Holocaust studies.

Published:

Holocaust Representations in History (2nd Edition),
Daniel H. Magilow and Lisa Silverman
Postwar Germany and The Holocaust, Caroline Sharples
The Holocaust in Eastern Europe, Waitman Wade Beorn
The United States and The Nazi Holocaust, Barry Trachtenberg
Witnessing The Holocaust, Judith M. Hughes
Hitler's 'Mein Kampf' and The Holocaust: A Prelude to Genocide,
John J. Michalczyk, Michael S. Bryant and Susan A. Michalczyk (eds.)
The Holocaust and Australia: Refugees, Rejection, and Memory,
Paul R. Bartrop

Anti-Semitism and The Holocaust (2nd Edition),
Beth A. Griech-Polelle

Forthcoming:

Sites of Holocaust Memory, Janet Ward
The Perpetrators of The Holocaust: The Folly of The Third Reich,
Nathan Stoltzfus
The Holocaust in Eastern Europe (2nd edition), Waitman Wade Beorn
The Roma and the Holocaust, María Sierra

Israel and the Holocaust

Avinoam Patt

BLOOMSBURY ACADEMIC
LONDON • NEW YORK • OXFORD • NEW DELHI • SYDNEY

BLOOMSBURY ACADEMIC
Bloomsbury Publishing Plc
50 Bedford Square, London, WC1B 3DP, UK
1385 Broadway, New York, NY 10018, USA
29 Earlsfort Terrace, Dublin 2, Ireland

BLOOMSBURY, BLOOMSBURY ACADEMIC and the Diana logo are trademarks of
Bloomsbury Publishing Plc

First published in Great Britain 2024

Cover design by Design Holborn, Photograph © Authors own image

A catalogue record for this book is available from the British Library.

A catalog record for this book is available from the Library of Congress.

ISBN: HB: 978-1-3501-8835-8
PB: 978-1-3501-8834-1
ePDF: 978-1-3501-8836-5
eBook: 978-1-3501-8837-2

Typeset by Newgen KnowledgeWorks Pvt. Ltd., Chennai, India
Printed and bound in Great Britain

To find out more about our authors and books visit www.bloomsbury.com
and sign up for our newsletters.

To the victims of the October 7, 2023 massacre.
May their memories be a blessing. Zikhronam livrakha.

CONTENTS

ILLUSTRATIONS

ACKNOWLEDGEMENTS

I write these lines two weeks after 7 October 2023, when the Hamas terrorist organization launched a full-scale surprise attack and invasion of Israel – infiltrating communities in Israel's south, massacring civilians, taking hostages and indiscriminately firing thousands of rockets and missiles at population centres throughout the country. Thus far we know over 1,400 Israelis have been murdered, nearly 3,000 have been wounded and over 200 people, including women, children and the elderly have reportedly been kidnapped and taken as hostages into Gaza. This is the deadliest attack against the Jewish people in a single day since the murderous onslaughts perpetrated by the Nazis during the Second World War. This book is first and foremost dedicated to the victims of this horrific attack; for those who perished, may their memories be a blessing and may the resilience of the survivors be a beacon of hope for us all.

When Rhodri Mogford approached me with the idea to add this book to the Perspectives on the Holocaust series, I was excited to take the project on. So much of my previous work has revolved around the relationship between the aftermath of the Holocaust and the creation of the state of Israel, along with the ways in which the Holocaust has been commemorated by Jews in Israel and America in the decades after the Second World War. I have benefitted from the shared wisdom of many teachers and colleagues who have assisted and encouraged me at various stages of my academic career and who have remained trusted interlocutors for years. Thanks, as always to David Engel, for the 'lifetime service contract', to Yael Feldman who introduced me to some of the Israeli literature examined in the pages that follow and to Deborah Lipstadt, who first introduced me to the field of Holocaust studies at Emory University and whose insights on the Eichmann Trial were especially helpful in this context. Many colleagues have served as sounding boards and writing partners for various segments of the material covered in the pages that follow. Laura Jockusch has been a close colleague and excellent writing partner on several occasions. Havi Dreifuss was incredibly generous in sharing her deep knowledge of Israeli historiography of the Holocaust and Boaz Cohen (currently in uniform in the reserves) has likewise been a pioneer in this field. Liat Steir-Livny is an incredibly productive and brilliant scholar, and a good friend, whose insights are also reflected at various points in the pages that follow.

This is a project which rests on the shoulders of many great scholars who have written major works in the field on Israel's relationship to the

Holocaust. Other scholars (and I apologize if I forget anyone) have offered insights, suggestions and comments at various conferences and meetings that have found their way into these pages one way or another. Over the past seventy-five years, multiple generations of scholars and survivors have preceded me in writing this history. To paraphrase Rabbi Moses Isserles, they have prepared the table, I have just come to lay a tablecloth. Among those scholars whose works have been consulted in the writing of this book are Yehuda Bauer, Israel Gutman, Tom Segev, Dalia Ofer, Hanna Yablonka, Anita Shapira, Tuvia Friling, Idit Gil, Dina Porat, Zeev Mankowitz, Evyatar Friesel, Idith Zertal, Hava Eshkoli, Mooli Brog, Ziva Shalev, Orly Lubin, Leora Bilsky, Judith Tydor Baumel, David Engel, Yoav Gelber, Hagit Lavsky, Arieh Kochavi, Aviva Halamish, Yechiam Weitz, Avihu Ronen, Sharon Geva, Bella Gutterman, Orna Kenan, Roni Stauber, Michal Arbell, Yael Feldman, Sidra DeKoven Ezrachi, Emmanuel Sivan, Gali Druker Bar-Am, Moshe Tlamim, Eliezer Don Yehiyeh, Micha Balf, Boaz Cohen, Rachel Rojanski, Doron Bar, Gershon Shaked, Dan Porat, Deborah Lipstadt, Havi Dreifuss, Irit Keynan, Dvir Abramovich, Kimmy Caplan, Tamir Hod, Jackie Feldman, Ephraim Sicher, Irit Milner, Dina Wardi, Ranan Omer-Sherman and Amos Goldberg. *Todah Rabah*. As always, while I am appreciative of the scholarship they have produced, along with their advice and support, any mistakes in the book (and I am sure there are some) are mine and mine alone.

Feedback at various conferences where elements of this research have been presented over the years has helped spur my thinking on various aspects of the project, including the annual or biannual conferences of the Association for Jewish Studies, the Association for Israel Studies, Lessons and Legacies, Beyond Camps and Forced Labour, a conference on the legacy of Rachel Auerbach at the Fortunoff Video Archives for Holocaust Testimony at Yale University, a University of Toronto conference on the aftermath of the Holocaust in 2018, the Future of Holocaust Testimonies conferences in Akko (2016 and 2022) and at the University of Virginia (2017), and a 2023 conference on the seventy-fifth anniversary of the Warsaw Ghetto Uprising hosted at the Simon Dubnow Institute in Leipzig.

In the Talmud (Ta'anit 7a), R. Chanina is quoted as saying, 'I have learned much from my teachers, more from my colleagues, but from my students I have learned more than from all of them.' I am grateful to many colleagues and students at New York University, the University of Connecticut, the University of Hartford, Clark University and Trinity College, where I have been privileged to teach classes on Jewish responses to the Holocaust, Jewish literature and Israeli history and culture, which have influenced some of the insights shared in this book. I have been privileged to hold the Philip D. Feltman Chair in Modern Jewish History at the University of Hartford and the Doris and Simon Konover Chair in Judaic Studies at the University of Connecticut. I appreciate their critical support of Judaic Studies as a respected discipline in American universities. I hope that this work makes the Feltman and Konover families proud.

As I reflect on the time I spent at the University of Connecticut while working on this book, I am especially grateful to my UConn colleagues who provided a warm and welcoming environment as part of HuskyNation. Two colleagues helped support the research and writing process for this book in various ways. Sierra McCaffrey always provided assistance whenever needed in her trademark cheerful way and I am forever grateful. Angelica Gimenez-Ravanelli served as a research assistant on this project, helping to compile a detailed bibliography of so many of the relevant works in this very rich field. Angie, I sincerely appreciate your dedication, diligence and hard work on this project. To my colleagues at the Center for Judaic Studies and across the university, including Sebastian Wogenstein, Sarah Willen, Jeremy Pressman, Stuart Miller, Arnie Dashefsky, Susan Herbst, Dan Weiner, Kathy Libal, Joscha Jelitzki, Susan Einbinder, Maha Darawsha, Jeffrey Shoulson, Yoni Miller, Jennifer Terni and Edina Oestreicher – *a sheynem dank*!

Thank you to the archival staffs at multiple institutions who offered invaluable assistance at various stages of the project (even in the midst of a global pandemic). Digitization projects at many of these institutions have made it possible to access and read materials that never would have been available otherwise. The Ghetto Fighters House Archive is a treasure trove and in many ways the materials housed there helped lay the foundation for this book. Thank you to Anat Bratman-Elhalel and the archival staff at Lochamei Ha-Geta'ot for the invaluable assistance. Thank you to Caroline Waddell and Ron Coleman at USHMM; Linda Levi, Jeff Edelstein, Misha Mitsel and Anat Kutner at the JDC Archives in New York and Jerusalem; Eliot Nidam-Orvieto and Sharon Kangisser-Cohen for assistance in locating materials at Yad Vashem; and to the Jewish National Library in Jerusalem for digitizing the Historical Jewish Press (another treasure trove).

To the copy editors and production designers at Bloomsbury Press and Newgen, thank you for your careful and detailed reading.

As the writing of this book was completed at the end of a global pandemic, the bonds of family were reinforced, even as we tried to transcend time and space virtually. Thank you to my parents, Nurit and Yehuda Patt, for instilling a lifelong love of history, for always being interested in my research and writing and for poring over lines of poetry by Natan Alterman, Dan Pagis and Avrom Sutzkever (and even enjoying it as much as me). And thank you for accompanying me on the field research for this book! To the Einstein, Weinstein and Neustat clans, thank you for the support and love. To my siblings, Iddo, Hanoch and Suzie Patt and your beautiful families, I have to think some of the questions posed here go back to those long discussions around the dinner table on Friday nights long ago. We were raised in a family culture of debate, discussion and intellectual curiosity. I hope we can continue this tradition for our families, too. To my amazing children, Maya, Alex and Micah – you have been surrounded by this history much too early and for far too long. Thank you for your patience, your love and your support (and for the much-needed grounding, distraction and occasional games of ping-pong). And finally to my beloved wife, Ivy, who has supported and encouraged me in countless ways since we first began discussing Jewish identity, Holocaust studies and much more at Emory University in Atlanta in 1996; words cannot express my gratitude for decades of love, support and inspiration (and for your 1992 March of the Living photos that found their way into this book).

Introduction: Between history and memory

Why is it that the Holocaust (or Shoah) has come to occupy an increasingly central role in the collective memory of Israel even as distance from the historical event continues to grow? Beyond frequent political invocations of the Shoah, educational trips to Poland and the prominent place accorded to Yad Vashem as a required destination for all political dignitaries (and the first stop for Yair Lapid, himself the son of a Holocaust survivor, on his first day as Israel's PM on 29 June 2022), survey data also supports the conclusion that more Israeli Jews identify 'Remembering the Holocaust' as an essential part of their Jewish identity than any other category.[1] Even so, the embrace of the Holocaust as a central component of Israel's national identity is not total and often qualified. Marking the eightieth anniversary of the Wannsee Conference in January 2022, then PM Naftali Bennett noted that a 'strong, secure, independent, thriving, diverse, free and united' state is needed to 'ensure the existence of the Jewish people'. At the same time, he emphatically declared: 'the State of Israel isn't ours "thanks to" the Holocaust, but because the Land of Israel was, is still and will always remain the home of the Jewish people.'[2]

Zionism, as an ideology, is predicated on the notion that Jewish life in the diaspora was harmful to Jews and therefore needed to be negated, that all efforts to achieve full emancipation and acceptance by the nations of the world would fail. And yet, the state of Israel exists in an uneasy relationship with the Holocaust, the ultimate manifestation of the negation of Jewish life in the diaspora. From its founding as a modern political movement, Zionist leaders argued that Jews are a nation, capable, in the words of Theodor Herzl, of 'forming a model state'. The Jewish people deserved their own Jewish state; in this sense, the Shoah was not a justification for the creation of the state, but almost prevented its creation. According to this line of thinking, from a classical Zionist perspective, the Jewish people deserve a state just as every other nation in the world deserve its own nation state. Justifying the existence of Israel with reference to the Holocaust therefore undermines that justification for the creation of the Jewish state. And yet, as historical distance from the end of the Second World War and the creation of Israel continues to grow, so does the centrality of collective memory of the Shoah in Israel's national identity.

What are the historical connections between the Holocaust and the creation of the state of Israel? For most casual observers of twentieth-century Jewish history, the two events would seem to be not only coincidentally separated by three years (1945–8), but surely such historic proximity would suggest a causal relationship. The intellectual distance to travel from the end of the Holocaust to the creation of the state of Israel is indeed not far. Certainly, from various religious perspectives, it is possible to trace a theological link between the two historical events. As Rabbi Yissachar Teichtal concluded in his volume *Eim HaBanim Samecha* ('A Joyous Mother of Children'), written in Budapest during the Second World War not long before his murder at the hands of the Nazis, *Restoration of Zion* was the only legitimate response to the Holocaust.[3] Witnessing the destruction of European Jewry at the hands of the Nazis, Teichtal reversed the anti-Zionist positions of his youth; true redemption would only come if the Jewish people united and rebuilt the Land of Israel. Writing from Mandatory Palestine in 1942 as the Nazi annihilation of the Jewish community of Europe reached its height, the noted Jewish historian Benzion Dinur (who would become the first director of Yad Vashem) concluded that 'the only path of escape from the fate of destruction is the return to the Jewish homeland'.[4]

In the aftermath of the Holocaust, it seemed apparent that survivors themselves had reached the same conclusion during the war, that the only response to the Holocaust was the creation of the state of Israel. In the words of Koppel Pinson (a sociologist who had been sent to the displaced persons (DP) camps in the American zone of Germany by the American Jewish Joint Distribution Committee (JDC) to assist in the formation of an education policy for the Jewish DPs):

> The events of 1939–1945 seemed to discredit completely those philosophies of Jewish life prevailing before the war which were not centered around Palestine. The Zionists were the only ones that had a program that seemed to make sense after this catastrophe .... Without Palestine there seemed to be no future for them. Anti-Zionism or even a neutral attitude toward Zionism came to mean for them a threat to the most fundamental stakes in their future.[5]

Or, in the words of Ze'ev Mankowitz, a historian who wrote extensively about the She'erit Hapletah, the surviving remnant after the Holocaust, 'from the outset the dream of a Jewish home in Palestine permeated the public life of the She'erit Hapletah'. In the wake of the Holocaust, he suggested, survivors understood that

> the creation of a Jewish state in the Land of Israel was taken to be the last will and testament bequeathed by the dead to the living … For many, their almost intuitive Zionism stood for the warmth, unquestioning acceptance and security of home; for the more politically minded it signified the only real hope for the rescue and rehabilitation of the little that remained of European Jewry and, in the longer term, the promise of the Jewish future.[6]

From its very inception, the founders of the newly created state of Israel pointed to a clear relationship between the Holocaust and Israel with survivors actively participating in the founding of the state. Israel's Declaration of Independence, read by David Ben-Gurion on 14 May 1948, asserted:

> The Nazi holocaust, which engulfed millions of Jews in Europe, was another clear demonstration of the urgency of the re-establishment in Eretz-Israel of the Jewish State, which would open the gates of the homeland wide to every Jew and confer upon the Jewish people the status of a fully privileged member of the comity of nations.
>   The survivors of the European catastrophe, as well as Jews from other parts of the world, continued to migrate to Eretz-Israel, undaunted by difficulties, restrictions and dangers, and never ceased to assert their right to a life of dignity, freedom and honest toil in their national homeland.[7]

Thus, in the self-understanding of many survivors as well as the founding fathers of the state, the founding of Israel was the uplifting, redemptive legacy of the Holocaust, engaging the Jewish people in a journey from catastrophe to rebirth, from crisis to redemption of the recent past. Even so, for the founders of Israel, the justification for Jewish sovereignty in the Land of Israel dated back millennia, not just a mere three years: 'the Land of Israel was the birthplace of the Jewish people. Here their spiritual, religious and political identity was shaped. Here they first attained to statehood, created cultural values of national and universal significance and gave to the world the eternal Book of Books.'[8]

But at the same time, Palestinians for whom the *Nakba*, or 'catastrophe,' began with the founding of Israel and the subsequent 1948 war, also link the creation of Israel to the Holocaust claiming that the Jewish people were given Israel as a reparation for the Holocaust by the international community who felt guilty for their inaction during the Holocaust, at the expense of the Palestinians living there. The Palestinians, they argue, are paying for what Germany did to the Jews. This argument is also made by others in the Muslim world and it is often linked to outright Holocaust denial and the denial of Israel's right to exist.[9]

It is striking then that both friends and foes of Israel alike often make the argument that Israel was founded *because* of the Holocaust, based on the assumption that temporal proximity indicates causality. But do either of the interpretations have a foundation in the historical record? Was there a causal connection? A closer analysis of the three-year period between the end of the Second World War and the creation of the state of Israel indicates the state was founded almost *in spite* of the Holocaust. The Zionist leadership of the Yishuv knew that it faced a massive demographic imbalance in Palestine before the Second World War and depended on Jewish migration from Europe; the annihilation of European Jewry in the Holocaust created an almost insurmountable demographic challenge.[10] The claim that Israel was a token of sympathy from the international community ignores the ancient cultural connection of the Jews to Eretz Israel, the continued existence of the Yishuv prior to the Second World War, and the longer history of the Zionist project. Moreover, the various previous partition plans, which, had they not failed, could have established Jewish *and Palestinian* statehood already in the 1930s, and then that Jewish state could have been a place of refuge for European Jews fleeing Nazism. Without the single-minded dedication of Yishuv leadership to the creation of a state *and* the continued failure to solve the Jewish refugee crisis in the aftermath of the war, it is quite likely the state may not have ever come into existence.

For the Zionist movement the option of state sovereignty had been on the agenda long before the Holocaust, but the Holocaust enhanced the determination to pursue sovereignty over no matter how small a piece of land, because a state was now deemed an existential necessity. The Holocaust experience might have convinced Jews in the diaspora, especially in the United States, which now had the largest Jewish community in the world, of the need for a Jewish state. But ultimately, the timing of the founding of Israel had less to do with what the Zionist movement or Jews in the world wanted, but with *Realpolitik* decisions of the international political power players of the day: while the British wanted out of Palestine as fast as possible since their empire was collapsing all around, the Americans sought to find a settlement for the 250,000 Jewish DPs in their occupation zones in Germany and Austria.

Even if there is no direct causal connection between the Holocaust and the founding of the Jewish state there is a deep emotional, psychological and cultural connection. Since its founding (and even before the establishment of the state) the memory of the Holocaust has been a constant presence in Israeli politics, culture and society. By tracing the evolving relationship to the memory of Shoah, however, we can also trace shifting conceptions of Israeli self-understanding and identity, Israel's relationship to the wider world, its neighbours, the Jewish diaspora and the Jewish past.

From the beginning of the state, the Holocaust played a central role in Israeli public memory. In the early years of the state, Labor Zionist governments wanted to craft a certain memory of the Shoah that maintained emotional distance from diaspora history and reinforced the classic Zionist notion of *shlilat ha-golah* (negation of the diaspora), while taking all pragmatic steps to bolster the fledgling state and emphasize a heroic memory of the catastrophe. Nonetheless, it is clear that the political leadership's efforts to craft a specific type of Holocaust memory that conformed to Labor Zionist ideology was also in tension with a far more contested popular understanding of Holocaust memory shaped by the experiences of a large number of survivors who had settled in Israel before and after the creation of the state, along with the tremendous losses experienced by Jews who had migrated from Europe before the war. If in the earlier years of the state, the Zionist establishment sought to 'control the narrative' and demonstrate that the Jewish people had the power to 'triumph over history,' we can also trace a shifting relationship to the memory of the Holocaust in the period before and after the Eichmann trial in 1961 that would parallel an increasing sense of vulnerability on the part of Israelis, especially after the Yom Kippur War in October 1973. After Menachem Begin's rise to power in 1977, a broad-based growing sense of collective memory of the Shoah became a more prominent part of public life and would be expressed more directly in political life, too. As survivors and children of survivors began to share private memories more publicly in the 1980s, it would also make sense that as we have seen the rise of post-Zionism and a questioning of the ideological underpinnings and founding mythology of the state, the belief that the Jewish people are constantly threatened and can only protect themselves in their own state against enemies always arrayed to 'destroy us' has become the predominant one. In this world view, memory of the Holocaust both serves as a justification and a confirmation for such a relationship to the rest of the world, while also serving as a unifying principle in a divided society.

The simplest explanation for why memory of the Holocaust has come to occupy such a central place in Israel's national identity might be to point to the ways in which politicians have sought to control memory of the Holocaust for political purposes from 1948 to present. But in fact, what we see is a much more complicated process that functions on various levels of Israel society (and is paralleled in the wider world). Because Israel was born in the aftermath of the Holocaust, its history is inextricably linked with the Shoah; at the same time we can analyse the changing memory of the Holocaust in Israeli society with the parallel evolving memory of the Holocaust in general. Collective memory of the Shoah evolves both within and between generations, alongside complex social, political and cultural developments in the wider world. Even so, despite the evolving relationship between Israeli society and the memory of the Shoah, one feature has remained relatively constant: the memory of the Holocaust has been interpreted through a particular Jewish lens with lessons of special significance to the Jewish people, rather than a universal lens with lessons of global significance for all mankind.

Over the last three decades, in some ways responding to critiques of the so-called New Historians, there has been much greater interest in the place of the Shoah in Israeli collective memory and its influence on Israeli politics, society and culture. It should be acknowledged that much of the scholarship in the field has developed largely in response to the publication of Tom Segev's groundbreaking *The Seventh Million: Israelis and the Holocaust* and his allegations that the Yishuv did not do everything it could have done to rescue European Jewry and responded to survivors in Israel with little empathy or compassion. In the book, Segev argued,

> After the war a great silence surrounded the destruction of the Jews ... then came moral and political conflicts, including the painful debate over relations with Germany, which slowly brought Israelis to recognize the deeper meaning of the Holocaust. The trial of Adolf Eichmann served as therapy for the nation, starting a process of identification with the tragedy of the victims and survivors, a process that continues to this day.
>
> The most fateful decisions in Israeli history, other than the founding of the state itself – the mass immigration of the 1950s, the Six-Day War, and Israel's nuclear project – were all conceived in the shadow of the Holocaust ... As the Holocaust recedes in time – and into the realm of history – its lessons have moved to the center of a fierce political struggle over the politics, ideology, and morals of the present.
>
> *The Seventh Million* concerns the ways in which the bitter events of the past continue to shape the life of the nation. Just as the Holocaust imposed a posthumous collective identity on its six million victims, so too it formed the collective identity of this new country – not just for the survivors who came after the war but for all Israelis, then and now. This is why I have called them the seventh million.[11]

According to historian Dalia Ofer, in many ways, Segev's work reflected a new vein of post-Zionist historiography, comfortable in critiquing the historical development of the Zionist movement and the Yishuv leadership, attempting to study the history from an 'objective,' non-Zionist viewpoint capable of incorporating the viewpoints of other groups (namely Holocaust survivors themselves) who had been largely co-opted by the state in previous historical treatments.[12] While some critics have dismissed Segev as a journalist and not a historian (for what it's worth, he does possess a PhD from Boston University in history) his book has been incredibly influential and seen the development of an entire generation of scholarship in one way or another engaged in debate with his analysis of Israel's historical relationship with the Holocaust. At the same time, his provocative argument raises a fundamental question: can the history of Israel be separated in any way from the memory of the Holocaust? Or does the fact that the cataclysmic, earth-shattering events of the Second World War preceded the creation of the state by a mere three years and had such profound implications on the subsequent history of the Jewish state make it impossible to separate the history of Israel from the memory of the Shoah? And if so, what then have been the impacts of the memory of the Holocaust on the development of Israeli politics, society, culture and so on?

Over the last three decades, triggered by the publication of Segev's book and broader post-Zionist critiques, research on the place of the Shoah in Israeli collective memory and its influence on state, society, culture and national identity has emerged as a vast field, accompanied by intense historiographical debate.[13] These scholars have investigated the Yishuv's responses to the destruction of European Jewry and attitudes of Israeli society to Holocaust survivors in the first decades of the state, while also highlighting the roles that survivors played in building the state and shaping its society. Scholars also studied the impact of certain critical events – such as the debate over reparations from Germany and Holocaust-related trials in Israeli courts – on Israelis' perceptions of the Holocaust, and the ways collective memory of the Holocaust has shaped Israel's politics, diplomacy and military activity.[14]

As Yael Zerubavel argues in her study of Israeli national tradition, collective memory is shaped in negotiation between the present and the past, between

> available historical records and current social and political agendas. And in the process of referring back to these records, it shifts its interpretation, selectively emphasizing, suppressing, and elaborating different aspects of that record. History and memory, therefore, do not operate in totally detached, opposite directions. Their relationships are underlined by conflict as well as interdependence, and this ambiguity provides the commemoration with the creative tension that makes it such a fascinating subject of study.[15]

Thus, according to Zerubavel, history and memory are in a fluid relationship, operating not in a linear direction, with history shaping memory, but functioning in a dynamic, interdependent manner. There are many different ways in which a society can integrate a foundational, even traumatic, event into its national memory and there are multiple political, social and cultural factors which influence the formation of that collective memory. To what extent has the collective memory of the Shoah in Israel been shaped by the complex interaction between the experiences of the victims and survivors and the desire of Israeli political elites to craft a collective memory in what they perceived to be the best interests of the state? At what point can we see these two narratives converging, reflecting a shift in the Zionist ethos of the state?

This book will demonstrate that the ways that Israeli society engaged with Holocaust memory are not just determined by political elites, but also complemented by broad societal engagement, spearheaded by survivors and their families. While Labor Zionist politicians gave an ideological reading of the Holocaust towards a justification of how history could be 'overcome' by national sovereignty and determined how the European Jewish catastrophe should be remembered, the political right since Menachem Begin has further politicized Holocaust memory by invoking the traumatic event for all its political decisions (foreign policy, military strength, diaspora relations, and relations to the Palestinians and the Arab world). Yet politicians are only one of several agents in Israeli Holocaust memory in a dynamic interaction with other agents in the courts, media, literature, culture, education and elsewhere. Throughout Israel's existence there has been an interplay between top-down attempts to control Holocaust memory and bottom-up engagement with it. The latter has been part and parcel with global trends in memorial culture and the elevation of survivors since the 1990s beyond the political sphere. This book traces how memory of the Holocaust in Israel and the debate over how central it should be changes over time and how the Holocaust and its survivors moved from the periphery to the centre of Israeli identity. It is indeed possible to trace a shift in Israel's collective national identity through the changes in its relationship to the memory of the Shoah, from a focus on celebrating ideals of heroism and denigrating collaboration, to a broader identification with victimhood and survival as the Shoah continues to occupy a central place in Israelis' collective memory and national identity.

1

Nazism, the Holocaust and the creation of the state of Israel

Zionism and Nazism

Although prayer for a return to Zion had always been a central component of the Jewish religion, the connection to the land had largely remained a passive one for centuries. While Jewish communities existed in the Land of Israel, most Jews prayed for a return to the land that would occur in the messianic age. In the nineteenth century, however, the challenges of modernization, secularization and continued antisemitism led a number of Jewish political thinkers to seriously consider the creation of a Jewish national home as a solution to the twin problems of assimilation and antisemitism, a Jewish home that would offer a new Jewish identity compatible with modern existence and a refuge for Jews suffering from persecution. After a wave of pogroms in the Russian Empire in the 1880s and under the influence of early Zionist thinkers who began to seriously consider 'Love of Zion' as a way to solve the problem of Jewish statelessness, approximately 25,000 Jewish immigrants from Eastern Europe joined the 'First Aliyah' to Palestine between 1881 and 1904. Under Theodor Herzl's leadership the Zionist movement took on the trappings of a modern political organization, with the formation of a worldwide network to support the movement along with an economic apparatus to better facilitate land acquisition. During the Second Aliyah (1904–14), socialist Zionist immigrants (including David Ben-Gurion, eventually the first prime minister of Israel) imbued the movement with a more rigid ideological framework, believing that only through a 'return to the land' could the Jewish people negate the harmful effects of diaspora passivity, while also creating a new Jew who through his or her connection to the soil could be 'built and rebuilt'. And yet, the ability of the movement to realize its aspirations to create a national home that in the words of Theodor Herzl would create a 'model state' were limited: without the support of one of the 'Great Powers' the movement would be powerless to establish a state on its own. While Theodor Herzl sought to secure the support of such a global leader before his death in 1904 (visiting Kaisers, Sultans, Kings and other assorted royalty), the First World War and the British conquest of Palestine from the Ottoman Empire presented the opportunity the movement needed to obtain great power support. In the context of the war, Chaim Weizmann, a Russian-born chemist and leader of the General Zionist council who provided scientific assistance to the British war effort in England, successfully lobbied British leaders to voice support for Zionist national aspirations in Palestine, leading to the Balfour Declaration of 2 November 1917:

> His Majesty's Government view with favour the establishment in Palestine of a national home for the Jewish people, and will use their best endeavours to facilitate the achievement of this object, it being clearly understood that nothing shall be done which may prejudice the civil and religious rights of existing non-Jewish communities in Palestine, or the rights and political status enjoyed by Jews in any other country.[1]

After the war, with the British granted the mandate for Palestine, the Zionist movement continued to advance in its goals to establish the Jewish national home in Palestine, even as tensions with the local Arab population, weary of increased Jewish migration, continued to grow. During the war, the British had made secret agreements with the French to carve up the Middle East, while also assuring Prince Feisal, son of the Sharif Hussein of Mecca, that if he supported a revolt against the Turks, he would become ruler of a Greater Syria that would include Palestine. Eventually Feisal would become king of Iraq after the French expelled him from Syria.

Under the British mandate, the Yishuv, or Jewish settlement in Palestine, successfully developed all of the instruments of a state-in-the-making, under the apparatus of the quasi-governmental Jewish Agency for Palestine, the Jewish National Fund (for land purchases), the Histadrut labour federation, the Hebrew University in Jerusalem and more. The Jewish Agency for Palestine, established by the World Zionist Organization in 1921 as the 'Palestine Zionist Executive', was recognized by British authorities in Palestine as representing the Jewish community in the mandate and became a de facto Jewish self-government in Palestine. The Jewish Agency also established offices in Jerusalem, London and Geneva to facilitate emigration (Aliyah) to Palestine. From 1935 to 1948, David Ben-Gurion served as head of the Jewish Agency.

And yet, despite such achievements, the greatest obstacle to the formation of a Jewish state was a demographic one: Jews in Palestine were outnumbered by Muslim and Christian Arabs more than two to one and without a massive influx of Jewish immigrants, Zionist goals of establishing a Jewish majority state would be hard to realize. Over the course of the 1920s, Arab nationalist sentiment in Palestine continued to grow and the Mufti of Jerusalem, Hajj Amin al-Husseini, positioned himself as leader of a Pan-Arabist nationalism that would elevate the significance of Jerusalem and the Palestinian Arabs in confronting British colonial power in general and Zionist migration to Palestine in particular. The Mufti helped organize bloody riots that targeted Jewish communities in Palestine in 1929 (and again in 1936). As the security situation deteriorated in Palestine after the 1929 riots, the Passfield White Paper of 1930 initially limited Jewish migration; after vigorous protest by Chaim Weizmann and the Zionist movement, the MacDonald letter of 1931 clarified and reiterated the double-bind which the British had created for themselves in Palestine:

> Under the terms of the mandate his Majesty's Government are responsible for promoting the establishment of a national home for the Jewish people, it being clearly understood that nothing shall be done which might prejudice the civil and religious rights of existing non-Jewish communities in Palestine or the rights and political status enjoyed by Jews in any other country.
>
> A double undertaking is involved, to the Jewish people on the one hand and to the non-Jewish population of Palestine on the other; and it is the firm resolve of his Majesty's Government to give effect, in equal measure, to both parts of the declaration and to do equal justice to all sections of the population of Palestine. That is the duty from which they will not shrink and to discharge of which they will apply all the resources at their command.[2]

Continued migration to Palestine would become even more critical after the Nazi rise to power in 1933 as Jewish refugees seeking to flee Germany found few countries willing to accept refugees during the global economic crisis that followed the Great Depression. (Likewise, US immigration policy had become severely limited after the passage of legislation in 1924.) This context helps to explain why, in 1933 when the Nazis came to power in Germany, the Zionist leadership in Palestine would take the controversial decision to not boycott the most ardently antisemitic party to ever have been elected, but instead to offer tacit support for the so-called transfer agreement in order to facilitate the immigration of German Jews to Palestine. The *Ha'avara* (Transfer) Agreement, concluded in August 1933 between the German Zionist Organization and Third Reich officials, facilitated the passage of close to 40,000 German Jewish émigrés headed for Palestine by enabling them to retain sufficient assets to qualify for visas (most German Jewish émigrés surrendered nearly all their assets before departure from Germany), while leaving some assets for the *Reichsvertretung* (the Reich Representation of German Jews) to perform relief work with German Jews. The agreement also provided a market for German exports, which were purchased in Palestine with the proceeds used to pay costs for new emigrants. Forty years after the Second World War, a group of post-Zionist historians began to write a new vein of historiography sharply critical of the Yishuv in Palestine's instrumentalist view of European Jewry, its relationship with Nazism and what they perceived as its failure to do more to rescue European Jewry during the Holocaust. Some reiterated 1930s' era critiques that accused Zionists of ideological identification with Nazism, working contacts with Nazis in defiance of the boycott and a narrow focus on the needs of the Yishuv in building the 'Jewish state' at the expense of a German Jewry suffering under Nazi rule.[3] Israeli scholars like Tom Segev in *The Seventh Million* pointed to the *Ha'avara* (Transfer) Agreement as a prime example of the Yishuv leadership sacrificing the interests of German and world Jewry for those of the Yishuv in seizing upon the 'complementary interests of the German government and the Zionist movement'.[4]

According to scholar Hava Eshkoli, however, German Jewish leaders also feared that support for the boycott of Germany would in turn lead to reprisals against the beleaguered Jewish community in Germany:

> Generally speaking, the Zionist institutions and the *Yishuv* establishment opposed the anti-German boycott even before the issue of the transfer agreement was raised. Their stance was shaped by the influence of lobbyists from German Jewry and Zionist leaders of German origin, who feared the boycott would provoke the Nazi regime to institute harsh measures against German Jews and the German Zionist movement, whom they portrayed as hostages. We must note, moreover, that this view was in harmony with Zionist priorities, which awarded precedence to the realization of Zionist goals and the building of Palestine over the struggle to preserve Jewish civil rights in the Diaspora.[5]

The Ha'avara Agreement – and violent reactions against it – reflected the range of attitudes to Nazism and the persecution of Jews in Europe, from a pragmatic willingness to negotiate with Germany to further the interests of the Jewish state project (with a belief that the creation of the state was ultimately the best way to help Jews anywhere in the world), to a militant opposition to any contact with Germany. Haim Arlosoroff, a member of the Zionist Executive and head of the Jewish Agency's political department, was one of the architects of the agreement, which he negotiated with Nazi leaders in Germany in June 1933. Two days after his return to Tel Aviv, Arlosoroff was shot to death during a night-time walk on the beach with his wife, on 16 June 1933. To this date, it is not known whether he was assassinated by political opponents of the agreement, Nazi operatives, or murdered by criminals on that beach.[6] Nonetheless, the agreement that he negotiated facilitated the migration of thousands of German-Jewish refugees to Palestine in the 1930s. In between, an ambivalent middle ground sought to balance the unpopularity of the scheme among large segments of the Jewish public with the pragmatic benefits (which would enable Jews to escape Germany while also providing much needed capital infrastructure purchased from the Germans – using seized Jewish assets!)

In truth, there were limits on Jewish power before (and during) the war, and the relationship between the Zionists and the Nazi movement was inherently unequal; in every single step along the way, the range of options for the German Zionists and the Yishuv leadership was limited by this great power imbalance. Whereas Herzl believed that Zionism would ultimately succeed in eliminating antisemitism, the Nazis believed that Zionism could be used in their effort to ultimately eliminate the Jews from German soil. The coalescing of Nazi and Zionist policy at key points around a shared goal of Jewish immigration from Germany gave preference to certain German Zionist objectives and, regardless of whether such was the intent or not, by allowing thousands of Jews to reach Palestine in this way, saved their lives before the Second World War. Still, the Zionist movement gave immigration preference to those who had undergone Zionist training programmes, thereby reflecting a continued prioritization for building the Jewish national home over rescue operations.

It is worth noting, however, that the Nazi rise to power in 1933 helped lead to greater Jewish migration to Palestine, which in turn exacerbated the security situation in the Yishuv. Against this backdrop, the Arab population of Palestine, angered by continued Jewish migration and what they perceived as an insufficient British response to their rising grievances, launched the Revolt of 1936–9, which included a general strike, boycott of Jewish goods in Palestine and violence against Jewish targets. The British colonial office responded by sending 20,000 troops to quell the violence (quite brutally) and began to consider restricting Jewish immigration to Palestine. The Peel Commission, appointed by the British government in May 1937 to investigate causes of unrest, found that the Palestine mandate was impossible to sustain because of unyielding mutual hostility and conflicting demands for statehood. For the first time, the commission recommended the partition of Palestine into separate independent Arab and Jewish states with the British securing holy sites. Palestinian Arabs were opposed to partition; the Jewish response was more tentative and divided, indicating acceptance in principle with a demand for larger borders. As the British attempts to quell the revolt failed, from September 1937 to January 1939 Arab attacks grew much more violent, with British officials targeted. In response Jews in the Yishuv bolstered training for self-defence units to protect Jewish settlements. The Haganah (literally 'defence', a paramilitary organization that would become the predecessor to the Israel Defence Force) initially followed a policy of restraint (*havlagah*) and cooperated with British forces; special Jewish units were formed under the leadership of the British officer, Orde Wingate. The Revisionist Zionist Irgun was also formed in 1937 and initiated retaliatory operations against Arabs. The continued unrest in Palestine, coupled with increasing Nazi aggression in Europe and the growing likelihood of war, led the British government to issue the May 1939 White Paper, which severely limited Jewish migration to Palestine just at a time where the Jewish refugee crisis in Europe had grown increasingly urgent. Why such a stunning reversal of the policy stated in the Balfour Declaration? As a new European war seemed imminent, the British could not risk an Arab revolt that would put their control of the Suez Canal in danger or drain troop resources to quell unrest in Palestine. The 17 May 1939 White Paper called for severe restrictions on Jewish immigration and guaranteed the creation of an independent state in Arab Palestine in 10 years: 'His Majesty's Government believe that the framers of the Mandate in which the Balfour Declaration was embodied could not have intended that Palestine should be converted into a Jewish State against the will of the Arab population of the country.'[7] The White Paper called for the establishment of a Jewish national home in an independent Palestinian state with Jewish immigration allowed to continue at maximum of 15,000 for 5 years and afterwards with only Arab agreement. Both Arabs and Jews rejected the 1939 White Paper, with David Ben-Gurion famously declaring: 'we must aid the [British] army as if there were no White Paper, and we must fight the White Paper as if there were no war.'[8]

As noted by scholars Dina Porat and Dalia Ofer in their research on the Yishuv during the Second World War, the ambivalent Zionist leadership was caught between *Scylla and Charibdis*, forced to choose between Zionist interests (fighting the British blockade at all costs) and Jewish ones (helping the British in support of the war effort, 1939 White Paper notwithstanding). The Yishuv in Palestine needed to support the British in their struggle to fight Nazism; at the same time, the creation of a Jewish state in Palestine remained the ultimate goal of the Zionist movement. Nonetheless, the 1939 White Paper reflected a stunning crisis for the Zionist movement. At the Twenty-first Zionist Congress held in Geneva from 16 August to 26 August 1939, meeting just one week before the Nazi invasion of Poland, the tone was sombre and representatives debated how to respond to the British White Paper.[9] Chaim Weizmann, who would remain president of the World Zionist Organization throughout the war, warned that while 'darkness' would soon descend on Europe, he expressed hope that those who survived would continue to work towards a better future:

> There is darkness all around us, and we cannot see through the clouds. It is with a heavy heart that I take my leave. If, as I hope, we are spared in life and our work continues, who knows – perhaps a new light will shine upon us from the thick black gloom. ... We shall meet again. We shall meet again in common labor for our land and people. ... There are some things that cannot fail to come to pass, things without which the world cannot be imagined. The remnant shall work on, fight on, live on until the dawn of better days. Toward that dawn I greet you. May we meet again in peace.[10]

With the outbreak of the Second World War in September 1939 not only was European Jewry on the precipice of destruction but the creation of a Jewish national home in Palestine seemed imperilled, just as the world would be plunged into global conflict. For the Zionist movement, the White Paper indicated that British support for the creation of a Jewish state was completely contingent on other geopolitical factors; it also convinced the movement to look elsewhere for international support (and after the Second World War, especially to the United States).

As noted, the question of whether or not the Yishuv did enough (or could have done more to save European Jews) has been the topic of intense historical and political debate in Israel. Tom Segev and others charged that the Yishuv was indifferent to the suffering of European Jewry; in the words of historian Shabtai Tevet, the official biographer of David Ben-Gurion and one of his staunchest defenders, the post-Zionist historians alleged that 'in their supposedly single-minded focus on the creation of a Jewish state in Palestine, [Yishuv leaders] were willing to sacrifice the non-Zionist Jews of Europe in furtherance of their goal'. Even worse, according to the most extreme version of this allegation, they cynically allowed European Jews to go their deaths so that Christian Europeans would feel guilty and support the creation of the state, and then in the aftermath of the war, the Yishuv leadership exploited those who survived and tried to make use of 'human material' to solve the demographic challenges that faced the creation of the state.[11] Defenders of the Yishuv's wartime policies point out that not only was the Zionist movement largely dependent on British policy at the time, but that they did in fact make efforts to engage in rescue and relief throughout the war.[12]

The Yishuv backed Britain in the fight against Germany; although Jewish soldiers in Palestine advocated for the creation of a Jewish battalion to fight the Nazis, the Jewish Brigade would not be deployed to Europe until the very end of the war, after most of the fighting was over. As an outgrowth of their opposition to the British mandate and the Zionist movement, the Palestinian Arabs backed the Axis powers. The Grand Mufti of Jerusalem, Hajj Amin al-Husseini (who had been expelled from Palestine by the British in 1937), made an agreement with Hitler and Mussolini: in exchange for Arab support, the Arabs requested Axis recognition of independence and sovereignty of Arab countries, elimination of Jewish National Home in Palestine. As noted in a summary of the meeting between the Mufti and Adolf Hitler in Berlin on 28 November 1941, Hajj Amin al-Husseini explained to Hitler:

The Arab countries were firmly convinced that Germany would win the war and that the Arab cause would then prosper. The Arabs were Germany's natural friends because they had the same enemies as had Germany, namely the English, the Jews and the Communists. Therefore they were prepared to cooperate with Germany with all their hearts and stood ready to participate in the war, not only negatively by the commission of acts of sabotage and the instigation of revolutions, but also positively by the formation of an Arab Legion.[13]

Palestine occupied a highly strategic location at the crossroads between Africa, Asia and Europe, along with its proximity to the Suez Canal in Egypt; in the first half of the Second World War, until the defeat of General Rommel's German forces at El-Alamein in November 1942, Yishuv leadership even devised contingency plans for a dramatic last stand in the mountains near Haifa should the Germans break through British defence and overrun Palestine, imperilling the 500,000 Jews living there. At the same time, Yishuv leaders desperately sought ways to counter the British White Paper and facilitate Jewish immigration to Palestine to rescue Jews who could escape from Europe. While the White Paper limited Jewish migration to 15,000/year between 1940 and 1945, the Zionist movement tried to counter the White Paper through 'illegal immigration' or *Aliyah Bet*. Such efforts were extremely difficult to organize and highly dangerous. For example, in the fall of 1940, 3,600 Jewish refugees from Austria, Czechoslovakia and Poland set out on three ships from the Romanian port of Tulcea in an attempt to break the British blockade and reach Palestine. The British intercepted two of the ships, the *Pacific* and the *Milos*, and transferred the passengers to the *Patria* in the Haifa harbour in November 1940, along with passengers from the *Atlantic* which had also been intercepted. In an act of sabotage intended to disable the SS *Patria* and force the British to allow the passengers to disembark in Haifa, a Haganah bomb inadvertently sunk the ship, killing 267 people including passengers and members of the British crew. After the sinking, the British allowed the *Patria* survivors to stay in Palestine, but the remaining 1,560 refugees from the *Atlantic* were transported to Mauritius in the Indian Ocean near Madagascar.[14]

In December 1941, another refugee ship disaster highlighted the tragic plight of Jews seeking to escape Nazi-occupied Europe for refuge in Palestine. Seven hundred and sixty-seven Jews boarded the *Struma* at the Romanian port of Constanta on the Black Sea, hoping to sail from there through Istanbul where they would obtain visas enabling them to continue their journey across the Mediterranean to Palestine. Even though the ship was unsafe, overcrowded, mechanically unsound and lacked adequate sanitary facilities, the ship reached Istanbul on 16 December 1941. At the port of Istanbul the passengers were informed they would not get visas to enter Palestine and, furthermore, would not be permitted entry into Turkey. After two months in the Istanbul harbour, Turkish police towed the boat out to sea on 23 February 1942; the next day, on 24 February, the boat sank, possibly after being mistakenly torpedoed by a Soviet submarine. David Stoliar, a nineteen-year-old Romanian Jew on board, was the sole survivor.[15] Even so, emissaries from the Yishuv continued to try to use Istanbul as a staging ground to facilitate the rescue of European Jews. Called the Rescue Committee of the Jewish Agency in Turkey, representatives of the Jewish

Agency were active in Istanbul from late 1942 to 1944. Their mission was to establish lines of communication with the Jews living in Nazi-occupied Europe and to implement aid and rescue operations. According to the research of Corey Guttstadt, in the years from 1940 to 1944, a total of 13,240 Jews passed through Turkey in flight to Palestine with visas or tacit Turkish approval; Dalia Ofer lists a total number of 16,474 migrants who passed through Turkey, including 3,234 Turkish-Jewish emigrants who left their home country of Turkey.[16] Throughout the war, desperate refugees who managed to reach the Mediterranean attempted the dangerous crossing to British-controlled Palestine. According to data compiled by the US Holocaust Memorial Museum, sixty-two such voyages were carried out from 1937 to 1944. From January 1939 to December 1944, 18,879 Jews reached Palestine by sea, while approximately 1,400 travellers may have drowned en route.[17]

Other rescue efforts organized by the Yishuv were more successful. In the spring of 1942, with the authorization of Soviet authorities, over 100,000 Polish refugees and personnel from the Anders Army escaping the German invasion made their way through the Soviet Union to Iran. Among the Polish civilians were approximately 1,000 Jewish children, who came to be known as the 'Tehran Children'. Even before the transports of Polish civilians began to arrive in Iran, representatives of the Jewish Agency negotiated with the Polish-Government-in-Exile to ensure the inclusion of Jewish children in the transports. Between April and August 1942, over 700 children arrived in Tehran, where they were sheltered in a refugee camp that became known as the 'Tehran Home for Jewish Children', operated with the assistance of the Jewish Agency, the JDC, Hadassah and the local Jewish community. Travelling for almost six weeks via Pakistan, around the Arabian Peninsula and through the Red Sea to the Egyptian city of Suez, then crossing the Sinai Desert by train, the Tehran children arrived at the Atlit refugee camp in northern Palestine on 18 February 1943. A second transport of 110 children travelled overland (via Iraq), arriving in Palestine on 28 August 1943. In all, some 870 'Tehran children' were resettled by the Yishuv on kibbutzim (collective farms) and moshavim (cooperative farming villages) in Palestine.[18]

In the first part of the war, the Zionist movement's foreign policy continued to focus on 'fighting the White Paper as if there is no war' while also engaging in acts of rescue when possible. With the fighting in Europe making it impossible for the World Zionist Organization to hold its annual Zionist Congresses, the Biltmore Conference was held in May 1942 at the Biltmore Hotel in New York City as a replacement for the Zionist Congress. Meeting before the full scope of the destruction in Europe was known, the conference declared its devotion to the cause of democratic freedom and international justice in its declaration of support for the allied war effort, while also expressing solidarity with 'fellow Jews in the ghettos and concentration camps of Hitler dominated Europe'. At the same time, the Biltmore Conference called for the fulfillment of the original purpose of the Balfour Declaration and the Mandate which recognizing the historical connection of the Jewish people with Palestine was to afford them the opportunity, as stated by President Wilson, to found there a Jewish Commonwealth. The Conference affirms its unalterable rejection of the White Paper of May 1939 and denies its moral or legal validity. The White Paper seeks to limit, and in fact to nullify Jewish rights to immigration and settlement in Palestine, and, as stated by Mr. Winston Churchill in the House of Commons in May 1939, constitutes 'a breach and repudiation of the Balfour Declaration.' The policy of the White Paper is cruel and indefensible in its denial of sanctuary to Jews fleeing from Nazi persecution; and at a time when Palestine has become a focal point in the war front of the United Nations, and Palestine Jewry must provide all available manpower for farm and factory and camp, it is in direct conflict with the interests of the allied war effort.

In calling for a repudiation of the 1939 White Paper, the Biltmore Conference expressed its belief that full victory in the war would not be achieved until the problem of Jewish homelessness was solved.

The Conference declares that the new world order that will follow victory cannot be established on foundations of peace, justice and equality, unless the problem of Jewish homelessness is finally solved. The Conference urges that the gates of Palestine be opened; that the Jewish Agency be vested with control of immigration into Palestine and with the necessary authority for upbuilding the country, including the development of its unoccupied and uncultivated lands; and that Palestine be established as a Jewish Commonwealth integrated in the structure of the new democratic world. Then and only then will the age old wrong to the Jewish people be righted.[19]

The declaration of the Biltmore Conference also reflected the outcome of an internal debate within the Jewish Agency and the Zionist movement as a whole: should they end all dependence on the British and work to create a Jewish state through direct action (Ben-Gurion, head of the Jewish Agency in Palestine's view) or should the movement continue diplomacy and continue to rely on British support for their goals (the view of Chaim Weizmann, head of the world Zionist organization)? The Biltmore Conference reflected a shift that would presage more direct confrontation with the British as an obstacle to the creation of the state and the need to continue the struggle for statehood even after the war. Even so, such debates over how to approach the British White Paper also reflected a general ignorance in early 1942 of the scope of Nazi plans for the annihilation of European Jewry, just as the Nazi plans for the Final Solution and the total extermination of European Jewry accelerated.

On 29 August 1942, Rabbi Stephen Wise, president of the World Jewish Congress (WJC), received a copy of a telegram sent from Gerhart Riegner, the WJC representative in Switzerland, that explained Riegner had 'received alarming report that in Fuhrer's headquarters plan discussed and under consideration all Jews in countries occupied or controlled Germany number 3–1/2 to 4 million should after deportation and concentration in East at one blow exterminated to resolve once for all Jewish question in Europe'.[20] Despite Riegner's alarming telegram, Rabbi Wise did not publicize the report, yielding to a request by the US State Department to wait until the shocking news could be confirmed.[21] News of the Final Solution would thus not be reported until the end of November 1942, some three months later. In the Yishuv, on Thursday, 26 November 1942, the banner headline atop the front page of *Davar* (the daily publication of the Labour movement) read: *Nikmat Dam Yeled Katan Od Lo Bara Ha-Satan* (Satan has not yet created a fitting revenge for the blood of a small child). The next day's paper called for three days of mourning in the Yishuv to mark the destruction (*hurban*) of European Jewry. On Sunday, 29 November 1942, all rabbis of the Yishuv would lead days of prayer accompanied by shofar blasts and rending of garments. Days of mourning would last until the beginning of Hanukkah (3 December 1942) as Jews in the Yishuv were called upon to avoid excessive enjoyment. *Davar* also reported on efforts in New York to organize labour unions to apply pressure by all means possible to allied governments to stop the slaughter of European Jewry. The front page of *Davar* on Thursday, 3 December 1942, detailed the cries of anger and mourning that had spread throughout Palestine, in services held in Jerusalem, Haifa, Tel Aviv, Petah Tikva, Rehovot, Netanya and elsewhere. David Remez, secretary of the Jewish Labor Federation, the Histadrut, called upon the Yishuv to rouse the world out of its silence to move to action – but in truth there was little the Yishuv could do. As Dina Porat's groundbreaking study *The Blue and Yellow Stars of David* details, the vast disparity between the might of the German machinery of destruction and a Yishuv community with meagre resources constrained by British policy meant that the general attitude of the Yishuv leadership was both one of helplessness and despair, even as newspapers reported one hundred thousand people participated in memorial services from 30 November to 2 December 1942.[22] The statement of the Jewish Agency executive about the systematic murder taking place in Europe and the extermination of millions of Jews along with the three days of mourning became 'a watershed in the Yishuv's consciousness. It was a dividing line between the first three years of the war, during which the Yishuv was unaware of what was happening in Europe, and the three subsequent years'.[23]

By the spring of 1943, as Jews in America and the Yishuv began to transition to mourning the destruction of European Jewry, Jews in the Yishuv read in the press and in other publications the last letters from members of Zionist youth movements in Europe. Bracha Habas, a prominent journalist, author and editor of multiple collections for a broad audience, collected and published 250 letters from youth movement members in a volume titled *Mikhtavim min hageta'ot* (Letters from the ghettos).[24] Included in the Habas collection was a letter from Tosia Altman, pre-war Hashomer Hatzair activist and wartime underground courier (who had by 1943 already become a household name in the Yishuv). Tosia Altman's last letter was anything but a battle cry for freedom, instead expressing the bitterness of a Jew in occupied Europe who felt abandoned by the rest of the Jewish world:

> I think you'll agree with me [she wrote to her unidentified addressee in a kibbutz] that one shouldn't draw strength from a poisoned well. I am trying to control myself not to vent the bitterness that has accumulated against you and your friends for having forgotten us so utterly. I blame you that you didn't help me with a few words at least. But today I don't want to settle my accounts with you. It was the recognition and certainty that we will never see each other again that impelled me to write … . Israel is vanishing before my eyes and I wring my hands and I cannot help him. Have you ever tried to smash a wall with your head?[25]

While news could flow out of occupied Europe beginning to convey the depths of the destruction, Jews in the free world, from New York to Tel Aviv, felt largely powerless to do anything to stop it as news reports were often filtered through pre-existing political frameworks. Even the Warsaw Ghetto Uprising of April–May 1943, the largest mass revolt in Europe to take place during the war, which would later become a rallying cry for the Zionist movement in its struggle to create the Jewish state, was filtered through partisan frameworks, with Jewish socialist members of the Bund in New York taking credit for organizing the revolt in the first year after the uprising and Zionists in the Yishuv hesitant to embrace the event, until they were certain that it was members of Zionist youth movements who had in fact organized the revolt (which they had, working together with Jewish socialists of the Bund).

In the Yishuv, even before the identities of the fighters had been ascertained, the Warsaw Ghetto Uprising was seen as the last stand of an embattled community, as 'the Masada of Warsaw'.

> The Masada of Warsaw Has Fallen – The Nazis Have Set Fire to the Remnants of the Warsaw Ghetto. (*Yediot Ahronot* on 16 May 1943)

> The Jews of Warsaw made their last stand today, abandoned and alone. They have sanctified the name of their tortured and downtrodden people with their blood, and renewed the tradition of the Zealots of Jerusalem and Masada, the heroes of Bar-Kokhba and other Jewish struggles. (Yitzhak Greenboim, chairman of the Va'ad Hatzala rescue organization)

> We cannot ignore the desperate heroism of the defenders of the ghetto, which is incomparable in history, since the days of **Masada**. This heroic

war stirred the hearts of the entire Yishuv, in particular, the hearts of the youth and our soldiers, who to the front and protect the land, and it is a source of comfort and pride for the entire nation. (Yitzhak Ben-Zvi, as chairman of the Va'ad HaLeumi (National Council), 1943; emphasis in original)

Azriel Schwartz (editor of the poetry collection *Plucked Leaves: Poems of Nations at War*, 1943) sought to correct premature comparisons of Warsaw to Masada.

There are those who seek to compare Warsaw to Masada, however, inasmuch as Masada fought opposite a destroyed Jerusalem (today) Warsaw fights opposite a Jerusalem that is rising and being built. We also could have been the last ones. We were saved by a miracle. We have remained the first to redemption and the heavy and growing responsibility falls upon us—we have been made the bearers of the banner of Israeli hope.[26]

On 6 June 1943, HeHalutz and Kibbutz HaMeuchad held a memorial service at Kibbutz Yagur to remember the 'ghetto fighters (who) saved the honor of the Jewish people', singling out specifically Zivia Lubetkin (of the Dror youth movement) and Tosia Altman (Hashomer Hatzair). The speakers who eulogized them noted that the 'ghetto rebels saved the honor of Israel and created with their lives one of the tales of greatest heroism of our time … On this new Masada generations will be built'. The two women, described by Reuters as the two 'Joans of Arc' were rapidly transformed into symbols of loss and suffering, as well as models of incredible self-sacrifice in a manner that was clearly gendered.[27] Zivia Lubetkin and Tosia Altman came to stand in for the death and suffering of millions of Jews in a way that male fighters did not; while Mordecai Anielewicz and Yitzhak Zuckerman would eventually become known as the leaders of the revolt in Zionist circles, Zivia came to represent the sacrifice of the Jewish people and their resurrection.[28]

On 14 June, the Jewish National Council in Palestine organized a 'Day of Protest against Allies' Indifference to Jewish Tragedy', proclaiming that day 'a day of solidarity with the heroic stand taken by the Jews in the Warsaw ghetto as well as an expression of protest on the part of the Palestine Jews against the indifference of the Allied Nations to the unprecedented Jewish tragedy'.[29] The Zionist leadership issued a remarkable statement that expressed admiration for those leading the fight in Poland, and a complete identification between the Zionist struggle in the ghettos of Poland and the struggle for national liberation in Palestine.

Today the Yishuv will demonstrate, the avant-garde of the nation fighting for its redemption, its identification with the enslaved and depressed diaspora … in the countries of occupied Europe in the hands of the Nazis, with the diaspora in Poland standing in the last remnants of its strength on its soul and on the honor of Israel … . today the Yishuv will … demand that Allies fighting against the evil Nazis rescue the 'surviving remnant' of the Diaspora in Europe, the heroes on the Jewish front that has risen in Poland … . The Jewish front that has been established through their heroism in the streets of the Warsaw ghetto and in the ghettos of other cities unites and joins with the fronts of our battles against the Nazi evil, one shoulder together with the Allied Nations, with the front in the war for the building of the homeland for establishment and for freedom. Jerusalem, 11th Sivan 1943 (signed by the 'Zionist leadership')[30]

Beyond an expression of pride in the actions of the Zionist underground and the call for rescue issued by the leadership, one can read here, too, admiration for the Zionist heroes who had joined the fight against the Nazis, a fight Jews in the Yishuv had been unable to join but whose time 'too will come'. In expressing pride in the Zionist leaders of the resistance in Poland, this fight became the fight of the Zionist movement in the Yishuv, too. Heeding the call of the leadership, hundreds of thousands in the Yishuv would sign a declaration calling for rescue and join a general strike in solidarity with European Jewry.[31]

The Jewish Agency, which had focused on continued immigration/aliyah of those who could obtain certificates to Palestine in the early part of the war, indeed transitioned to more focused rescue efforts after November 1942, with the realization that Nazi policy intended to exterminate European Jewry. By and large, this realization came too late to aid the vast majority of European Jewry. Following frantic reports from Richard Lichtheim, the Jewish Agency representative in Geneva, the Yishuv first attempted to channel public pressure onto lifting the British blockade of Palestine (the White Paper policy of 1939), before focusing on rescue through offices in Istanbul and Tehran. According to Tuvia Friling, from late November 1942, when the systematic annihilation of Jews in Europe was officially disclosed, the Yishuv pursued relief and rescue along two main avenues:

(1) 'Grand rescue' or 'grand projects'—actions meant to rescue Jews by extricating them from the occupied areas. This aggregate included programs for the rescue of children and at least three ransom schemes: the Transnistria Plan, the Slovakia Plan (and its derivative, the Europa Plan), and the 'goods for blood' proposal, delivered from Hungary by Joel Brand.

(2) 'Small rescue' or 'small projects'—sundry efforts geared mainly to helping Jews survive the war in the occupied areas: sending money, dispatching parcels of food, clothing, medicines, and forged papers, and arranging 'excursions'—smuggling Jews from one dangerous place to another less dangerous place.[32]

The Jewish Agency established the *Va'ad ha-Hatsala be-Kushta*, the Joint Rescue Committee in Istanbul from late 1942 through 1944. The Rescue Committee in Istanbul focused on making contact with the Jewish communities in Nazi-occupied Europe and worked to implement aid and rescue operations. Among the activists in Istanbul were Chaim Barlas and Melekh Neustadt. Barlas (1898–1957) had served as director of the Palestine office of the Jewish Agency in Warsaw from 1919 to 1925 and was director of the Agency's Immigration Department from 1926 to 1948, as well as its representative in Geneva (1939–40) and Istanbul (1940–5).[33] Neustadt was a Mapai party leader and member of the Zionist Actions Committee active in the Histadrut (Federation of Labour). In 1942, Neustadt went to Istanbul on behalf of the Histadrut to try to contact members of HeHalutz in occupied Europe. Much to his surprise he discovered in the summer of 1942 that it was indeed possible to still contact the movement in occupied Europe and urged the Histadrut and WJC to open offices in Istanbul in June 1942. By the end of the summer of 1942, however, reports soon spread regarding the physical extermination of Polish Jewry—it was too late. Even so, Neustadt worked into 1943 to try to organize rescue out of the Istanbul office. After the revolts, Neustadt tried to convince the surviving ghetto fighters to leave occupied Poland, to survive as the last remaining eyewitnesses to what had transpired, but the activists refused to leave.[34] The Jewish Agency's Rescue Committee used Istanbul's proximity to the Balkans to make contact with Jews in occupied territories and exchange information with them – transferring funds to the Jewish communities for various uses (such as for the Europa Plan, in which the Jewish communities of Europe tried to ransom Jewish lives by paying the Germans large amounts of money) – and tried to carry out immigration to Palestine. The committee still considered any type of movement to Palestine to be the most reliable way of rescuing Jews.[35]

Failure to organize major rescue operations did not mean that rescue and relief for the surviving remnant in occupied Europe did not take place in remarkable ways even after 1943, including the efforts of Joel Brand and Rudolf Kasztner in Hungary. One of the more controversial rescue operations of the war (as discussed in the next chapter), the Kasztner train also represented a successful effort to rescue nearly 1,700 Jews through negotiations with the Nazis. After the German invasion and occupation of Hungary in March 1944, Kasztner and Brand entered into negotiations with Dieter Wisliceny and Adolf Eichmann of the SS, with the hope of suspending deportations of Jews from Hungary in exchange for trucks and other military equipment to be delivered to the Nazis. In June 1944, Kasztner convinced Eichmann to allow a train of nearly 1,700 Jews to escape Hungary and deportations to Auschwitz in exchange for a ransom to be paid per person. The list of 1,686 Jews slated for release included wealthy Jews, Zionist leaders, prominent rabbis (including the Satmar Rebbe, Joel Teitelbaum) and perhaps most controversially Kasztner's own friends and family members.

On 30 June 1944, the 'Kasztner train' left Budapest, carrying 1,686 individuals in exchange for an unclear sum of money, gold, stock and other valuables. After imprisonment in Bergen-Belsen, the transport eventually reached Switzerland in December 1944. Kasztner was assassinated in Israel in 1957 after being accused of collaboration with the Nazis.[36]

News of revolts by members of the Jewish underground in Warsaw, Bialystok, Sobibor and Treblinka only added to the determination of soldiers from the Yishuv to join the war effort in some way. Throughout the war, Jews from the Yishuv had lobbied the British Army to join the fighting in Europe. The British Army would eventually allow for the formation of a Jewish Brigade in September 1944 that would include more than 5,000 Jewish volunteers from Palestine organized into three infantry battalions and several supporting units under the command of Brigadier Ernest Benjamin. Although the Jewish Brigade struggled to join the war until the very end of fighting in Europe, Brigade soldiers fought against the Germans in Italy from March 1945 until the end of the war in May 1945. While Brigade soldiers played an important role in the immediate aftermath of the war, especially as some of the first Jews from the outside world to make contact with the surviving Jewish population, it was another group of Jewish soldiers from the Yishuv who would in fact occupy a more central place in collective memory of the Yishuv's contributions to the war effort.

Between 1943 and 1945, a group of 250 Jewish men and women from Palestine volunteered to join the British army on a mission to organize resistance to the Germans and aid in the rescue of Allied personnel. From the original group of 250 volunteers, 110 underwent training; of those, 32 would eventually parachute into Europe and another 5 managed to infiltrate the target countries by other routes.[37] The parachutists who had been selected for training had immigrated to Palestine from Europe, spoke the native languages fluently and held a native knowledge of the countries to which they were supposed to infiltrate. Ultimately, three of the parachutists infiltrated Hungary, five joined the Slovak national uprising in October 1944 (Rafi Reiss, Haim Hermesh, Zvi Ben-Ya'akov, Haviva Reik and Abba Berdiczew) and another six reached northern Italy. Other parachutists managed to reach Yugoslavia, Romania, Bulgaria, France and Austria. The Germans captured twelve and executed seven of the thirty-seven parachutists sent into occupied Europe, including three in Slovakia, two in Hungary and one in northern Italy.

Hannah Szenes, one of the best-known of the parachutists, was seized in German-occupied Hungary and executed in Budapest on 7 November 1944 at the age of twenty-three. Born in Hungary in 1921, she immigrated to Mandatory Palestine in 1939 and became one of the founders of Kibbutz Sdot Yam. In 1943 she volunteered to join the British Army for the secret mission to parachute behind enemy lines. While her courage and native Hungarian made her an ideal candidate for the secret initiative, the mission was ill-fated and ill-conceived from the start. In March 1944, together with

Reuven Dafni, Yona Rosen and Abba Berdichev, Szenes (code name 'Hagar') parachuted into Yugoslavia near the Hungarian border. After meeting local partisans in Croatian territory, she crossed the border into Hungary in June 1944. She was soon captured by Hungarian soldiers patrolling the border and brought to Budapest where she was severely tortured but refused to divulge details about the mission. In November 1944, the 23-year-old Szenes was executed, both as a British spy and a Hungarian 'traitor'.[38] After the war, remains of the seven parachutists who lost their lives during the war, including Szenes, were interred in the National Military Cemetery overlooking Jerusalem in Israel. Szenes, in particular, assumed legendary status and her poetry and songs ('Blessed is the Match' and 'The Walk to Caesarea' became extremely popular in Israel).

Despite efforts at rescue and resistance initiated by Jews from the Yishuv, the truth is the Zionist movement and the Jewish Agency were largely powerless to respond to the Nazi threat. They depended on Allied powers to intervene in rescue, efforts that one scholar has summarized, even in the case of the United States, as 'little and late'.[39] Nonetheless, among the surviving population, the notion that the only fitting conclusion once the war came to an end would be the creation of a Jewish state became a strong animating principle. Even before liberation, surviving ghetto fighters like Yitzhak Zuckerman and Zivia Lubetkin from the Warsaw Ghetto along with political representatives on the Jewish National Committee published leaflets, one of which (issued on 22 August 1944, under the title 'A Voice from the Depths') linked the continued struggle against Hitler and Nazism with the creation of a Jewish state in the Land of Israel:

And so, Hitler has not attained his objective. And he shall not be able to attain it. The Jewish people lives! Out of 17 million, over 5 million have been exterminated. But the Jewish people of 12 million fights with greater determination and force for its existence and for its better future. The Jewish masses throughout the world share our tragedy with us; they suffer together with us, and are doing all they can to arouse the whole world concerning our situation and coming to our help. They are fighting with great energy and enthusiasm in order to re-establish Jewish life anew and to bring about an economic and social resurrection. Only one, sole historic compensation can be considered after the flood of Jewish blood that has been spilled: an independent, democratic Jewish State in which the tortured Jewish people will have an unrestricted opportunity for development and productive existence.[40]

When Zuckerman and Lubetkin arrived in Lublin on 20 January 1945 following the liberation of Warsaw, they discovered there was a general consensus on the need for the Zionist solution among a group of early leaders of the surviving Jewish population from the Zionist underground and partisan groups, and agreement was reached on the official formation of a Bricha

FIGURE 1.1 *Hannah Szenes in the garden of her home in Budapest, c. 1937.*

FIGURE 1.2 *Group of Jewish paratroopers. From right to left, top row: Reuven Dafni, Zadok Doron and Abba Berdichev. Bottom row: Sara Braverman, Arieh Fichman and Haviva Reik.*

FIGURE 1.3 *Graves of seven parachutists from Palestine killed in action in Europe, Mount Herzl Cemetery, Jerusalem.*

movement to facilitate 'escape' from Eastern Europe, with a coordinating committee led by the partisans Mordechai Rosman, Nisan Resnik and ŻOB veteran fighter Stefan Grajek.[41] While the members of this initial group in Lublin were split over the need for immediate or gradual departure, those who remained in Lublin and later in Warsaw focused their efforts on the organization of the Jewish people for departure from Poland. Abba Kovner, who had been the leader of the Jewish underground in Vilna and then fought with partisans, argued that any effort to reestablish Jewish institutions on the accursed European soil would be a betrayal of the Jewish dead.[42] While Zuckerman agreed with Kovner over the need for departure from Poland, he rejected immediate departure and Kovner's ideas for revenge. Instead, Antek argued that youth movement activists could not desert the Jewish public and needed to remain behind in order to assist in organization.

And indeed wartime leadership in the resistance movements helped the surviving ghetto fighters and partisans play a key role in organizing the

Bricha and convincing Jews liberated in Poland and returning from the far reaches of the Soviet Union to escape from Poland and journey towards the DP camps in Germany, Austria and Italy on their path towards the Land of Israel. Abba Kovner, on the other hand, came to Palestine in 1945 on a mission to organize a massive revenge operation to kill six million Germans by poisoning the water system of several major cities in post-war Germany. As Dina Porat has persuasively argued, Yishuv leadership disagreed with Kovner's grandiose plans for revenge, believing that the creation of the Jewish State would be the most fitting historical revenge for the destruction of European Jewry. What was Kovner's plan? In a nutshell, after liberation, when he discovered the levels of destruction not only in the killing fields of Vilna and Ponar, but in the extermination camps of Poland, Kovner's desire for revenge became all-consuming. Arriving in Lublin in January 1945, Kovner founded a secret organization of likeminded people called *Nakam* (Revenge). As he articulated in a series of principles developed for the group in Bucharest in April or May 1945:

> We have taken it upon ourselves not to let the world forget by performing the necessary act: Retribution. It will be more than revenge; it must be the law of the murdered Jewish people! Its name will therefore be DIN [the acronym of *Dam Israel Noter*, meaning the 'blood of Israel is vengeful' – and '*din*' itself means 'judgment'] so that posterity may know that in this merciless, uncompassionate world there is both a judge and judgment.[43]

The group hatched a grandiose plan to poison the water system in several major German cities after the war, aiming to kill six million Germans in retaliation for the murder of six million Jews. While plan A for mass revenge never came to fruition, on 13 April 1946, members of the *Nakam* group carried out plan B, poisoning bread meant to feed SS-unit prisoners in Stalag 13 Langwasser Camp in Nuremberg, which was under American authority at the time. The *Nakam* group infiltrated the kitchens of the POW camp and brushed 3,000 loaves of bread with arsenic, causing many of the prisoners to fall ill. In her analysis of this remarkable story, Dina Porat argues that while Abba Kovner and his group had the determination and the wherewithal to carry out their grandiose plans for mass revenge, they did not have the support of the Yishuv leadership, which tried to strike a delicate balance in the aftermath of the war. They did not want to dismiss Kovner entirely, but, at the same time, they wanted to make sure that plan A would neither materialize nor get out of control, putting various mechanisms in place to ensure that they could maintain supervision over the Avengers. Porat highlights a meeting between Pasha Avidov of the Nakam group and David Ben-Gurion at the November 1945 conference of Jewish fighters in Paris, where, in a very brief encounter, it became clear that the future prime minister of Israel did not support Avidov's revenge ideas. 'I cannot promise you what will happen if you do not cancel your plan. Now is the time to build a country and now is not the time to deal with less important things', Porat writes, paraphrasing Ben-Gurion. As Porat notes, Ben-Gurion made clear, 'if revenge could not bring back six million Jews, he was not interested in it'.[44] Eventually, Kovner was captured by the British on his way back to Europe from Palestine; he dumped all of the poison overboard just before his arrest. Kovner would spend several months in prison in Cairo and Jerusalem, while his comrades moved onto plan B, the plan to poison the bread of the SS prisoners near Nuremberg. While Yishuv leaders could not support a massive revenge operation that would endanger the possibility of creating a Jewish state, there is evidence to suggest plan B had their approval. After the war, even if the Jewish public in Israel and its leadership believed in the need to take revenge on the Germans, this idea was set aside in favour of the very real need to rescue the survivors and bring them to Israel, and the need to establish the state, which would then be the ultimate response. Thus the building of the state became the approved form of collective, national revenge.

The aftermath of the Holocaust and support for the creation of a Jewish state

The outcome of the war was catastrophic. European Jewry had been destroyed and notwithstanding bold wartime proclamations, the Yishuv had been largely powerless to do anything to save European Jewry. The experience of the war had also reinforced the dependence of the Yishuv on global powers to realize their state aspirations. Even so, the Yishuv had a demographic problem; the British White Paper was still in effect, the blockade had not been removed and Jews in Palestine were outnumbered two to one. If anything, the likelihood of forming a Jewish state seemed more remote than ever. So how is it that in three short years after the liberation of the camps, the state would come into existence? To understand this surprising turn of events, we must look not at the connections between the Holocaust and the creation of the state, but between the aftermath of the Holocaust, the plight of the DPs and the diplomatic steps that would lead to UN support for the partition of Palestine in November 1947.

At the end of the war, members of the Jewish Brigade journeyed north through Italy, reaching newly liberated Jewish inmates from concentration camps in Austria and Germany. There was little they could do but distribute rations and offer moral support and the encouragement of seeing soldiers with stars of David emblazoned on their trucks next to slogans like *Die Juden Kommen!* (The Jews Are Coming!) written in chalk. But the end of the war revealed the depths of the devastation and destruction of European Jewish civilization.

Soon after liberation, Jewish survivors began to search for surviving family members almost immediately, although most Jews found that few had survived. Those survivors who remained in the hastily erected DP camps faced deplorable conditions: poor accommodations, no plumbing, no clothing, rampant disease, continuing malnourishment and a lack of any plan on the part of the Allies. Jewish chaplains serving with the American military were among the first Jews to encounter the survivors in the camps (along with the occasional Jewish Brigade soldier).[45] While the JDC sought to gain access to the camps as early as May 1945, the JDC's first organized group did not enter the American zone of occupation until August 1945, some three months later.[46] This meant that in the earliest stages after liberation, the survivors depended on the US Army and UNRRA (United Nations Relief and Rehabilitation Administration) for relief, and on a small group of Jewish chaplains who played an especially significant role in tending to the needs of the survivors. One particularly active American Jewish chaplain, Rabbi Abraham Klausner, aided in the early political organization of the She'erit Hapletah (or the Surviving Remnant) and created a tracing service for survivors to find one another.[47] Klausner reported to his superiors in the United States on the situation facing Jews in post-war Germany after visiting thousands of DPs scattered across the American zone of occupation in the first month after liberation. He summarized his 24 June 1945 report to Philip Bernstein, executive director of the National Jewish Welfare Board committee on Army-Navy religious activities, stating, 'Liberated but not free, that is the paradox of the Jew':

There seems to be no policy, no responsibility, no plan for these … stateless Jews … Twelve hours a day I tell my lies. 'They will come,' I say. 'When will they come?' they ask me. UNRRA, JDC, Red Cross – can it be that they are not aware of the problem? It is impossible … Of what use is all my complaining; I cannot stop their tears. America was their hope and all America has given them is a new camp with guards in khaki. Freedom, hell no! They are behind walls without hope.[48]

Organizing among themselves, Jewish DPs voiced their frustration in letters to military authorities and world Jewish organizations (such as the WJC and the JDC), pleading for assistance from the US military government and UNRRA to rectify their miserable situation.[49] Expecting to be welcomed by the world with open arms, liberation was a rude awakening, as Jewish DPs continued to struggle to obtain bearable living conditions and yearned for contact with the rest of the Jewish world, which had still largely been denied access to the DP camps by military authorities seeking to establish order on the chaotic post-war situation. With the JDC denied access to the military zone of occupation, survivors worked together with GIs (short for "government issue," a common term for American soldiers) and Jewish chaplains to organize help for themselves. Klausner met Zalman Grinberg, a doctor and a survivor from Kovno, who had commandeered part of a Benedictine monastery at St Ottilien for use as a Jewish DP hospital after liberation, and who would become a close colleague in the rebuilding of Jewish life in post-war Germany during his early work in Bavaria.[50] As Grinberg wrote to the WJC in May 1945, disappointment with the slow arrival of relief was evident:

> It has been four weeks since our liberation and no representative of the Jewish world, no representative from any Jewish organization has come to be with us after the worst tragedy of all time, to speak with us, to give us help, and to lighten our burden. We must, ourselves, with our own diminished strength, help ourselves.[51]

Chastened by the absence of any assistance from world Jewry, Grinberg and Klausner, with the assistance of other survivors and representatives from the Jewish Brigade, decided to take matters into their own hands, establishing the Central Committee of the Liberated Jews (CCLJ) in the US Zone of Germany on 1 July 1945, as the official representative body of the Jewish DPs.[52] The purpose of the Central Committee was to champion the interests of the Jewish DPs and to draw attention to their plight before the US Army and UNRRA just as other national groups of DPs had done. The CCLJ would eventually gain official US Army recognition as 'the legal and democratic representation of the liberated Jews in the American zone' in September 1946. The Central Committee focused its work on the survivors' immediate needs, including food, shelter, medicine and security and addressed the question of emigration, soon reaching a consensus that Zionism represented the best solution for the stateless surviving population and that they should be encouraged to prepare themselves for immigration to Palestine at the earliest point possible.[53] The CCLJ appointed Rabbi Abraham Klausner honorary president and elected Dr Grinberg as chairman of the executive committee. Josef Rosensaft, a survivor of Auschwitz and several other camps who had been liberated from Bergen-Belsen, became leader of the Central Committee of Liberated Jews in the British zone.[54]

As scholar Ze'ev Mankowitz has argued, 'the creation of a Jewish state in the Land of Israel was taken to be the last will and testament bequeathed by the dead to the living ... . it signified the only real hope for the rescue and rehabilitation of the little that remained of European Jewry and, in the longer term, the promise of the Jewish future'.[55] The early political leadership of the She'erit Hapletah, composed of many former members of Zionist youth groups who had chosen to remain in Germany rather than return to Eastern Europe, was overwhelmingly attuned to the needs of the youth in the DP camps.[56] From an early point in time, the Jewish DP leadership espoused a strong Zionist position. In many cases it was the surviving members of Zionist youth movements and political parties who undertook the self-help work and in turn became most active among those seeking to convince survivors to avoid a return to Eastern Europe. These were generally youth movement leaders who had experience leading and organizing Jewish youth both before and, in some cases, during the war. This experience made them well-suited to lead the younger Jewish population that had survived life in German concentration camps. For the young Jewish survivors in the DP camps (primarily under the age of thirty-five), regardless of whether they had experience in a Zionist youth group before the war, such kibbutz groups emerged as attractive options, providing them with the camaraderie, support and replacement 'family' they so desperately craved. Zionism filled a crucial function for the Jewish DPs and proved appealing to a number of groups in post-war Germany, who all supported the Zionist project for differing reasons. This support would lead to the creation of a flourishing Zionist network in the American zone of Germany where survivor youth could continue the process of Zionist immersion within the framework of kibbutzim and *hakhsharot* (agricultural training farms) that did in fact ultimately aid in the creation of the state of Israel.

The reports of continuing deprivation and poor organization of recovery sent by the DPs and Jewish chaplains eventually prompted American officials to take a greater interest in the problem of the DPs. President Truman dispatched Earl Harrison (dean of the University of Pennsylvania Law School and former US commissioner for immigration and naturalization) to survey conditions in the DP camps. In his scathing report back to Truman, Harrison concluded that we are 'treating the Jews as the Nazis treated them except that we do not exterminate them'. He proposed that Jews be separated in their own camps – until then they had been forced to live with other national groups and former collaborators – and, to resolve their refugee status, he proposed that one hundred thousand immigration certificates to Palestine be granted immediately to the Jewish DPs. Following Harrison's report, American authorities, under the leadership of General Eisenhower, worked to ameliorate conditions for Jewish DPs, moving Jews to separate camps and agreeing to the appointment of an adviser for Jewish affairs.

In October 1945, Ben-Gurion, in his capacity as head of the Jewish Agency, visited the DP camps in Germany, where the Jewish DPs welcomed him as 'the personal embodiment of all their hopes for the future'.[57] Major Irving Heymont, responsible for the administration of the Landsberg DP camp, described Ben-Gurion's visit to Landsberg on 22 October 1945 and the excitement the visit engendered among the camp population. The camp was already abuzz, for the day before the first election of the camp committee had occurred with the *Ichud* Zionist slate of Samuel Gringauz emerging victorious.

As Heymont related,

To add to the excitement of election day, the camp was visited by Mr. David Ben-Gurion — the head of the Zionist organization if Palestine. *To the people of the camp, he is God. It seems that he represents all of their hopes of getting to Palestine* ... . I don't think that a visit by President Truman could cause as much excitement.[58]

Through his meetings with General Eisenhower and General Walter Bedell-Smith, Ben-Gurion learned that the US Army authorities did not intend to stop Jewish infiltrees from Eastern Europe from entering the American zone; sensing an opportunity, he outlined a plan that was to bring as many Jews as possible into the occupation zones that were under US command.[59] In the wake of the Harrison report, in which American authorities had been excoriated for poor treatment of Jews, American officials provided separate camps for Jews and were determined to improve conditions for Jews in the US zone. Furthermore, Ben-Gurion submitted a number of suggestions to Eisenhower on how to improve the morale of the Jewish DPs, which included allowing the Jewish DPs to govern themselves, subject to the ultimate authority of the US Army, and providing agricultural and vocational training on confiscated Nazi farms.[60]

Over the course of 1945 and into 1946, with continued antisemitic violence, economic hardship and increasingly restrictive new Communist regimes, many Jews, who were not liberated on German soil, escaped Poland and other Eastern European countries with the aforementioned *Bricha* organization formed by surviving underground activists in Poland (Bricha is Hebrew for 'flight', the clandestine Zionist organization that conducted the underground immigration of European Jews to Palestine). They believed that there was no future for them in Europe and that entering the Western occupation zones of Germany would allow them to continue their route overseas.[61]

With the arrival of more than one hundred thousand Jews fleeing continued persecution and antisemitism in Eastern Europe with assistance from the *Bricha*, the Jewish DP population reached 250,000 in Germany, Italy and Austria by the beginning of 1947. Approximately 185,000 were in Germany, 45,000 in Austria and 20,000 in Italy. Young adults constituted a disproportionately high percentage of the surviving population: reports and surveys consistently estimated the proportion of Jewish DPs between the ages of fifteen and thirty at more than half and often above 80 per cent of the total Jewish population.[62] In the absence of families, many survivors quickly created new families, as evidenced by the many weddings and the remarkable birth rate among the surviving population in the first year after liberation. The nature of the surviving population also shifted as many more Jews who had survived the war in far-flung exile in the Soviet Union began to arrive in the DP camps. Upon repatriation to Poland, with the realization that their families, communities and homes had been destroyed, they decided to move further west. Because the DPs were a population in constant transition – highly mobile, hoping for departure, waiting for immigration options, this notion of a post-war community of survivors was in flux – the She'erit Hapletah existed as a collective, but the individuals who composed it were constantly changing.[63]

While still living in a transitional situation, hoping for the possibility of emigration, DPs succeeded in creating a vibrant and dynamic community in hundreds of DP camps and communities across Germany, Italy and Austria. With the assistance of representatives from UNRRA, the JDC, the Jewish Agency and other organizations, they established schools throughout the DP camps. As the population of young people in the Jewish DP camps increased with the arrival of more Bricha 'infiltrees', the educational system expanded, with most classes focused on preparing Jewish youth for a future in the Land of Israel, teaching Hebrew language, Jewish history, Jewish literature and more. Despite some outside observers who objected to the concentration on Zionism, this approach reflected a consensus among Jewish DPs, who consistently articulated an emphatic and vocal desire to make Palestine the collective solution to the problem of Jewish statelessness, even for those who did not plan to go to Palestine individually.

The largest camps, including Landsberg, Feldafing and Föhrenwald in the American zone of Germany and Bergen-Belsen in the British zone, boasted a vibrant social and cultural life, with a flourishing DP press, theatre life, active Zionist youth movements, athletic clubs, historical commissions and yeshivot testifying to the rebirth of Orthodox Judaism.[64] The DPs took an active role in representing their own political interests: political parties, mostly Zionist in nature – with the exception of the Orthodox Agudat Israel and the remnants of the Jewish socialist Bundist party still working to build a future for Jewish workers in the diaspora – fought over camp committees and met at annual congresses of the She'erit Hapletah while advocating the immigration of survivors to Palestine. The Zionist youth movements, with the assistance of emissaries from Palestine, created a network of at least forty agricultural training farms throughout Germany on the estates of former Nazis and German farmers, demonstrating their ardent desire for immigration to Palestine and performing an act of symbolic revenge against the Germans. As noted earlier, from an early point in time, the Jewish DP leadership espoused a strong Zionist position. In many cases, it was the surviving members of Zionist youth movements and political parties who undertook the self-help work and in turn became most active among those seeking to convince survivors to avoid a return to Eastern Europe. For the young Jewish survivors in the DP camps (primarily under the age of thirty-five), regardless of whether they had experience in a Zionist youth group before the war, such kibbutz groups emerged as attractive options, providing them with the camaraderie, support and replacement 'family' they so desperately craved. On the diplomatic level, the high visibility of the kibbutzim and hakhsharot (agricultural training farms) and their manifestations of Zionist enthusiasm demonstrated to outside observers a perceived state of 'Palestine passion' on the part of the Jewish DPs. While Zionism could allow them to transcend their current situation through a focus on the future, when they did face Germany and Nazism they were now armed with the tools to do so. At the same time, the young farmers could take pride in their collective accomplishments, as farming provided some tangible product for their time and efforts in Germany, as they waited for departure on aliyah. Indeed, in numerous ways, the demonstrations of a Jewish presence in post-war Germany, the baby carriages testifying to the 'baby boom' in the DP camps, the focus on the education of Jewish youth and the statement made by the survivors in Germany that *Mir Zaynen Do* ('We Are Here', the refrain of the Jewish Partisans Hymn) were a poignant affirmation of Jewish resilience and a defiant declaration that even after the destruction of the Holocaust, the Jewish people and the eternal Jewish spirit could not be eliminated.

The apparent importance of Zionism for the increasing numbers of arriving DPs confirmed the necessity of the Zionist solution for representatives of the Anglo-American Committee of Inquiry (AACI), created after the Harrison Report to come up with a diplomatic solution to the Jewish refugee problem in post-war Europe. After beginning their work in Washington and London in January 1946, members of the commission visited the DP camps and Poland to assess the Jewish situation beginning in February. Notwithstanding some concerns over Zionist propaganda, on 20 April 1946, the AACI recommended '(A) that one hundred thousand certificates be authorized immediately for the admission into Palestine of Jews who have been the victims of Nazi and Fascist persecution; (B) that these certificates be awarded as far as possible in 1946 and that actual immigration be pushed forward as rapidly as conditions will permit'. This was the conclusion that the committee came to not only because of a lack of any other options but also because the committee genuinely believed that this was the truest expression of the Jewish DPs' desires. 'Furthermore, that is where almost all of them want to go. There they are sure that they will receive a welcome denied them elsewhere. There they hope to enjoy peace and rebuild their lives.'[65] The committee based these findings in part on surveys conducted among the DPs. However, the committee also firmly believed that based on what it had observed among the Jewish DPs, they were a group ardently preparing themselves for a Zionist future.

The Harrison Report served to link the resolution of the Jewish DP situation with the situation in Palestine, thereby elevating the diplomatic implications of the Jewish DP political stance. International observers from the Anglo-American Committee of Inquiry and the United Nations deemed DP Zionist enthusiasm central to the resolution of the political conflict over the land of Palestine. By February 1947, the British had referred the problem of Palestine to the United Nations. As their stay dragged on in Europe, DPs staged mass protests condemning the British blockade of Palestine and participated in the illegal immigration (aliyah bet) movement to Palestine, most noticeably in the Exodus Affair of 1947. Over the first four months of 1947, the British government had intercepted eight vessels carrying a total of 9,237 persons. On 11 July 1947 a ship carrying 4,052 men, women and children departed the French port of Sete on a mission to break the British blockade of Palestine.[66] On the way to Haifa, the ship's name was changed to *Exodus 1947* (*Yetziat Eyropah 1947*). The ship was intercepted by British warships, and the passengers fought them until they were subdued. The British resolved to teach the illegal immigration movement a lesson, and rather than allow the passengers to disembark in Palestine or even Cyprus, they decided to force the DPs to return to France. The transfer of the DPs to prison ships in Haifa harbour took place within full view of the United Nations Special Committee on Palestine (UNSCOP) commissioners touring Palestine at the time, a notable diplomatic coup on the part of the Zionist enterprise. Although the prison ships were returned to France, the passengers refused to disembark and the French refused to force them to do so. The passengers even went so far as to stage a hunger strike to arouse sympathy for their plight. The ship's passengers were finally returned to Hamburg, a practical defeat for the DPs in their effort to depart German soil, but one of the greatest victories for the Zionist movement in their ongoing diplomatic struggle against the British blockade. The symbolic value of Holocaust survivors being forced to return to former Nazi soil was not lost on the world press or on the UNSCOP commissioners debating the future of Palestine. Following the drama of the Exodus Affair in the summer of 1947, and the work and report of the UNSCOP, the United Nations voted for the partition of Palestine on 29 November 1947, recommending that the problem of the 250,000 Jewish DPs be dealt with through the partition of Palestine.

The announcement was greeted with great enthusiasm in the DP camps, and the Central Committee declared that

> on the ruins of the Diaspora will arise the Jewish state, which will represent the most beautiful ideals of our people and will give the possibility to return the Jewish masses of the historical past and the coming future. With the help of the Jewish state the Jewish camps in Germany will be liquidated and the Jewish people will return to the family of free nations after 2000 years.[67]

Following the passage of the UN partition plan (29 November 1947) and the creation of the state of Israel in May 1948, approximately two-thirds of the DP population immigrated to the new state, with a sizable percentage of the younger segment participating in the fighting in the 1948 war. Most of the remainder immigrated to the United States, which had only become a realistic immigration option following passage of the Displaced Persons Act in 1948 and the amended DP Act of 1950, which authorized two hundred thousand DPs (Jewish and non-Jewish) to enter the United States. By 1952, more than eighty thousand Jewish DPs had immigrated to the United States under the terms of the DP Act and with the aid of Jewish agencies. Almost all of the DP camps were closed by 1952, with the exception of Föhrenwald, which remained open until 1957.

What then is the nature of the historical relationship between the Holocaust and the creation of the state of Israel? As Yehuda Bauer has argued, we must distinguish between the Holocaust itself and the post-war consequences of the Holocaust. While at the moment of liberation it may have seemed even more unlikely that the state would come into existence, the state was established both as a result of the struggle of the Yishuv in the context of the Zionist settlement of Palestine *and* by the struggle of the Holocaust survivors and the Jews who returned from the Soviet Union, who helped to create American pressure on the British.[68] It seems clear that a combination of factors: the post-war statelessness of the surviving population, the failure of the international community to address the Jewish refugee crisis, the embrace of Zionism by a large segment of the surviving Jewish population and the shrewd activity of the Zionist leadership in Palestine and Europe to take advantage of all of these factors created a situation which led to United Nations support for the partition of Palestine in November 1947.[69] And of course, all of this depended on the viability of the facts on the ground of a state-in-the making in Palestine, coupled with the necessary diplomatic support for the partition of Palestine in 1947. Nonetheless, the ways in which the aftermath of the Holocaust would come to be inextricably linked with the creation of the state, also meant that the state would exist in an uneasy relationship with the memory of the Holocaust for decades.

2

The state of Israel and the memory of the Holocaust, 1948–61

The Holocaust took a prominent place in the public life of the state of Israel early on, although there was a constant tension between the top-down crafting of Holocaust memory by the political leadership of the new state and the bottom-up, grassroots-level activities of the survivors who sought to establish themselves in Israel. Those who had spent the war in Mandatory Palestine only had a limited understanding of the destruction of European Jews and tended to interpret it through the lens of Zionist ideology. Both political leaders and the wider public engaged in a polarized discourse pitting 'heroes' and 'victims' against one another. On the one hand, the few surviving Jewish partisans and fighters from the Zionist ghetto undergrounds, among them Chajka Klinger from Będzin, Rozka Korczak, Vitka Kempner and Abba Kovner from Vilna and Zivia Lubetkin and Yitzhak Zuckerman from Warsaw, were welcomed in the Yishuv with great excitement and respect. They provided first-hand testimony to members of the Labour Movement, the Haganah, the Palmach and the political leaders of the Yishuv, were given public attention and prominent press coverage and were encouraged to tell their stories.[1] At Zivia Lubetkin's testimony at Kibbutz Yagur on 8 June 1946 (almost exactly three years after she was eulogized there in 1943), at least three thousand were in attendance to hear Zivia describe the destruction of Warsaw for eight straight hours. While other survivors had already reached Israel and shared testimonies on the Shoah, leaders of the Yishuv like Eliyahu Dobkin of the Jewish Agency Executive and Yitzhak Tabenkin, one of the heads of Labor Zionism and the kibbutz movement, often believed they were hearing exaggerated reports. Perhaps by June 1946, one year after the end of war, the Yishuv was prepared to believe, which is why Lubetkin's testimony set off such a shockwave.[2] During the war, the

Zionist movement struggled to make sense of the enormity of the catastrophe within the context of the continued drive to create the Jewish state. After the war, the Yishuv in Palestine embraced the leading role of Zionist youth in the revolt in Warsaw and other ghettos, as the surviving members of the Jewish Fighting Organization argued that the wartime struggle continued as part of the struggle to create the Jewish state. The Warsaw Ghetto Uprising became the prism through which Jews in the Yishuv chose to remember the Shoah, even as it fulfilled an ideological function in the Zionist narrative by pitting heroes and victims against each other, blaming the victims for their alleged passivity.

The *mordim* (resisters) were referred to as *giborim* (heroes) and valourized for having 'saved the honour' of the Jewish people. For political leaders and the former fighters alike, the fight against the Nazis was intrinsically connected with the ongoing struggle to create the Jewish state. On the other hand, survivors who could not pride themselves in armed resistance met a wall of silence, disinterest, even impatience from 'veteran' Israelis who believed that the majority of European Jews had either collaborated with the Nazis – as members of the Jewish councils, ghetto police and as kapos – or gone passively to their deaths 'like sheep to the slaughter'. There was a strong element of blaming the victims for their own destruction. Had they understood better, such thinking went, they would have distinguished themselves either as ardent Zionists who immigrated to Eretz Israel before the Holocaust or had understood that the only 'correct' response to Nazism was armed underground resistance. Aharon Megged's short story 'Yad Vashem' (1955) clearly represented this attitude of the native-born Israelis to that diaspora history. Like the official Holocaust memorial and museum dedicated in 1953, Yad Vashem means a 'monument and a name'. In the story, a young Israeli-born couple about to have a baby confront their grandfather's desire to have the baby named after a grandson murdered by the Nazis and their Ukrainian collaborators. The name of that boy was Mendele, a Yiddish name in its affectionate, diminutive form. The couple refuse to name their child Mendele, which the granddaughter calls 'a Ghetto name, ugly, horrible'. They want a Hebrew name for their son, like the Biblical name 'Ehud' (meaning united or strong), which corresponded with the widespread Israeli custom of reinventing or rediscovering Hebrew names to replace those names that had an old-world flavour to them. Learning of his grandchildren's refusal to continue the Jewish tradition of naming after the deceased, Grandpa Zisskind (literally, sweet child) cannot contain his anger:

> 'What do you know about what was there? What do you know of the people that were there? The communities? The cities? What do you know of the life they had there?'
> 'Yes', said Yehuda, his spirit crushed, 'but we no longer have any ties with it'.

'You have no ties with it?' Grandfather Zisskind bent towards him. His lips quivered in fury. 'With what ... with what do you have ties?'

We have ... with this country, said Yehuda and gave an involuntary smile.

'And you – you're ashamed to give your son the name Mendele lest it remind you that there were Jews who were called by that name. You believe that his name should be wiped off the face of the earth. That not a trace of it should remain ...'

'O children, children, you don't know what you're doing ... You're finishing off the work which the enemies of Israel began. They took the bodies away from the world, and you – the name and the memory ... No continuation, no evidence, no memorial and no name. Not a trace ...'

And indeed the child would be named Ehud and it was the grandfather who would remain alone, 'an orphan in the world'.[3]

For many of the Israeli-born sabras, however, the task of building the new country took precedence. They had been raised on an ideology that encouraged them to create a 'new Jew' in the Land of Israel, a new Jew divorced from the diaspora past, who could triumph over two thousand years of powerlessness and passivity that they believe characterized Jewish life in the diaspora. Ideologically, the need to divorce the Zionist future from the Jewish past meant distancing from the Jewish civilization that had just been destroyed in order to start a new one. As stated by Yudka, the little Jew, in the Haim Hazaz story 'The Sermon', written in 1942 at the peak of the destruction of the Jewish diaspora, what was the point of remaining connected to the diaspora past?

> I want to state ... that I am opposed to Jewish history ... because we didn't make our own history, the goyim made it for us ... . What is there in it? Oppression, defamation, persecution, martyrdom. And again oppression, defamation, persecution, and martyrdom ... I would simply forbid teaching our children Jewish history. Why the devil teach them about their ancestors' shame?[4]

For the Sabras raised on the ideal of *anu banu artzah livnot u-lehibanot* ('we have come to the land to build and to be rebuilt') it seemed impossible to build a future that maintained any nostalgic connection to a destroyed civilization. What good could come from remembering a history of shame?

This polarized view of survivors and their diaspora past also found expression in the terms used to describe them. The survivors were commonly referred to as *nitsolei shoah* those who 'were rescued from the destruction' or *sordei shoah*, those who 'outlived' the destruction (in both cases seemingly without their own agency). When referring to the dead, the Jewish masses passively 'perished' (*nispu*) in the Nazi genocide, while ghetto fighters 'fell' (*naflu*) in battle. There were also such derogatory terms for the dead such as *avak adam* (human dust) and *sabonim* (soaps), signifying the supposed passivity of European Jews who 'allowed' themselves to be murdered and turned into bars of soap (*sic*) by the Nazis instead of fighting them. This view resulted from a number of factors: lack of knowledge of the complex nature of the Holocaust, as well as an ideological view that saw diaspora Jews as 'passive' and rejected diaspora life. Accordingly, the Holocaust was not a crime *sui generis*, but just another example of antisemitic violence that had been inherent in the condition of exile (*galut*) for centuries and could only be resolved through national sovereignty for Jews.[5] The lack of nuance in the perception of the European Jewish catastrophe also resulted from psychological inhibitions; the focus on heroic resistance was a defence mechanism, when many who lost relatives in the catastrophe struggled with the shock of an event too difficult to confront, along with feelings of guilt and a sense of shame that the Yishuv had not done enough to rescue European Jews.[6]

It is also important to note that just at the time that the state in the making would have been absorbing large numbers of survivors and assimilating information about their devastating wartime experiences, the country quickly became entangled in an existential struggle for survival. After the UN voted in favour of partition on 29 November 1947, the British began to prepare for withdrawal from Palestine. Skirmishes between Palestinian militias and the Haganah began even before the withdrawal of British forces on 14 May 1948. When David Ben-Gurion proclaimed the creation of the 'The State of Israel' in Tel Aviv on 14 May 1948, five Arab armies from Egypt, Syria, Lebanon, Jordan and Iraq, along with Palestinian militias had already invaded. For many survivors of the Holocaust, who longed for the creation of the Jewish state as the obvious conclusion to the wartime destruction of European Jewry, it was the outbreak of another war that would enable their departure from Europe.

Recently some Israeli historians have begun to address the experience of Holocaust survivors in the War of Independence, focusing on the most direct link between the Holocaust and the establishment of the state, that being the use of survivors as a vital manpower reserve in the War of Independence. In her study on the participation of the Holocaust survivors in the war, Hanna Yablonka reveals the difficulty with which they experienced integration into Israeli society, detailing the barriers that existed in making their arrival in Israel such a disappointment for both the survivors and the Yishuv.[7] A substantial number of the enlisted frontline Jewish fighters in the War of Independence were survivors recruited in the DP camps in Germany, Austria and Italy making a journey from liberation and survival in Europe straight into another conflict. Hanna Yablonka estimates that between March 1948 and May 1949, out of 82,000 total Jewish soldiers in the war, just over one-quarter, or 22,330, were survivors of the Holocaust.[8] While their contribution was extremely significant, it is not the case that these 1948 conscripts were merely sent to die as 'cannon fodder' dying in numbers that surpassed those of native-born Israelis as some historians have suggested.[9] On the other hand, participation in the struggle to create the state as soldiers in the newly formed Israel Defence Force (IDF) offered many survivors a chance to assimilate into the new society, even as many struggled to learn a new language and handle a weapon.[10]

Beyond the battlefield, survivors played a direct role in translating the meaning of the Shoah for soldiers engaged in the existential struggle for Israel's survival in 1948. After Abba Kovner's capture at sea by British forces and his imprisonment in Egypt and Jerusalem, he played a prominent role during the 1948 war inspiring IDF soldiers in battle. Between June 1948 and May 1949, he wrote thirty battle missives distributed among the soldiers, distinguished by both their poetry and emotionally evocative pathos and their violent rhetoric. As a veteran of battles in occupied Europe, Kovner, 'through his gory battle missives ... sought to cleanse the fighters of the guilt and shame of bloodshed and to give words to an unspoken trauma'. In his poetic language, scholar Michal Arbell argues, Kovner made a direct link for the soldiers fighting the Egyptian enemy – at times equating the Egyptians with the Nazis, as in a poem from a missive published in July 1948. The poem urged Jewish soldiers to fight for 'our homes, for the lives of our children', as 'the souls of six million – the souls that did not get to see the day – call us from the ground: let the great revenge come – let the people of Israel be free, forever!'[11] Despite contributions by survivors to the War of Independence, the literature of the 1948 generation, however, did little to dispel disparaging opinions of the newly arrived survivors who were often represented as weak, passive and confused.[12]

The newly arrived survivors, drafted through conscription campaigns in the DP camps, struggled to obtain a place in the Israeli collective memory of the 1948 war. Emmanuel Sivan has analysed the role of the literary elite and public and private commemorative rituals in the creation of the image of 'the silver platter upon which (we) have been given the Jewish state' (from the poem of Natan Alterman, which assumed a predominant role in early commemorations of *Yom HaZikaron*, Israel's Memorial Day). As Sivan notes, 'the predominant myth related to the war losses is that of the 'sabra' as the emblematic fallen soldier, the native-born carrying the brunt of the burden on the firing line'.[13] Why did the 'sabra' become equated with fallen war-heroes of 1948, even though some 22,000 *gahal* (acronym for *giyus hutz la-aretz* or foreign conscription) recruits made up one quarter of all soldiers? According to Sivan, literature was one 'potent vehicle' in the propagation of this myth, with the publication of such works as Moshe Shamir's *Chapters of Elik* and *He Walked in the Fields*, as well as S. Yizhar's *Days of Ziklag*, Anda Amir's *Figures from the War of Liberation* and Yitzhak Ziv Av's collection of war correspondence, *The Price of Freedom*. Also central in this regard was the official government publication of *Gevilei Esh* (*Scrolls of Fire*), an anthology of the writings of the war dead.[14] Thus, as Sivan notes, for a variety of reasons both demographic and ideological, 'the term 'sabra' became all but synonymous with the combat soldiers of 1948'.[15]

In the novel, *He Walked Through the Fields*, written by Moshe Shamir and published in 1947 (later turned into a movie in 1967), the protagonist, Uri, represents the prototypical sabra willing to sacrifice his own individual needs for the good of the nation. Forced to choose between his love for his girlfriend, Mika, a Polish Jewish survivor and one of the 'Tehran children' and his obligation to the Palmach (an elite fighting force of the Haganah), Uri chooses his duty to the Zionist cause over his family (even after he finds out his girlfriend is pregnant). Uri dies sabotaging a bridge, a diversion that enables a shipload of Holocaust survivors to reach the shores of Palestine with the *ha'apalah*. The sabra sacrifices himself heroically to create a place of refuge for the survivors, while his son will be born, carrying his name and his legacy. Shamir's works were representative of the Palmach generation, highlighting the sacrifice of the Sabra for the greater good, while counterposing his heroism with the passivity of the newly arrived survivors.

As noted in this volume's introduction, in Israel's Proclamation of Independence, read by David Ben-Gurion on 14 May 1948, Israeli political leaders made a causal connection between national destruction in Europe and sovereignty in Eretz Israel, emphasizing,

> the catastrophe which recently befell the Jewish people – the massacre of millions of Jews in Europe – was another clear demonstration of the urgency of solving the problem of its homelessness by re-establishing in Eretz-Israel the Jewish State, which would open the gates of the homeland wide to every Jew and confer upon the Jewish people the status of a fully privileged member of the comity of nations.[16]

Such self-representation as a place of refuge also reflected certain demographic realities in the new state. According to Hanna Yablonka, 70,000 survivors immigrated to Israel between 1945 and 1947, 280,000 between 1948 and 1951 and another 100,000 in the second half of the 1950s. By 1960, 25 per cent of the Israeli population was made up of Holocaust survivors.[17]

Even before the state was created, attempts to reconnect families torn apart by the war were a constant part of daily life in pre-state Israel. The newspaper *LeKarov vela-Rahok* (published by the search bureau for missing relatives) appeared from the end of June 1945 until September 1947. A total of 73 issues were published, listing the names of 260,000 survivors of the Holocaust. According to statistics kept by the bureau for missing relatives presented at the 22nd Zionist Congress (held in Basel, Switzerland in December 1946), the bureau had managed to connect 30,000 inhabitants of Palestine with up to 60,000 survivors still living in Europe.[18] Throughout the 1950s, the radio programme 'looking for lost relatives' was broadcast

FIGURE 2.1 *Search bureau for missing relatives, 1947 (public domain).*

twice daily, as households throughout Israel would go silent, listening for the names of missing relatives to be read on the radio.

Among the first pieces of legislation passed by the newly created state after the end of the war was *The Law of Return 5710 (1950)*.[19] While very practically granting the right of immigration to every Jew anywhere in the world to make *Aliyah* as a symbolic gesture in the aftermath of the Holocaust, the law indicated that no Jew need be a stateless refugee ever again, declaring 'every Jew has the right to come to this country as an oleh'. In response to the 'urgency of solving the problem of homelessness' noted in the Declaration of Independence, which prevented rescue for millions of Jews during the Holocaust, the Law of Return was a clear statement that for any Jew (later to be defined as anyone with a Jewish grandparent) the Jewish state would serve as a refuge. The law also retroactively granted citizenship to any Jews who had come as an *oleh* even before the state had been created: 'every Jew who has immigrated into this country before the coming into force of this Law, and every Jew who was born in this country, whether before or after the coming into force of this Law, shall be deemed to be a person who has come to this country as an oleh under this Law.'[20]

In the first decade of statehood the Israeli government passed several laws to cement and ritualize Holocaust discourse in Israel, laws which continued to reflect the state's polarized views on the Holocaust and its survivors. In August 1950, the Knesset passed the 'Nazi and Nazi Collaborators Punishment Law'. Israeli lawmakers created a specific legal category 'crimes against Jews' that complemented war crimes and crimes against humanity; the law was intended to prosecute Nazi war criminals (although it was clear that these would remain out of reach) and those Jews who allegedly had helped the Nazis in their genocide (Jewish council members, Jewish police, Kapos).[21] That Israeli lawmakers saw a pressing need for such a law tells us something about their misguided perception that a large number of survivors only got out because they had 'collaborated' not realizing that the Nazi regime had made its victims accomplices. On the basis of this law, Israeli courts tried some forty survivors for collaboration between 1950 and 1973 (most in the 1950s and early 1960s).

The second piece of legislation was the Holocaust Memorial Day Law, passed in several steps between 1951 and 1959. In April 1951, the Knesset passed a resolution to establish the national Holocaust Remembrance Day (*Yom HaShoah*) – literally *Yom Hazikaron la Shoah ve-Mered ha-geta'ot*, Holocaust and Ghetto Revolt Memorial Day – to be held on the 27th day of the Hebrew month of Nissan on the Jewish lunar calendar. Previous commemorative events had been on 10th of Tevet (a minor fast day commemorating the siege of Jerusalem by Nebuchadnezzar II of Babylonia which would ultimately lead to the destruction of the First Temple, usually in December/January) and the 14th of Nissan (the date of the outbreak of the Warsaw Ghetto Uprising on 19 April 1943, which coincided with the first night of Passover). The 27th of Nissan was one week after the end of Passover, but still corresponded to the timing of the Warsaw Ghetto Revolt, which lasted four weeks. By placing Yom HaShoah one week before Israel's National Memorial Day or Yom Ha-Zikaron (commemorating fallen soldiers) leading into Israel's Independence Day, the state had established a commemorative cycle on the calendar that enshrined a national narrative arc leading from destruction to war and finally, to national rebirth. It took until April 1955 to pass the Martyrs' and Fighters' Remembrance Day Law (*Yom Ha-shoah ve-hagevurah*), and only in April 1959 did the Knesset pass another law decreeing a specific ritual: a two-minute moment of silence with a siren at sundown and 10 am the next day, suspending all work and traffic; commemorative programmes at educational institutions and the radio; flags on government buildings flown at half-mast; and a central, government-sponsored memorial service at Yad Vashem.[22]

In April 1951, the Jewish National Fund also dedicated a 'Martyrs' Forest' in the mountains outside Jerusalem, and the Ministry of Religious Affairs created a genizah (a storage area for holy books) on Mount Zion for Torah scrolls desecrated by the Nazis.[23] Prime Minister David Ben-Gurion shared remarks at the dedication ceremony at the Martyrs' Forest, while Zivia Lubetkin spoke in person, noting the appropriate symbolism of locating the forest in the hills on the path to Jerusalem.[24] In her remarks at the dedication of the Martyrs' Forest, Zivia Lubetkin recalled that

> two things unified our brothers as they walked the final path, and this was in fact their epitaph: to take revenge and to remember, to remember not to forget … . And all of those who remain alive from the troubles of the Nazi period know and feel this. Bless the Jewish National Fund for establishing two monuments to the living and the silent: the Ghetto Fighters kibbutz in the north and here near Jerusalem – the Martyrs' Forest, a forest which will take root and remind all who pass of the horrors of the Holocaust and the destruction and the secret of bravery. On this day we will remember not only the horrors of the Shoah in the millions who were burned in the ovens and in the gas chambers, but we will also remember those who fought alone in battle. Without weapons, with no ground beneath their feet, no sky above their heads. Although they were not able to save the lives of millions, they were able to save their honour. And it is not coincidence, that this holy forest will be planted on the path to Jerusalem. Not only that the eyes of all those perished looked to Jerusalem, but also this generation that looked at the depths of destruction and was able to witness the establishment of Israel must remember that the path to independence leads along the path of the forest of the martyrs.

As Lubetkin explained, it was fitting that the destruction and the rebirth would be linked; all who journeyed to Jerusalem would remember that the path to independence passed through the depths of destruction. The statue of Mordecai Anielewicz was also dedicated on the site of the destroyed (and soon to be rebuilt) Kibbutz Yad Mordecai on 19 April 1951. Nathan Rapoport, who had moved to Israel not long after the dedication of the Ghetto Heroes Monument in Warsaw, was commissioned to create it. While the kibbutz had been named after Mordecai Anielewicz in 1943, after its destruction in 1948 the leaders of the kibbutz insisted they would rebuild the new kibbutz around the statue that Rapoport would build. Symbolically, then, Kibbutz Yad Mordecai would rise again as a testament to the strength of Anielewicz. Rapoport's monument, twelve feet high, modelled after Michelangelo's David, showed a figure armed with a single hand grenade instead of David's stone for his sling. Anielewicz's David turned to face the Nazi Goliath. At Yad Mordecai, however, his backdrop would not be the ruins of the Warsaw ghetto – instead, the ruins of the kibbutz water tower destroyed by Egyptian shelling would become the backdrop and foundation for the young fighter, now transformed into a muscular and determined kibbutznik.[25] Isaac Schwartzbart (of the WJC) titled his remarks prepared for the dedication of the statue, 'The Lasting Significance of the Warsaw Ghetto Uprising'.[26]

> On April 19, at the 'Yad Mordecai' Kibbutz of Hashomer Hatzair in Israel, there will be unveiled a monument to Mordecai Anielewicz, the commander of the Warsaw Ghetto Uprising in 1943. Kibbutz Yad Mordecai lies at the entrance to the Negev wilderness which is gradually being transformed into fertile land for the Jewish people. The settlement is situated not far from famous Negbah, very near to the Mediterranean, and not far from Gaza, the strip of Israel land held by Egypt. More than 50 chalutzim fell in the battle of Yad Mordecai during the Arab-Jewish hostilities in 1948. And now a monument is about to be unveiled there which is to perpetuate the memory of the uprising of the remnant of the Jews in the Warsaw Ghetto, where thousands of Jews, men and women, fell in the battle for the honor of the Jewish people and for the idea of freedom for all people as against the atrocious barbarism perpetrated by Nazi Germany in World War II. Will the uprising of the Warsaw Ghetto find an eternal monument in the history of the Jewish people and in the hearts of generations, present and, to some, throughout the centuries? Today we can only wish so.

Again, the defence of the ghetto would be connected symbolically with the defence of the state.

In August 1953 the Knesset decreed the building of the central Holocaust memorial Yad Vashem, the Martyrs' and Heroes' Remembrance Authority on the western slope of Mount Herzl outside of Jerusalem through passing the Yad Vashem Law. The idea of a centralized memorial had been developed by Mordechai Shenhavi as early as 1942 but had not been a priority of the Yishuv leadership during the war. In the early years of the state, however, as competing institutions such as the 'Chamber of the Holocaust' memorial on Mount Zion (established in December 1949 by the Ministry of Religion) and European Jewish memorial projects emerged, the idea for a national Holocaust memorial was taken on by lawmakers in a struggle over hegemony over memory and research in the framework of a state-sponsored centralized (secular) memorial and research institution.[27] [The term 'Yad Vashem,' literally a memorial and a name, was taken from the book of Isaiah 56:5 'To them I will give within my temple and its walls a memorial and a name better than sons and daughters; I will give them an everlasting name that will endure forever'.]

The Yad Vashem law, signed by Moshe Sharett, Ben-Zion Dinur and Yitzhak Ben-Zvi, stated this clearly, fulfilling Shenhavi's vision of a memorial authority in the Land of Israel that would commemorate 'the heroic stand of the besieged and fighters of the ghettoes, who rose and kindled the flame of revolt to save the honour of their people'.[28] As Ben-Zion Dinur had argued

FIGURE 2.2 *The monument to Mordecai Anielewicz at Kibbutz Yad Mordecai.*

before the Knesset, Yad Vashem could play a central role in shaping the collective memory of the nation; as he expressed it: 'The I of the nation only exists to the extent that it possesses a memory'. The Labor Zionist publication *Davar* based its support for Yad Vashem on the fear that the 'ghetto fighters struggle could be distorted by the rewriters of history in Poland and their fellow travelers in the country ... who combine even the memory of sublime national heroism with their absurd, sycophantic refrain about the battle cry of the faithful of the revolution'.[29] Nonetheless, in the early years of Yad Vashem, a struggle unfolded over how to write the history of 'most recent destruction' between the professional historians like Dinur, and the survivor historians, like Rachel Auerbach, Nachman Blumenthal and Josef Kermisz who argued for the need to incorporate eyewitness testimony, but were dismissed as 'too close to the material' to write such history in an objective, academic matter.[30] While Yad Vashem acquisitioned documentation collected by historical commissions abroad it only employed a few survivors and those who worked in its library, archives and testimony department had to fight for recognition. Dinur prioritized working with graduates of the Hebrew University and claimed that survivors lacked scholarly expertise; the survivors found that Dinur and his disciples were lacking any knowledge and experience in researching the Holocaust. In 1959 Dinur stepped down as the survivors in his employ won the battle over public opinion. This struggle would climax around the time of the Eichmann trial, when Auerbach's push to include survivor testimony in the understanding of this history would be incorporated in the Trial.

In the early years of the state, perhaps no event reflected the encounter between the top-down pragmatic approach to mastering the past and the bottom-up emotional reaction to German crimes than the intense debate over reparations from Germany. Israeli negotiations with Germany also reflected an early example of the actual politicization of Holocaust memory: how could political leaders wrestle with the meaning of the Holocaust in both political and economic terms? In the aftermath of the 1948–9 war and the absorption of hundreds of thousands of immigrants from Europe, the Middle East and North Africa, Israel was on its knees economically. In those circumstances, David Ben-Gurion turned to West Germany to try to secure money to help the absorption process. Just the idea of entering into negotiations with the West German government aroused intense and passionate, indeed violent, confrontations in Israeli society. In the aftermath of the Second World War, Israelis continued to maintain a visceral revulsion to expressions of German culture through a rejection of symbols like the operas of the antisemitic composer Richard Wagner and Israeli passports which expressly forbade travel to Germany.

Michael Amir, the Israeli consul in Brussels, Belgium, expressed the government's pragmatic, rational approach to negotiations in November 1950, arguing that the continued boycott of Germany meant that this Israeli government, while staking out a fine moral position, would be missing out on the limited window to demand compensation from West Germany before the country had been fully rehabilitated and accepted back into the family of nations:

> Do not say that I am trading in blood and that I am haggling over the cruel crimes of which humanity has never seen the like ... I do not make light of reparations from one nation to another, from one state to another. *At the stage of historical decisiveness at which we now stand, that may be able to aid, to a great extent, the building of our land.*
>
> There is a great struggle within me as I write these lines. I see before me at this very moment the tragic marches to the gas chambers and I ask myself, of course, if I am not alienating myself from those millions of victims. Yet I always come back to the opinion, expressed by [Ernest] Renan: 'Whoever wishes to make history is obligated to forget history'. I do not forget, but we, in the State of Israel, are obligated to take a realistic political line ... *I will admit without shame that it grates on my deepest emotions, but policy is not a matter of emotion.* (emphasis added)[31]

In March 1951, the Israeli government made a claim to the four powers occupying post-war Germany for compensation and reimbursement, based on the fact that Israel had absorbed and resettled 500,000 Holocaust survivors. They calculated that since absorption had cost $3,000 per person, they were owed 1.5 billion dollars by Germany. While arguing that the

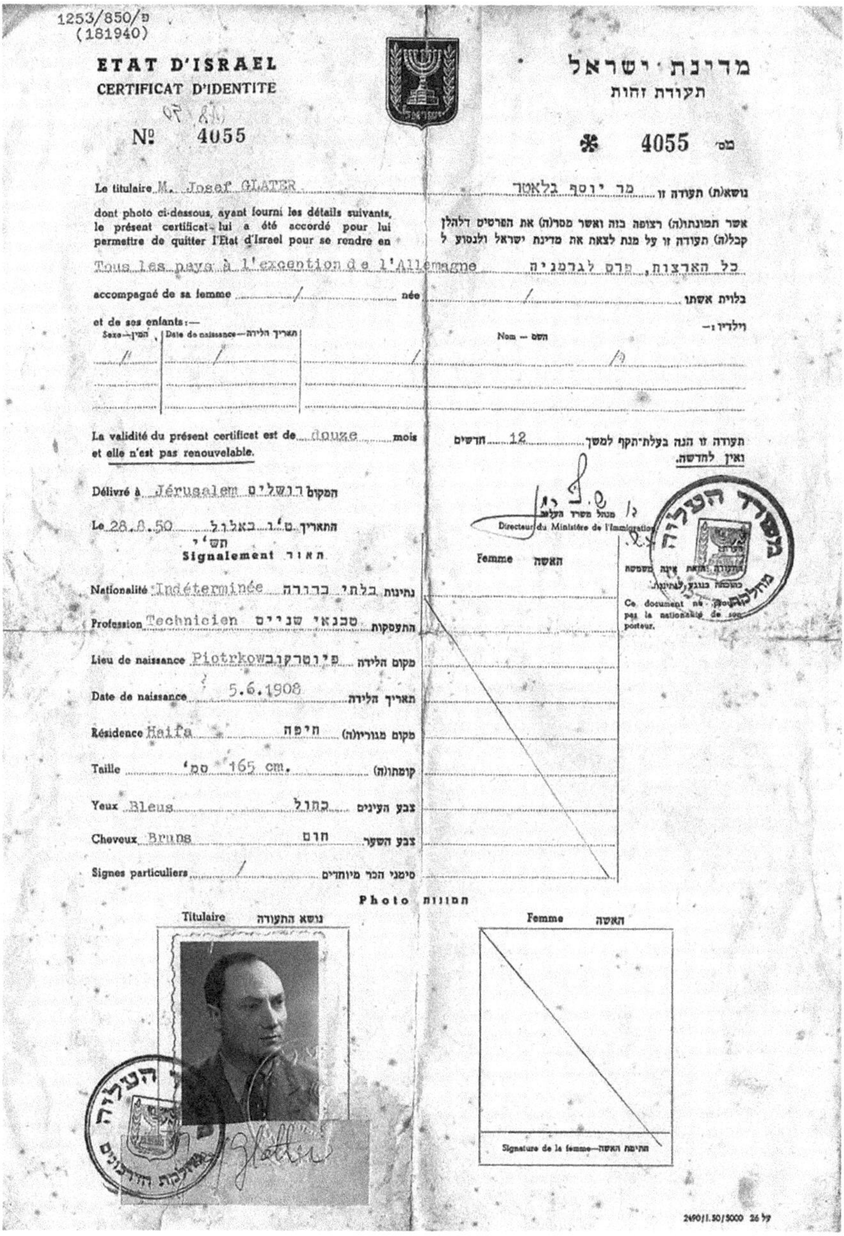

1253/850/פ
(181940)

ETAT D'ISRAEL
CERTIFICAT D'IDENTITE

N° 4055

מדינת ישראל
תעודת זהות

מס' 4055

Le titulaire M. Josef GLATER

נושא(ת) תעודה זו מר יוסף גלאטר

dont photo ci-dessous, ayant fourni les détails suivants, le présent certificat lui a été accordé pour lui permettre de quitter l'Etat d'Israel pour se rendre en

אשר תמונתו(ה) רצופה בזה ואשר מסר(ה) את הפרטים דלהלן קבל(ה) תעודה זו על מנת לצאת את מדינת ישראל ולנסוע ל

Tous les pays à l'exception de l'Allemagne

כל הארצות, פרט לגרמניה

accompagné de sa femme / née

בלוית אשתו /

et de ses enfants:—

וילדיו:—

Sexe—המין	Date de naissance—תאריך הלידה	Nom — השם
/	/	/

La validité du présent certificat est de douze mois et elle n'est pas renouvelable.

תעודה זו הנה בעלת־תקף למשך 12 חודשים ואין לחדשה.

Délivré à Jérusalem ירושלים המקום

Le 28.8.50 התאריך ט"ו באלול תש"י

Directeur du Ministère de l'Immigration

מנהל משרד העליה

Signalement תאור

Nationalité Indéterminée בלתי ברורה נתינות

Profession Technicien טכנאי שניים התעסקות

Lieu de naissance Piotrkow פיוטרקוב מקום הלידה

Date de naissance 5.6.1908 תאריך הלידה

Résidence Haifa חיפה מקום מגוריו(ה)

Taille 165 cm. ס"מ קומתו(ה)

Yeux Bleus כחול צבע העינים

Cheveux Bruns חום צבע השער

Signes particuliers / סימני הכר מיוחדים

Femme האשה

Ce document ne prouve pas la nationalité de son porteur.

Photo תמונות

Titulaire נושא התעודה

Femme האשה

Signature de la femme—חתימת האשה

2490/1.50/5000 26 קל

FIGURE 2.3 *1950 Israel travel identity document issued to those lacking an official passport granting the holder admission to any country in the world, except Germany.*

Germans could never atone for what they did with any type of material recompense and refusing to negotiate over the value of human lives lost, they argued that restitution was owed just based on the fact Germany had plundered at least $6 billion worth of Jewish property.

In a speech to the Bundestag in September 1951, West German Chancellor Konrad Adenauer, a devout Catholic who had been mayor of Cologne before the war and was himself a target of the Nazis during the war, admitted Germany's guilt and wanted to take this chance to atone for it. In addition, Adenauer understood that paying reparations would help accelerate West Germany's return to the family of nations and facilitate acceptance by the Western powers. In his 27 September 1951 speech, Adenuaer recognized that 'unspeakable crimes [against Jews] have been committed in the name of the German people' during the time of the Third Reich and the Holocaust and offered to negotiate with Israel and representatives of world Jewry over compensation.[32]

Within Israel, the reparations issue provoked heated debate. Many survivors strenuously opposed accepting any money from Germany, claiming that nothing could ever even begin to atone for the suffering imposed on them by the Nazis. David Ben-Gurion and his government argued that the reparations were essential to absorb the hundreds of thousands of survivors who had been displaced by the war, their assets and property stripped as a result of German aggression; furthermore, the Israeli treasury was almost completely bankrupt in the aftermath of the war.

Nonetheless, Mordecai Nurock (a Member of Parliament from the Religious Zionist party Mizrachi, who had lost his wife and both of his children in the Holocaust) expressed a widely held belief that not only was any money from Germany stained with Jewish blood, but there was no guarantee that the Germans would abide by any negotiated agreement.

> Any direct contact is a desecration of the memory of the martyrs and the heroes of the ghettos and a severe blow to the moral dignity of the Jewish people. We will not receive money at all, but we will become a distributor of German goods from which Jewish blood is still dripping. And soon a neo-Nazi government will be formed that will abrogate all the agreements – just as the accursed 'Fuehrer' did with regard to the great powers after we give our agreement to the recovery and cleansing of that unclean country now advancing the hypocritical slogan, 'Peace with Israel', in order to serve its own interests. From the moral aspect this is a national calamity, a great spiritual-moral catastrophe for the Jewish people, one never before witnessed. The murderers destroyed one third of the nation's body, they plundered everything from us, but not our honor, and now, with our own hands, we are offering them the honor and the soul of the Jewish people. We cannot force those who hate us to love us, but we can force them to act respectfully towards us.[33]

Critics of negotiations with West Germany argued that any money received from the Germans was 'blood money' intended as an expiation for their crimes. At any rate, such was the accusation hurled at the government by the opposition parties led by Menachem Begin's Herut party when the proposed *Shilumim* or Reparations agreement came to the Knesset in 1952. The 7 January 1952 issue of *Herut* called on Israelis to 'Remember What Amalek Has Done Unto You', labelled the negotiators as traitors, and included artwork and photographs of murdered Jews who reminded readers that there could be no reparations for those already murdered. Calling on its readers to remembers those murdered in the death camps for eternity, the newspaper announced a massive demonstration in Zion Square, Jerusalem, scheduled for the same day, featuring Menachem Begin and Prof. Josef Klausner to protest the reparations from Amalek and any contact with the hated Germans.[34]

Begin engineered riots and attacks on the Knesset in which a hundred policemen were injured. The *Jerusalem Post* described the chaotic scene outside the Knesset on 8 January 1952, as they debated the proposed agreement, as

> an atmosphere of violence unprecedented in Israel parliamentary life. The shouting of a mob not far off, the intermittent wail of police cars and

FIGURE 2.4 *Menachem Begin leading the demonstration at Zion Square, Jerusalem, January 1952. The banner reads, in part, 'Our Honour will not be sold for money...wipe away the shame'.*

Source: Screengrab from YouTube.

ambulance sirens, sporadic explosions of gas grenades and the glow of flames from a burning car came through the windows of the Knesset building, and later the window panes were splintered by rocks, and fumes of tear-gas bombs from the battle-scarred street outside permeated the chamber. One member was hit in the head by a stone.[35]

Begin threatened that this would be his last appearance in the Knesset and made what most listeners thought was a threat to go underground if an attempt was made to negotiate with Germany: 'Some things are dearer than life. Some things are worse than death. We are willing to leave our families and die … . People went to the barricades for lesser things … I know that we will be dragged to concentration camps … . We will die together'. Nevertheless, despite protests and demonstrations organized by Begin's Herut party, the government entered into negotiations with Chancellor Adenauer and the West German government, which in the context of the Cold War was eager to re-enter the family of allied nations.

After the near riot described above, the Israeli parliament (by one vote) approved negotiations with Germany; Israel started with a demand of 1.5 billion dollars, including an additional .5 billion dollars demanded by the newly formed Conference on Jewish Material Claims Against Germany, to represent 'World Jewry'. Negotiations began at the end of March 1952 at an undisclosed location in Holland but did not go smoothly. Israeli representatives, many of whom spoke German fluently, refused on principle to speak German; negotiations were conducted in English. Six months later, however, on 10 September 1952, the negotiating representatives signed the agreement in Luxembourg: Moshe Sharett, as the Israeli foreign minister, Nahum Goldmann, representing the Claims Conference, and Konrad Adenauer, as foreign minister and chancellor of the Federal Republic. According to the agreement, West Germany committed to supply the state of Israel with goods and services valuing 3 billion marks over a period of 12 years. Part of the agreement was the German assurance to enable personal reparations too, paid directly to survivors and their families, as well as the return of property to its legal owners.[36] Against the fierce protest of large segments of the population, the Israeli government made the pragmatic decision that the Jewish people were better served by building the infrastructure of its state than letting the past stand in its way. As intense as the opposition to negotiating with Germany had been, the infusion of money and natural resources was critical for the nascent Israeli economy and the opponents of reparations moved on to other issues more internally focused on Jewish behaviour during the war.

As much as the Israeli government sought to control the parameters of public debate and commemoration, indeed even the writing of the history of the Shoah, this top-down, state-sanctioned process of engaging with the past came into direct conflict with a bottom-up, organic process of remembering developed by the survivors themselves.

Survivor organizations and hometown societies, *landsmanshaftn*, created alternative memorial ceremonies that commemorated the destruction of their communities. In 1961 the Association of Immigrants from Poland in Israel described itself as an umbrella organization for 104 hometown *landsmanshaftn*, of which one-half to two-thirds had been founded after Israel gained independence.[37] They also engaged in the writing and editing of memorial books, *Yizkor* books. Israel became the most prolific centre of publication of hundreds of such books in Yiddish and Hebrew. According to Rosemary Horowitz and Michlean Amir, 75 per cent of all *Yizkor* books were published in Israel and 62 per cent in Hebrew.[38] In the Yiddish press, too, as Gali Drucker Bar-Am has shown, the publication of specific sections dedicated to memorializing destroyed Jewish communities, as, for example, in the Yiddish newspaper *Letste Nayes*, created 'a sense of community cohesion and shared fate among readers'.[39] Moreover, survivors played a fundamental role in turning Tel Aviv into a vibrant Yiddish literary centre, among other things through publishing reflections on the Holocaust in literary periodicals such as *Di goldene keyt* edited by the poet and partisan from the Vilna ghetto, Avrom Sutzkever. As noted in Drucker-Bar Am's research on the memorial practices of Yiddish-speaking Holocaust survivors in Israel in the 1950s, the approximately 500,000 survivors who reached Israel in its first decade of existence (approximately 70 per cent of all new immigrants to the country at the time) developed unique modes of Holocaust remembrance (in Yiddish) which did not conflict with their attempts to acculturate into their new Hebrew-speaking homeland.[40]

Even so, this sometimes created friction between them and the host institutions, which considered the Yiddish language a vestige of the diaspora (*galut*), 'the Jewish exile that the immigrants should "forget" while acquiring the new national identity'. Nonetheless, as Drucker Bar-Am convincingly demonstrates in the 1950s, 'the remembrance patterns of *olei sheyres-hapleyte*, in contrast, grew from the grassroots and thrived within the unique subculture of Yiddish speakers'. This grassroots survivor-driven memorial culture typified by commemorations in the Yiddish Press, formation of *landmannschaftn*, publishing of Yizkor books and dedication of memorials contrasted with the state-sponsored commemorations, which continued to privilege the ghetto fighters and partisan heroes, while 'among the survivors a broader grasp of heroism, including manifestations of culture and humanity in wartime, is evident. The survivors also took a broader view of the loss, one that sanctified not only the people murdered but also their culture, which had been murdered as well, and of course Yiddish, the language of the victims and the survivors.'[41] Special sections of the Yiddish newspaper *Letste Nayes* called '*Yizker iber shtet un shtetlekh*' (Memorials for Cities and Towns), or '*Di fartilikte yidishe kehiles*' (The Destroyed Jewish Communities) and later renamed '*Tsum ondenk fun fartilikte yidishe kehiles*'(In Memory of the Destroyed Jewish Communities) helped create 'a sense of community cohesion and shared fate among readers'.[42] This sense

of a common community of suffering among survivors found expression in
the pages of the Yiddish press, along with alternative memorial sites that
differed from those established by state institutions. For example, the Holon
cemetery, south of Tel Aviv, would come to be the home of an elaborate array
of nearly 800 memorial gravestones erected for destroyed communities in
Europe (created by survivors and descendants of that community).

In using the Yiddish language to craft alternative commemoration
practices and carve out a literary memorial space, however, the work of the
renowned Yiddish poet Avrom Sutzkever was second to none.[43] Sutzkever,
who was already a well-known young Yiddish poet before the war, had been
a member of the 'Paper Brigade' in the Vilna Ghetto during the war that
worked to rescue the treasures of Jewish civilization from certain destruction
in the Jerusalem of Lithuania.[44] Sutzkever continued to write Yiddish poems
during the war, poems that reflected on the loss of his mother and child,
as well as his hope for Jewish resistance and the search for an absent God.
After escaping from the ghetto to join the partisans in the forests, the famous
poet was airlifted to Moscow and was one of the only Jewish witnesses
to testify at the Nuremberg trials after the war, recounting in detail the
extermination of Vilna Jewry and several of the acts of murder that he had
personally witnessed and the humiliation that he himself had undergone.
In 1947 Sutzkever came to Palestine.[45] In his first book of poetry in Israel,
In fayer-vogn (In the Chariot of Fire), Sutzkever wrote a separate section of
poetry dedicated to the Holocaust called '*Di karsh fun dermonung*' ('The
Cherry of Remembrance'). In his poetry, Suztkever reflected on the challenge
of no longer using words to portray what he saw before him; now his words
would be refracted through the prism of memory. While during the war he
may have written a 'with a piece of coal, a poem on the paper corpse of
my neighbor', in the aftermath of the war, 'there is not even a corpse', only
'disgraced whiteness, draped with soot'.[46]

In the early 1950s Sutzkever wrote a series of prose poems called *griner
akvarium* (Green Aquarium), again reflecting on the notion that like the
glass through which one has to look to see inside an aquarium, so too would
the poet have to be the lens through which the reader would witness the
memories of the recent past. As explained by scholar Avraham Novershtern,
such a process, however, was not without its dangers as Sutzkever noted: 'walk
through words as through a minefield: one false step, one false move, and all
the words you strung in a lifetime on your veins will be blown apart with
you'.[47] The poet captured the dilemma of remembrance in a new land in
verse: how to remember the destruction of a civilization, of communities, of
loved ones in a ruptured word, separated not only by physical distance, but
by language and time?

Despite such challenges, survivors also played a key role in shaping
commemoration practices in Israel through the establishment of museums
and other public education spaces. Yad Vashem was not the first Holocaust
memorial museum to be established in Israel; the Ghetto Fighters House

FIGURE 2.5 *Memorials to the Jewish communities of Lodz (top) and Wlodawa/ Sobibor erected in the Holon cemetery by Landsmannschaftn in the 1950s.*

Source: Photos by author.

had been established on 19 April 1949 (the sixth anniversary of the Warsaw Ghetto Uprising) near Acre at Kibbutz Lochamei Ha-Getaot by surviving Warsaw ghetto fighters Yitzhak Zuckerman, Zivia Lubetkin and other members of the Jewish underground who had been granted permission to form a kibbutz populated entirely by survivors (a very rare exception at the time). Although the actual cornerstone for the first blocks of living quarters for the new kibbutz was laid on 10 February 1949, the Kibbutz HaMeuchad movement decided that the actual settlement ceremony should take place on the sixth anniversary of the Warsaw Ghetto Uprising, next to photos from the Holocaust and the uprising. The manuscript from Yitzhak Katznelson's 'Song of Lament' and pages from the diaries of the ghetto fighters were included in a special exhibition, in addition to photos. *Davar* announced the establishment of the kibbutz – 'The Ghetto Fighters Settle in the Galilee on the Anniversary of the Warsaw Revolt' (*Davar*, 19 April 1949) – where, strung between 'two cypress trees, hung a banner: 'the desperate heroism of Israel has not yet ceased.' The crowd of thousands, which included leaders of the revolt, partisans, leaders of the workers movement, staff from the Polish consulate and representatives of Polish Jewry, as well as large numbers of residents from surrounding kibbutzim and many soldiers, heard speeches from prominent Yishuv leaders and former ghetto fighters and watched musical performances concluding with the singing of the 'Partisans Song', before the playing of 'Hatikvah' on the flute.[48] The commemoration ceremony was also a dedication, which captured the transition from remembering the past to building for the future. Both symbolically and physically, the ghetto fighters seemed to proclaim, those who struggled to create the state and establish new homes there continued the struggle commenced by the fighters in the Warsaw ghetto. One year later, on 19 April 1950, the cornerstone was laid for the permanent building of the Ghetto Fighters House Museum, which would be funded by Kibbutz HaMeuchad (meaning that the museum would focus primarily on the activity of the Dror movement, much to the chagrin of members of Hashomer Hatzair and other movements).[49]

While Lochamei Ha-Geta'ot celebrated heroic Jewish resistance, the Holocaust Cellar on Mount Zion constituted a sacred memorial site, located as close to the holiest site in Judaism as possible in 1949 (the Old City and the Western Wall remained under Jordanian rule from 1949 to 1967). General director of the Religious Affairs ministry, Shmuel Zangwill Cahana, supported the site as an alternative cemetery for victims of the Shoah who were not buried and the goal was to create in the cellar tablets in memory of every city whose residents were massacred. Reflecting a bottom-up approach to grassroots commemorative practices, the survivors who reached the cellar began to bring artefacts that survived the destruction with them, and in addition jars with ashes from the camps were brought, along with destroyed Torah scrolls covered in blood. In this way the site also turned into a museum that honoured spiritual resistance and the struggle of Jews and Judaism as a religion to endure, despite all forms of Nazi persecution. From the beginning the site possessed a religious character, which focused on the destruction of the communities, the recording of names of those killed, recitation of the Shma and reading of *mishnayot* and prayers. The goal was to demonstrate that Jews continued to keep the mitzvot even in the camps and that their Jewish national spirit was not broken during the suffering of the Shoah.

The Chamber of the Holocaust does not mention the Zionist movement or the state; instead the line that connects the past and the present for the Jewish people is the Torah. Until today, the chamber is still administered by a Haredi group, the Diaspora Yeshiva. It includes 10 different rooms, 2,000 plaques, filled with a heavy, damp air – almost a 'holy' air. The museum tries to provide a proper burial for the ashes and the Torah scrolls, including a Torah scroll from Wengrow covered in the blood of Jewish martyrs: 'their holy blood was spilled *al kidush hashem*.' On display are bars of soap mistakenly labelled as Jewish fat (Yad Vashem has insisted the chamber correct this error but they refuse to do so). Other artefacts that attest to 'spiritual resistance' included miniature tefillin secretly used in camps, a narrow shofar smuggled and used in camps and a 'coat of revenge' made of parchment from a Torah scroll. Rabbis featured including Elhanan Bunem Wasserman and Kalonymus Kalman Shapira – again emphasizing the cellar as a space to solemnly commemorate those who died to sanctify God's name, demonstrating the eternal strength of the Jewish people and the Jewish religion. Above the entrance to the cellar is a quote from Ovadiah: 'there will be a sanctuary for survivors and it will be holy.'

According to historian Doron Bar, in the first decade of the state, the cellar's very traditional commemorative activities differed completely from those carried out in other memorial sites, specifically in Yad Vashem, where the more nationalistic and secular aspect of memory were the main focus. 'The contrast between these two institutions ... reveals an inner struggle in Israeli society during the 1950s regarding the memory of the Holocaust ... one of the central issues between Israeli National Religious Party-leaning public and the religious Zionists ... and other Israeli political groups.'[50] According to Bar the different ways of commemoration also allude to different world views:

> While the Holocaust Cellar drew its claim to authenticity from the east, namely from the Temple Mount, the Old City of Jerusalem, and David's Tomb, Yad Vashem based its authority mainly on the west: the 'Zionist' part of Jerusalem and the 'sacred' Zionist-national space that evolved during the same period in western Jerusalem and included Herzl's Tomb, the Military Cemetery, and Yad Vashem.[51]

Likewise, Bar argues, this difference was also clear in the different architectural designs of both memorials, represented in what would be the modern and monumental Yad Vashem in opposition to the ancient building and caves of the Cellar on Mount Zion. Yad Vashem, which focused on individual Jewish experiences in the Shoah, while pointing to the creation of the Jewish state as the only response to the destruction of the Jewish diaspora became a monumental site that came to espouse the political and pedagogical values of the state. The Holocaust Cellar, in contrast, had a local character, which made it popular among the more traditional Holocaust survivors and was the reason why the site became so successful, in its own way, in the 1950s. Nonetheless, over the course of the 1950s, as Yad Vashem began to receive increased budgetary support and greater international recognition, its viewpoint, which emphasized the heroic values of Jewish resistance as an affirmation of the Zionist world view, came to predominate.

In addition to the efforts of Sutzkever and the publishers of the Yiddish press which served as a forum for early reflections on the Holocaust, survivors also wrote fictional accounts of the Holocaust, most notably the novels and novellas that appeared under the nom de plume *Ka-Tsetnik* 135633. Born in Poland as Yehiel Feiner, upon arrival in Israel, the writer Hebraicized his name to Yehiel De-Nur but remained anonymous, taking on the pen name *Ka-Tsetnik*, or concentration camp inmate, in Yiddish. The Auschwitz survivor was the author of *Salamandra* (1946) and *House of Dolls* (1955, known for its graphic description of the sexual enslavement of Jewish women in the Nazi camp system) and *Pipel* (1961, about the sexual abuse of a Jewish boy). Katsetnik's writings inspired a strange genre of

FIGURE 2.6 *Chamber of the Holocaust, urns containing ashes from victims of the Holocaust, and memorial plaques to destroyed Jewish communities (below).*

Source: Photos by author.

pornographic pocketbooks called *Stalag*, which especially attracted younger Israelis and was technically the only pornography available in Israel in the early 1960s. As Elie Wiesel described his work,

> Katsetnik is no ordinary writer, and many of his books are not ordinary novels. Katsetnik's words encompass the ruins of past worlds. His images are figures in shattered mirrors. What he has to say about people no one has as yet said and no one will say. He was a witness in the highest sense of the word, a witness who took with him a bit of the flames from the Holocaust ... . His heroes were purified in fire, before they appeared before the reader who feared suddenly to stare them in the face. If they ever met, they would never depart.[52]

Ka-Tsetnik (whose true identity would not be revealed until he testified at the Eichmann trial) wrote his first book, *Salamandra*, over the course of two weeks as he recovered in a British hospital after liberation; it was published in 1946. Just as the salamander is legendary as a creature that can live through fire, so too did Ka-Tsetnik see himself as a salamander who had survived the worst fires imaginable, living to depict his experiences for the world. As noted by Omer Bartov, Yechiel Feiner changed his name to Di-nur, or 'of fire' in Aramaic when he arrived in Palestine.[53] *Salamandra*, which would become the first volume of six connected books published between the 1940s and 1980s, tells the story of Harry Preleshnik, along with his fiancée and future wife Sonia Schmidt, and some members of his family. *Salamandra* (based very much on the experiences of Yehiel Feiner) begins just before the war and ends with Harry's final escape from the Germans at the very last phases of the war. It is worth noting that at a time when the Israeli public had limited historical knowledge, books like *Salamandra* and *House of Dolls* became the primary sources for the reading public to gain an understanding of the Holocaust, making Ka-tsetnik's depictions rather significant at the time. In *Salamandra*, Ka-tsetnik included scenes of Jews betraying one another to survive (including a man turning over his sister-in-law and baby to the SS) and a group of Jews strangling a baby to avoid capture by the Gestapo. The members of the Judenrat are depicted in a very negative manner, eager to take advantage of their power over their fellow Jews. Such negative depictions of Jewish behaviour during the Shoah served as an important counterpoint to the glorification of Jewish heroism in the Warsaw Ghetto Uprising (also depicted in *Salamandra*), especially at a time when the young Jewish state wanted to hold up the heroism of the ghetto fighters as the paragon of Jewish action during the Holocaust.

Ka-tsetnik's second book, *House of Dolls* (1953), was far more successful than *Salamandra* and was eventually translated into a dozen languages. In the novel the protagonist's sister, Daniella, becomes a prostitute in a women's labour camp where she is forced to join the camp brothel and serve as a 'military whore' to the SS. Daniella has the words *feld-hure* tattooed between her breasts and along with the other women suffers under the cruel torture of Elsa who strips them naked and whips them. As noted by literary scholar David Mikics,

> For Israeli kids in the '50s and '60s – a rather puritanical era, devoted to the responsible building of a new society – this was exciting, illicit stuff. Often enough, they learned about sex from a novel about a Nazi death camp. Ka-Tzetnik's *House of Dolls* influenced the Stalag series of schlocky, sex-and-violence pulp novels featuring Nazis and Jews, popular among Israeli teenagers in the postwar era; eventually, it became recommended reading in Israeli high schools.[54]

Such depictions, written by a survivor himself, must be contrasted with Israeli literature of the time period, which, if mentioning the Shoah at all, tended to co-opt survivor experiences from the Holocaust to make them uniquely Israeli ones.[55] This made literature created by survivors especially significant because, as Yael Feldman suggests, the Israeli effort to 'assimilate the experience of the Shoah to its overall Zionist perspective' resulted in the appropriation of the Shoah for Zionist ideological purposes, turning the Shoah into the 'Sabra's story', rather than that of the survivor.[56] In this sense, the narrative of the Holocaust, as in stories such as Moshe Shamir's *He Walked Through the Fields* and the love story between the sabra, Uri and the Tehran Child, Mika, continued to be told through the eyes of the Israeli, reflecting the uniqueness of the Sabra experience at the expense of the survivor's voice (and, as Feldman emphasizes, written largely through the pen of the Israeli, by writers who never experienced the Holocaust first-hand). As the focus of Israeli literature and drama addressed the central tension implicit in the encounter between Sabra and survivor, it failed to address the survivor as subject, instead using the survivor as a mirror to reflect perceptions of Israeli society.[57] The Sabra, as the hero, remained the subject, while the survivor continued to fulfil the role of other, necessary as the Israeli's foil.[58] The encounter with the survivor, as a symbol of the Holocaust, could thus serve to doubly confirm the existence of Israel and the Israeli identity, first through a negation of the survivor's pre-Israeli existence and status as subject and second through a concomitant justification of the necessity for a Jewish state. Actually reading and listening to the stories told by survivors would challenge the 'sabra-centric' construction of the national narrative.

The legal realm provided a public space in which the state-sponsored official modes of addressing the Holocaust and its grassroots level counterpart converged. In August 1950, the Knesset passed the 'Nazi and Nazi Collaborators Punishment Law'. Israeli lawmakers created a specific legal category 'crimes against Jews' that complemented war crimes and crimes against humanity; the law was intended to prosecute Nazi war criminals (although it was clear that these would remain out of reach) and those Jews who allegedly had helped the Nazis in their genocide (Jewish council members, Jewish police, Kapos). As Israel's first minister of justice, Pinchas Rosen put it when presenting the legislation to the Knesset:

> We may assume that Nazi criminals ... will not venture to Israel, but the law also applies to those who implemented the Nazis' will, and unfortunately some of them may be in our midst ... Hopefully the proposed law will contribute to cleansing the air among the survivors who have immigrated to Eretz Israel. Anyone familiar with their problems understands the painful question of suspicion and mutual recrimination that still torment the survivors of the camps and ghettos ... The law is designed to punish the criminals, vindicate the innocent, and let our camp be purged.[59]

On the basis of this law, Israeli courts tried forty survivors for collaboration between 1950 and 1973 (most in the 1950s and early 1960s).[60]

Although it was not based on the Nazi and Nazi Collaborators Punishment Law, the so-called Kasztner Affair in 1954 was also an expression of the deep controversy over collaboration. In 1952, Malkiel Gruenwald published a leaflet charging that through his negotiations with Adolf Eichmann and Kurt Becher of the SS, in which they proposed exchanging people for military hardware and trucks, referred to as 'Blood for Goods', Rudolf (Reszo) Kasztner had not only participated in the destruction of Hungarian Jewry, but had personally benefited from his negotiations with the SS while failing to warn Hungarian Jews of the impending deportations. Gruenwald, a member of the religious-Zionist Mizrahi party and a Hungarian refugee who had lost most of his family in Hungary, not only sought to expose what he saw as Kasztner's crimes, but also hoped to denounce the governing Socialist Zionist Mapai party and force the government to appoint a commission that would investigate the events that led to the destruction of Hungarian Jewry. Kastzner subsequently sued Gruenwald for libel and, owing to his position as a government official (he was spokesman for the Ministry of Trade), was represented at trial by Haim Cohen, Israel's attorney general. Gruenwald's defence attorney, Shmuel Tamir, succeeded in turning what was supposed to be a libel trial against his client into an indictment of Kasztner and the Mapai party. Four key charges against Kasztner were outlined in Gruenwald's pamphlet: '1. Collaboration with the Nazis; 2. "Paving the way for the murder" of Hungarian Jewry; 3. Partnership with a Nazi war criminal [Kurt Becher] in acts of thievery; and 4. Saving a war criminal from punishment after the war [Kurt Becher]'.[61]

Beyond raising questions about whether Kasztner should have warned Hungarian Jews about impending deportations, the affair also triggered intense public debate about the role of the Jewish councils in not doing enough to challenge Nazi edicts, while preventing the Jewish underground from organizing resistance. Even though Kasztner himself had not been a member of the Judenrat, the debate over his choices during the war became a forum for broader questioning of the Jewish councils.[62] On the eleventh anniversary of the Warsaw Ghetto revolt (in the context of the Kasztner Affair), the Hebrew poet Natan Alterman was among the first to raise the question of whether the heads of the Jewish councils throughout Eastern Europe had in fact been justified in their efforts to *prevent* resistance. Perhaps the burden of the heretofore glorified ghetto fighters needed to account for the fact that the entire ghetto was destroyed as a result of their actions. What responsibility did the fighters bear for the ultimate fate of the ghetto?[63] And what was the relationship between the fighters who died for the Jewish nation and the rest of those who died? Alterman's poem, published in *Davar* on the same day the newspaper covered the ceremony at the Martyrs' Forest announcing the beginning of work at Yad Vashem, sparked a debate over the actions of the ghetto fighters and the centrality of the Warsaw Ghetto Revolt in Israeli memory of the Shoah.

Memorial Day – and the Rebels

And on Memorial Day the fighters and rebels said:
Don't set us on a bright pedestal to differentiate us
From the Diaspora. In remembrance we step down
To blend again in the dark with the House of Israel.
Said the fighters and rebels: This day is a true symbol,
Not a glorious barricade lost in flames, nor the image
Of a boy and girl thrusting to break through or die,
In the manner of pictures of ever-burning rebellion.
This is not history's quarry. Don't hoist battle flags here
As if they are the fulfillment, the honour, and the justice.
Said the fighters and the rebels: We are part of the nation,
Of its honour, heroism, and profoundly yearning weeping.

As the poem goes on, Alterman's nameless fighters and rebels give voice to questions raised by 'Jewish fathers [read Jewish elders, or the *Judenrate*, in the ghetto] who said the underground will bring destruction (Shoah) on all of us'. Those fighters who supposedly fought for the 'honour of the nation' suddenly raise a troubling suggestion in Alterman's poem: 'I fought and carried the banner of the miracle of the revolt … [but] the revolt is only one note in the tale, and was not a crossroads or the ultimate goal, and for its honor this nation will still yet compete with every other nation.' Had the fighters joined the fight as individuals and not as representatives of the nation? Was the revolt in fact the historical turning point it had been made out to be? Alterman challenged the heroic interpretation of the fighters' actions to save the 'honor of the nation', suggesting that both those Jewish elders and the Jewish boys and girls who walked to their final destination 'leaving only one white sock in the archive as a stone of memory' deserved a share of the heroism and honour of the Jewish nation.

Despite the controversy raised by this poem, the Israeli public was not prepared for a debate over the historical interpretation of the revolt, let alone the role played by the young Zionist leaders of the underground and the complexities of Jewish behaviour during the war. And the critique raised by Alterman was interpreted in a political sense anyway, as a challenge to the ghetto fighters specifically and the Zionist Left as a whole amidst the drama of the Kasztner Affair.[64]

In his judgment on 22 June 1955, Judge Halevi accepted most of Gruenwald's accusations against Kasztner, ruling that by saving the Jews on the Kasztner train, while failing to warn Hungarian Jews that 'resettlement' in fact meant deportation to the gas chambers, Kasztner had sacrificed the majority of Hungarian Jewry for a chosen few and had, in effect, 'sold his soul to the devil'. It also had become clear during the trial that Kasztner had indeed submitted testimony vouching for Kurt Becher after the war, a fact he had earlier denied. The verdict triggered the fall of the Israeli Cabinet after the government sought to appeal on Kasztner's behalf. The Supreme Court of Israel overturned most of the judgment in January 1958, stating that the lower court had 'erred seriously', but only after Kasztner had been shot near his home in Tel Aviv on the night of 3–4 March 1957 by Zeev Eckstein and died of his injuries twelve days later.

Despite the atmosphere of accusations against Kastzner and the campaign of provocation against Kasztner that continued after the Halevi verdict, the assassination came as a major shock for the Israeli public. In the newspaper *Al HaMishmar*, affiliated with the left wing *Mapam* (United Workers Party), originally Marxist-Zionist and affiliated with the Hashomer Hatzair movement, the tone shifted in the wake of Kastzner's assassination. Whereas in 1955, Kastzner had been labelled as a symbol of the diaspora shtadlan (the interceder with the Gentile powers), diametrically opposed to paragons of heroic resistance like Mordecai Anielewicz or Hannah Szenes, by 1957 his murder gave rise to soul-searching on the Left. In an editorial published in *Al HaMishmar*, three weeks after the murder, the novelist Moshe Shamir asked, 'at what point in our public consciousness the idea of the murder could have been embodied, if only in a microscopic manifestation, as a cell of a seed'. His answer was that 'the first seed of the idea of the murder' was embodied in the license we took upon ourselves 'to judge the survivors of the Holocaust and to divide them into heroes and traitors'; to judge those who had returned from the test of fire and fear and to divide them into good and bad.[65]

The 'Kasztner Affair' was as much about branding some survivors as collaborators who allegedly 'sold their soul to the devil' as about the deep rift between those who affiliated with David Ben-Gurion's ruling Socialist Zionist *Mapai* party and the right-wing revisionist *Herut* party under Menachem Begin. Only recently have Kasztner's efforts been more widely recognized as the largest rescue operation of the Holocaust and represented in exhibitions and the curriculum. The Kasztner Affair represents the encounter between the pragmatic, state-based approach to the past, the lack of understanding of the complexity of the Holocaust, and the emotional anger of survivors against powerless Jewish communal leaders and the deep sense of guilt for having survived while loved ones had not.[66] It also previewed the later encounter between these two approaches to engaging with the recent past at the Eichmann trial. By 1961, Israeli society seemed ready to enter a new phase in its relationship to the history of Jewish experiences during the Holocaust.[67]

3

From Eichmann to Begin, 1961–77

'Who is Adolf Eichmann?' asked many Israelis, survivors and sabras alike, when on 23 May 1960, Prime Minister David Ben-Gurion announced that Israeli agents had captured and kidnapped Eichmann in Argentina – in violation of international law – and brought him to Israel to stand trial. Eichmann was a mid-ranking SS officer, not perceived as a major decision maker with a public presence, but an able and ambitious bureaucrat who within the SS administration worked out the logistics of implementing the Final Solution. Eichmann was indicted in February 1961 and tried between April and August that year on the basis of the 1950 Nazi and Nazi Collaborators Punishment Law. He was found guilty and sentenced to death on 11 December 1961. Both the Israeli Supreme Court and President Yitzhak Ben-Zvi rejected an appeal for pardon and Eichmann was hung at midnight on 31 May 1962; he was cremated and his ashes were spread in the Mediterranean Sea outside of Israel's territorial waters.

Although a fair trial, it was a political trial with a clear ideological and political agenda. Prime Minister David Ben-Gurion saw the trial as an opportunity to convey a strong educational message to the broader Israeli public. Ben-Gurion first and foremost wished 'to teach the details of the horrors to the generation of Israelis who have grown up since the Holocaust'. 'I don't care whether they want to know them', he said, 'they ought to know them. They should be taught the lesson that Jews are not sheep to be slaughtered but a people who can hit back – as Jews did in the War of Independence'.[1]

Nonetheless, the Israeli judicial system strove to remain independent from the political sphere and worked to prevent the trial from simply devolving into a 'show trial'. Holding the trial in Israel was an expression of sovereignty and symbolized Israel's self-understanding as the representative of the victims of the Holocaust and the Jewish people as a whole. Therefore,

Ben-Gurion rejected the request by both the WJC and American Jewish leaders to hold an international trial because the victims had belonged to all kinds of nationalities. This was indeed part of a wider debate over whether Israel had the right to speak on behalf of all Jews. Beyond establishing and punishing Eichmann's guilt, the trial aimed to instruct Israelis and the world at large about antisemitism, while unifying Israeli society and teaching the younger generation a lesson about bravery and the harmfulness of diaspora life for Jewish existence.[2] Unlike the Nuremberg trials, the murder of European Jewry would be the central focus of the Eichmann trial.

Attorney General Gideon Hausner filled the role of chief prosecutor during the trial and the three judges Moshe Landau (of the Israeli Supreme Court), Binyamin Halevi (president of the Jerusalem district court) and Yitzhak Raveh (the Tel Aviv district court judge) presided over the trial. Halevi, who had issued the verdict in the Kasztner Affair declaring that Kasztner had 'sold his soul to the devil', was a somewhat controversial inclusion on the bench, especially as his appointment to this trial had been opposed by the minister of justice and the head of the Supreme Court (the three-judge panel overseen by Supreme Court justice Landau was something of a compromise). And in truth there would be considerable overlap between the two trials, especially when it came to examining Eichmann's role in the deportation of Hungarian Jewry in 1944, when the role of Kasztner and his contacts with Eichmann would surface again. Eichmann's defence would be led by Dr Robert Servatius, a German lawyer who had served in the Second World War but had never been a member of the Nazi Party. After the war, he had served as a criminal defence lawyer at the Nuremberg trials, where he represented Fritz Sauckel. After careful vetting of Servatius by the Mossad, Israel's law was changed to allow a foreign lawyer to represent a defendant and Servatius fees were in fact paid by the Israeli government (partly to ensure the defence would not be funded by neo-Nazis). Eichmann's defence would also be limited by the absence of defence witnesses, who could not be assured immunity should they come to Israel to testify on behalf of Eichmann.[3]

Hausner's carefully orchestrated case against Eichmann encapsulated the history of the Nazi mass murder of European Jews in its entirety and in that respect was the first 'Holocaust trial' in the history of criminal justice (while the Nuremberg trials tried twenty-two of Nazi Germany's leaders for crimes against peace, war crimes and crimes against humanity, the International Military Tribunal in Germany was not specifically focused on the Holocaust). The Eichmann trial also departed from previous war crimes trials in that the prosecution based its case on oral evidence from Holocaust survivors rather than perpetrator documents. Chosen carefully with the help of survivors such as Rachel Auerbach, director of testimony collection at Yad Vashem, and Michael Goldman-Gilead, Hausner's assistant, the life stories of 108 survivor witnesses represented different countries and diverse wartime experiences, establishing a general understanding of the scope and complexity of the Holocaust.[4] For Rachel Auerbach, it was essential that the trial incorporate the testimony of survivors to the greatest extent possible. Auerbach was in direct contact with Bureau 06 of the Israeli police, which directed the investigation and prepared the evidence, and afterwards with Gideon Hausner, as he prepared to prosecute the case. As noted by historian Boaz Cohen,

> She requested that the authorities bring 'not only those [witnesses] who saw Eichmann face to face', or those who could provide 'legal evidence only' of Eichmann's guilt. She wanted witnesses such as those 'who were in the middle of the horrors of the extermination and who survived nonetheless to tell the story' to be called to testify. Only they, she claimed, would be able 'to silence the doubts' about the horrors and scope of the Holocaust. It appears that Auerbach feared that 'one who was not there' could not accept the stories of the survivors and that the trial would be a golden opportunity to answer those doubts.[5]

Most survivors who took the stand felt empowered by speaking in the name of their murdered loved ones and being listened to for the first time.[6] But many were also tormented by testifying and feared that they would not be believed when trying to relate experiences from 'there' to those who had only experienced the 'here'. According to historian Deborah Lipstadt, the choice to add survivor testimony, to make the trial a portrait of 'gigantic human tragedy', while controversial from a legal perspective, made the trial

> monumental from a historical perspective .... their presence would transform the trial from an important war-crimes trial into an event that would have enduring significance. It would give a voice to the victims that they had not had before and would compel the world to listen to the story of the Final Solution in a way that it never had before.[7]

From the beginning of the trial, Hausner clearly embraced the all-encompassing approach suggested by Auerbach, presenting himself as the voice of the victims in the indictment of the accused:

> When I stand before you here, Judges of Israel, to lead the Prosecution of Adolf Eichmann, I am not standing alone. With me are six million accusers. But they cannot rise to their feet and point an accusing finger towards him who sits in the dock and cry: 'I accuse.' For their ashes are piled up on the hills of Auschwitz and the fields of Treblinka, and are strewn in the forests of Poland. Their graves are scattered throughout the length and breadth of Europe. Their blood cries out, but their voice is not heard. Therefore I will be their spokesman and in their name I will unfold the terrible indictment.[8]

The poet and journalist, Haim Gouri, who covered the trial for the paper *La-Merhav* and published his articles in book form once the trial was over, reflected the impact of the daily events of the trial on the broader Israeli public. Regarding Hausner's speech, he wrote:

> I know that I will remember this day my entire life. I write in my notebook: 17 April 1961 ... . Never has a human being said to another human being those things that Gideon Hausner said today to Adolf Eichmann. There took place today in Jerusalem a miracle that I hardly believed would ever occur.[9]

Ultimately, the attempt to hold Eichmann responsible for the Holocaust as a whole was perhaps legally counterproductive as most of the witnesses' testimony was not directly relevant to crimes committed by Eichmann. Yet the narratives were tremendously important for the historical understanding of the Holocaust, for survivors in Israeli society, for creating Holocaust consciousness in Israel and even globally, creating what Annette Wieviorka has called the 'era of the witness'.

Most survivors who took the stand felt empowered, which did not mean that they were not also tormented by testifying (famously through fainting, heart attacks and an inability to relate experiences from 'there' to those who had only experienced them 'here'; many witnesses were frustrated by the selectivity, harshness and impatience of the members of the court during questioning). Many witnesses felt that they could finally fulfil the duty entrusted on them by the dead. For example, Yehiel Dinur, known to the Israeli public only as the author *Ka-tsetnik*, when asked by Hausner, why he had 'hidden his identity' behind a pseudonym, replied:

> It was not a pen name. I do not regard myself as a writer and a composer of literary material. This is a chronicle of the planet of Auschwitz. I was there for about two years. Time there was not like it is here on earth. Every fraction of a minute there passed on a different scale of time. And the inhabitants of this planet had no names, they had no parents nor did they have children. There they did not dress in the way we dress here; they were not born there and they did not give birth; they breathed according to different laws of nature; they did not live – nor did they die – according to the laws of this world. They were human skeletons, and their name was the number 'Ka-Tzetnik'.

Shortly thereafter Dinur fainted on the witness stand.[10]

In using the trial as an educational opportunity for the broader Israeli public, Hausner also engaged in a process of appropriating the individual experiences of survivors into a Jewish national narrative, making the Holocaust a foundational Israeli experience. For example, in his questioning of Rivka Yoselevska, who survived a mass shooting near Pinsk after the

German invasion of the Soviet Union, Hausner declared her a symbol of Jewish survival and rebirth. Coverage of the trial also described this incredible witness as a symbol of the Jewish people. Until the trial Yoselevska was unknown. Her testimony lasted about an hour and a half and was given in Yiddish.[11] Under her photograph in its daily trial coverage, *Davar* described her as one who had: 'Risen from the Grave.'

As noted by Sharon Geva in her analysis of female witnesses at the Eichmann trial, one commentator from *Hatosfe* noted, 'the prosecution seems to have led us slowly. It presented witnesses who had stood at the brink of death and survived, whereas this one, Rivka Yoselevska, appeared from out of the pit. She survived not only the talons of death but death itself, from the death pit in which the wounded, the dying, wrestled with the massacred'.[12]

In his account of the trial, Haim Gouri wrote:

> Had it not been for her [Rivka Yoselevska], I would not know what happened one Sabbath in a town called Povost-Zagordski near Pinsk, where she was born and where her father had been a leather merchant. I would not know that she had two sisters, Haya and Feige, and a brother named Moshe, that she had married in 1934, or that by that marriage she had had a daughter named Marta. Had it not been for Rivka Joselewska [*sic*], I would not know what happened on the Sabbath of the New Moon of Elul in 1942 when the Jews were ordered to assemble, leaving all their possessions, taking neither food nor drink, but only their children. She ran after the truck filled with friends and neighbors, with Marta in her arms, until at last they got to the spot.[13]

For the Israeli audience, Yoselevska became someone who had miraculously emerged from the pit of death, a survivor of the mass shootings who suddenly came to represent the anonymous murdered masses. In her testimony at the trial, Yoselevska recounted in detail the march to the pit where they would be shot, even recounting the questions her daughter asked her along the way: 'Mother, why are you wearing your Sabbath dress? They are going to kill us.' Her daughter urged her to flee, but it was not possible. Her testimony reached its climax at the moment she climbed out of the pit:

> I fell down … I felt nothing. At that moment I felt that something was weighing me down. I thought that I was dead, but that I could feel something even though I was dead. I couldn't believe that I was alive. I felt I was suffocating, bodies had fallen on me. I felt I was drowning. But still I could move and felt I was alive … I had no strength left. But then I felt that somehow I was crawling upwards. As I climbed up, people grabbed me, hit me, dragged me downwards, but I pulled myself up with the last bit of strength. When I reached the top I looked around but I couldn't recognize the place. Corpses strewn all over, there was no end to the bodies. You could hear people moaning in their death agony.[14]

FIGURE 3.1 *Yehiel Dinur (aka Ka-tsetnik), prosecution witness at the trial of Nazi War criminal Adolf Eichmann, at Beit Ha'am in Jerusalem. Israel Government Press Office, 7 June 1961. Public domain.*

FIGURE 3.2 *Davar, 9 May 1961, p. 3. Rivka Yoselevska describes how she was miraculously saved from a mass grave near Minsk.*

Just as she reached the most gruesome and horrifying aspect of her testimony, including the ways in which those who died and those who were barely alive were extricated from the pit, Hausner interrupted her; it was too much: 'Please let us be brief, Mrs. Yoselevska. It is difficult to recount and difficult to listen to. Tell us.' Yoselevska continued to describe how she waited three days and three nights until nearby villagers had gone, so she would not be discovered alive and killed (again) and Hausner, eager to reach the conclusion, instructed Yoselevska to describe the aftermath of the massacre. 'When I saw they were gone, I dragged myself over to the grave and wanted to jump in ... Where should I go? What should I do?'

Q. And then a peasant passed by and took pity on you?

A. I remained not far from the grave. A peasant saw me. I had been wandering around there for several weeks. He saw me.

Q. He took pity on you and gave you food, and then you joined a group of Jews in the forest and stayed with them till the Soviets came?

A. Till the end I stayed with them.

Q. And now you are married and you have two children?

A. Yes.

Presiding judge: Do you have any questions to the witness, Dr Servatius? Dr Servatius: I have no questions.

As historian Sharon Geva argues, Hausner was eager to conclude her devastating testimony with a redemptive coda:

When Yoselevska's account reached the critical point – the injured mother searching for her daughter and spending three days and three nights sitting at the lip of the tomb – Hausner jumped to its consoling segment. This is an epitomic manifestation of the way Israeli society coped with a personal story that allowed for consolation only when it became a national story. The journalists corroborated this. 'In her horrifying personal tragedy, she symbolizes the entire Commonwealth of Israel', a Ma'ariv commentator wrote under the headline 'From the Death Pit – to New Life'.[15]

In his concluding argument Hausner again turned Yoselevska into a symbol of Jewish survival and rebirth:

Rivka Yoselevska embodies in her person, all that was perpetrated, all that happened to this people. She was shot. She was already amongst the dead in the funeral pit. Everything drew her downwards, to death. Wounded and wretched, with unbelievable strength she arose out of the grave. Her physical wounds healed, but her heart was torn asunder and broken forever. She found asylum in our country, established her home here and built her life anew. She overcame the evil design. They wanted to kill her, but she lives – they wanted to blot out her memory, but she has brought forth new children. The dry bones have been given sinews, flesh has grown upon them and they have taken on skin; they have been infused with the spirit of life. Rivka Yoselevska symbolizes the entire Jewish People.[16]

On the other hand as the testimony of the former Auschwitz Kapo Vera Alexander made clear, 'collaborating' with the Nazis by becoming a prisoner functionary could still mean trying to save fellow prisoners to mitigate their suffering. In her testimony, Alexander explained that she chose the position of 'kapo' which had heretofore been reviled in Israeli collective discourse as a form of despicable collaboration, in order to make a difference for her fellow Jews.
As Hausner questioned Alexander:

Q. Tell me, Mrs Alexander, how was it possible to be a Blockälteste in Auschwitz and to maintain the stance of being created in God's image and maintain the image of a human being?
A. It was not easy. One needed a lot of tact and much manoeuvring.
    On the one hand, one had to obey orders and to fulfil them, and, on the other hand, to harm the prisoners as little as possible and to assist them.
Q. How did you manage that?
A. Sometimes we received orders. For example, the women who were in the 'quarantine block' did not work. They were kept in the block all day, and they were forbidden to sit on their beds and, altogether, to go

near their beds. The bed had to be made up tidily. We posted one girl on guard in front of the entrance to the block, and we allowed these women to get on to their beds and to sit on them. The moment the girl standing on guard saw that the SS were approaching, we entered the block and had to make them get off the beds very quickly.

Q. We have been told that you saved women from being put to death. How did you do that? Tell us of some cases.

A. There were cases after a selection, where women were selected for death, and I knew which block they were supposed to enter. I tried, not always successfully, to remove them from the ranks. Sometimes I managed to place girls in a commando which was going out from Auschwitz to work. This was not heroism on my part – it was my duty. I don't remember all the instances, and I don't remember how I did it.[17]

The trial had begun to examine what Primo Levi would describe as the 'grey zone' reflecting on a deeper understanding of choiceless choices and challenges faced by Jews.

Only a handful of witnesses focused on armed resistance (Abba Kovner, Yitzhak Zuckerman, Zivia Lubetkin, Ruzka Korczak) and while a focal point for many in the Israeli public, who eagerly awaited their accounts, theirs was just one Holocaust experience among many. It also became clear from their testimony that armed resistance was not an option for everyone and that there were other forms of defiance apart from armed fight. As noted by Sharon Geva, the responses to Lubetkin's testimony were the strongest of those elicited by all the trial testimonies, reflecting the immense appreciation for armed resistance during the Holocaust – of which the valour of the Warsaw ghetto fighters was unsurpassed. 'From time to time, we felt like asking Hausner, "When are we going to get to the revolt?"', wrote the poet and intellectual Haim Gouri, then a journalist for the newspaper *La-Merhav*.[18] In her testimony on 3 May 1961, Lubetkin offered a Jewish perspective on the revolt; while at Nuremberg the story of the uprising was presented through German records, here Lubetkin described the Jewish ghetto inhabitants as determined fighters. For Lubetkin, the Jews of the ghetto faced impossible odds and had achieved a great victory.

> I saw the thousands of Germans who were surrounding the ghetto – with machine guns, with cannon – and thousands of them, with their weapons, as if they were going to the Russian front. And there we stood opposite them – some twenty young men and women. What were our weapons? Each one had a revolver each one had a hand grenade; the entire unit had two rifles, and in addition we had homemade bombs, primitive ones, the fuse of which had to be lit by means of a match, and Molotov cocktails. It was very strange to see that some Jewish boys and girls, confronting this enormous enemy with all his weapons, were joyful and merry. Why were they joyful

and merry? We knew that our end had come. We knew beforehand that they would defeat us, but we also knew that they would pay a heavy price for our lives. Indeed, they did. It is difficult to describe, and there will surely be many who will not believe it, that when the Germans came near the foot of one of our strong points and passed by in formation, and we threw the bombs and the hand grenades, and we saw German blood pouring in the streets of Warsaw, after so much Jewish blood and tears had previously flowed in the streets of Warsaw – we felt within us, great rejoicing and it was of no importance what would happen the following day.[19]

Lubetkin's testimony was followed by her husband Yitzhak Zuckerman, who had been the deputy commander of the Jewish Fighting Organization in the Warsaw Ghetto (and who together with Lubetkin was one of the founders of Kibbutz Lochamei Ha-Geta'ot). As noted by Hanna Yablonka, before the trial, a special connection was forged between Zuckerman, Lubetkin and the investigators of Bureau 06. As Yablonka argued, the members of Kibbutz Lochamei Hagetaot and especially Antek Zuckerman and his wife Zivia Lubetkin 'became the moral anchors for the Bureau 06 team, as well as for Gideon Hausner'.[20] Rachel Auerbach, who played such a prominent role in convincing Hausner to incorporate witness testimony into the trial was also scheduled to speak on the same day, originally before the two heroes of the revolt. Eventually her time was cut from ninety minutes to half an hour. Much to her disappointment,

> The night before her testimony she was told that she would speak after Lubetkin and in the morning she was told that her testimony had been postponed until after Zuckerman's testimony, scheduled in the afternoon. The meaning of this was, she said, that they did not allow 'me to speak at all, because they already knew 'all' about Warsaw and they did not have the patience to hear more.[21]

As Boaz Cohen explains, Auerbach was deeply offended by this turn of events, along with her treatment by Hausner and the trial judges. In a letter to Arieh Kubovi, chairman of Yad Vashem since 1959, she explained this was 'a wretched testimony – amputated and strangled ... [which] did not bring honour to Yad Vashem'. Regarding her feelings during the testimony, she wrote in a letter to Arieh Kubovi, chairman of Yad Vashem:

> And despite the questions which were asked of me, I was not granted the possibility of responding completely, because question after question came quickly and during this 'race' I suddenly felt a contraction of my heart muscles until my only thought at that moment was just to step down, to step down as soon as possible and only not to faint and not to become a subject of stupid sensation in the press ... I am very hurt and I will not recover easily or quickly from this.[22]

FIGURE 3.3 *Tzivia Lubetkin testifying at the Eichmann trial, 3 May 1961 (YouTube screengrab).*

FIGURE 3.4 *Attorney General Gideon Hausner listening to witness testimony (YouTube screengrab).*

FIGURE 3.5 *Witness Yitzhak Zuckerman testifies for the prosecution during the trial of Adolf Eichmann (USHMM: Photograph #65276).*

Nonetheless, Hausner understood that what mattered more than the specific historical details of the testimony was the impact that the spectacle of survivor witnessing could have on the general public. The trial received wide public attention and ordinary citizens from all walks of life lined up to watch the trial that took place at *Beit Ha-Am*, a concert hall/theatre that could accommodate 750 spectators; scores of people also gathered in public places to listen to the broadcasts from the courtroom and daily briefings in the press (while there was no television yet in Israel, it was televised around the world). Most people in attendance, especially those who had *not* been personally affected by the Holocaust, responded with profound shock and emotional turmoil to the excruciating accounts.

While Hausner sought to present Eichmann as a Jew-hating monster and mastermind of the Final Solution, many Israelis were actually struck by Eichmann's appearance as an 'ordinary guy', by his simplicity, uninventiveness, his lack of thinking behind his actions, very much in the vein of what Hannah Arendt in her controversial report on the trial for the *New Yorker* termed the 'banality of evil': evil that did not stem from ideological hatred but rather his lack of thought.[23] This defence would become a topic of major debate after the trial, especially as magnified by Hannah Arendt's hugely consequential account, *Eichmann in Jerusalem: A Report on the Banality of Evil*. Nearly sixty years later (in 2022) an Israeli documentary film by Yariv Mozer titled *The Devil's Confession: The Lost Eichmann Tapes* would air on Israeli television, featuring recordings of Eichmann a few years before the trial actually boasting about his accomplishments, proud of his significant role in planning and executing the Final Solution. The airing of these tapes, which for legal reasons had been kept out of the public trial, would undercut the persona Eichmann projected at the trial, suggesting just how successful his duplicitous defence strategy had been – not in preventing his execution, but in presenting a false narrative of his role as a minor cog in the machinery of destruction. If anything, his ability to underplay the depths of his evil only magnified its unfathomable reach.

For many Israelis, one of the most significant outcomes of the trial, however, was a much deeper understanding of the complexity of Jewish behaviour during the war, seen through the ambiguities presented in the testimony of ghetto fighters and partisans like Lubetkin, Zuckerman and Kovner who emphasized cultural resistance, while others spoke to the futility and impossibility of armed resistance. Moshe Beisky, a survivor from Płaszów rescued by Oskar Schindler, offered one of the most memorable responses to Hausner's questioning, which often challenged witnesses to make the points Hausner thought Israelis needed to hear. Later described by Hausner as bringing the trial to 'a new moral peak', Beisky was challenged by Hausner to explain why 15,000 prisoners assembled for a public execution in the concentration camp had not revolted against the Nazi guards.

> Fifteen thousand people stood there – and opposite them hundreds of guards. Why didn't you attack then, why didn't you revolt?

Beisky, who in 1961 was already a judge in the Tel Aviv magistrate court, seemed to be taken aback by the question, but offered three distinct answers to the question – a question Hausner knew was on the mind of the Israeli public:

> 'People [in the camps] were forced to do crushing labor and they [the Germans], as it were, needed their work. [And] something else: The belief in the fact that, despite everything, the war would somehow come to an end', and 'we should not, because of that, endanger 15,000 people'.

In addition, Beisky explained, the intense fear they experienced was paralyzing: 'In the end it was a terror-inspiring fear. People stand facing machine guns and the mere fact of gazing upon the hanging of a boy and his cries – and then, in fact, no ability remains to react.' Finally, Beisky explained, quite rationally, even if they did manage to revolt and escape in their prison garb, where would they go? 'Nearby was a Polish camp' whose conditions were no better than ours. The difference was 'one hundred meters beyond the camp they had a place to go – their homes. Yet I don't recall one instance of escape on the part of the Poles'.[24]

Hanna Yablonka notes that the testimony also aroused soul-searching among Israeli observers at the trial, including Haim Gouri, who wrote:

> We must beg forgiveness of those whom we judged in our hearts, we, who were not a part of them. And we judged them on more than one occasion, without ever asking ourselves what right we had to do so … more than once, we included those unfortunate ones in the arbitrary and judgmental generalization, 'like lambs to the slaughter'. Today we know more than ever before … what we did not know about the main issue.[25]

After the trial Hausner also explained how the testimony of the eyewitness helped to decrease the distance Israelis may have felt from the events experienced by their European Jewish brethren. 'For we and they [the murdered Jews] – are one. Not only might we have been there physically in their place, but if we indeed had been there, and they here, they would have surely set the Yishuv on its feet … (Had we been there in their place) would have suffered a fate not different from theirs, nor would our heroism have been greater than theirs.'[26]

As Hanna Yablonka summarizes: 'Hausner's words reflect the most substantial change effected by the trial – the establishment of a connection between the Jews of Israel and those in Europe, based on the realization that only an accident of chronology separated them, and no issue of value or quality.'[27] The result was that there was a more empathetic understanding of victimhood, more identification with those victims, which broke down the previous dichotomy of heroes versus victims or fighters versus martyrs.

The life stories that emerged from the courtroom had a profound effect, especially on Israel's younger generation, and created public awareness of the complex nature of the event and the multifaceted Jewish responses to it; it bled into a more nuanced understanding of victimhood, which refined and challenged the stereotypic view of Jewish victims who had simply marched like 'sheep to the slaughter'. The Israeli audience developed a deeper understanding of the complexity and scope of the events described as the 'Shoah' along with a deeper understanding that the Final Solution was not simply about the destruction of Jewish life in the diaspora, but an all-encompassing attempt to annihilate the entire Jewish people – hence Israelis who were non-survivors begin to feel a deeper connection to the victims.

The survivor as such began to be valued as a 'bearer' of a foundational history, no matter what his/her survival strategy or politics, lifting the survivors from a place of weakness and shame to a place of authority. Survivors, who as we have seen, were never silent about what they had experienced, finally felt listened to for the first time. And as Israelis began to internalize the meaning of this history, understanding the scope of death and destruction, they also began to increasingly identify Israeli vulnerability as a sign of the potential for a repeat of the Holocaust. While it is clear that memory of the Holocaust formed a constant part of Israeli public life in the 1950s, it is possible that the Eichmann trial signalled a shift on the part of the Israeli public in terms of a willingness to hear, absorb and internalize the meaning of the memories being shared by a broader spectrum of survivors. The Eichmann trial changed the nature of Israel's relationship to the Holocaust. For the first time, most Israelis witnessed the testimony of survivors who detailed the horrors of the war over the course of many months. Holocaust awareness rose to a new level in Israeli society. In the words of historian Hanna Yablonka:

> The trial turned the Holocaust into a Jewish story, a major – and at times also, the only – component in the Israelis' sense of identity. The Holocaust finally penetrated the Hebrew language, becoming part of the discourse between Israel and the rest of the world and among Israelis themselves. It left a sense of deep, existential fear and suspicion of the outside world. This has become a major element in Israeli policies with respect to the international community, and especially the Arab world. Finally, the survivors had been integrated into Israeli society, almost, one might say, as a sacred community. It is through the survivors that Israelis have been able to connect directly with the Holocaust.

While never the intent of David Ben-Gurion, Yablonka argues that inadvertently the trial signalled 'the end of the Israeli ideology within Jewish history'.[28] Rather than proving that Israel as a state and Zionism as an ideology had managed to conquer Jewish history, by leading to a greater identification with the history of the Holocaust, the trial taught Israelis that they stood very much within the broader scope of Jewish history and within the scope of Jewish interactions with the wider world.

As a legal proceeding the trial also succeeded in demonstrating Eichmann's very personal involvement in the 'Final Solution'. The prosecution presented more than 100 witnesses and 1,600 documents (some bearing Eichmann's signature) presenting each stage of the persecution of European Jewry from persecution to legislation, plunder, incarceration and mass murder. Beyond educating the public about previously unknown aspects of the Holocaust, the prosecution also successfully proved the degree to which Eichmann, as head of the Gestapo section for Jewish affairs, was personally responsible for aspects of the

Final Solution. Eichmann's defence that he merely followed orders as one small piece in the machinery of destruction failed; the court was convinced that Eichmann had not only fulfilled his role within the Third Reich, he had also pursued the mission of exterminating European Jewry with extraordinary zeal bordering on obsession to seek out every single Jew in Europe for destruction. This was especially the case in Hungary in 1944, where Eichmann was sent by Heinrich Himmler in 1944 to take personal charge of the deportation of that country's Jews to the extermination camps in Poland. On 15 December 1961, Presiding Judge Moshe Landau read the verdict, finding Eichmann guilty on all counts with a sentence of death.

> After considering the appropriate sentence for the Accused with a deep feeling of the burden of responsibility borne by us, we reached the conclusion that in order to punish the Accused and deter others, the maximum penalty laid down in the law must be imposed on him ..... .
>
> For the dispatch of each train by the Accused to Auschwitz, or to any other extermination site, carrying one thousand human beings, meant that the Accused was a direct accomplice in a thousand premeditated acts of murder, and the degree of his legal and moral responsibility for these acts of murder is not one iota less than the responsibility of the person who with his own hands pushed these human beings into the gas chambers.
>
> Even if we had found that the Accused acted out of blind obedience, as he argued, we would still have said that a man who took part in crimes of such magnitude as these over years must pay the maximum penalty known to the law, and he cannot rely on any order even in mitigation of his punishment.
>
> But we have found that the Accused acted out of an inner identification with the orders that he was given and out of a fierce will to achieve the criminal objective, and in our opinion, it is irrelevant even for the purpose of imposing a punishment for such terrible crimes, how this identification and this will came about, and whether they were the outcome of the training which the Accused received under the regime which raised him, as his Counsel argues.
>
> This Court sentences Adolf Eichmann to death, for the crimes against the Jewish People, the crimes against humanity and the war crime of which he has been found guilty. We shall not impose a penalty on him for membership of a hostile organization, of which he was found guilty.[29]

On the sentencing, Gouri wrote,

> The words 'to death' elicited a tremor among the public, which was standing silently on its feet. Even the death of the other arouses awe. Even the death of 'the great expediter of death'. But this was a unique sort of tremor ... We saw for the last time the face of the man whom we never

believed that we would see, that we would ever see his later pictures, after the pictures of the smiling Sturmbannführer wearing the cap of the SS, the overseer of the 'Final Solution'.[30]

After losing his appeal of the verdict to Israel's Supreme Court and following the denial of clemency by Israel's president Yitzhak Ben-Zvi, Eichmann was executed by hanging at midnight between 31 May and 1 June 1962. His body was cremated and the ashes scattered at sea, beyond Israel's territorial waters. Following the Eichmann trial, renewed interest in the prosecution of Nazi crimes also led to several subsequent trials of Nazi criminals still alive in Germany.

Beyond the legal approach employed at the trial, the historical approach employed – incorporating surviving testimony, along with a broader understanding of the range of Jewish experiences and Jewish responses to Nazi persecution – would have a profound approach on the developing field of Holocaust history and research. While Raul Hilberg had published his monumental *The Destruction of European Jews* in America in 1961 – a volume that relied primarily on German documentation to explain the 'machinery of destruction' – a new generation of young Israeli Holocaust scholars, some of whom were either survivors themselves or had been mentored by the survivor historians, began to approach the writing of Holocaust history with a conscious attempt to incorporate Jewish source material and survivor testimony.

The Ghetto Fighters House, founded on 19 April 1949, had worked to counteract the myth of Jewish passivity during the war by focusing on specific examples of Jewish resistance and Jewish heroism. The main goal of the Ghetto Fighters House was to expose Israel's population to the special aspects and broad scope of active Jewish self-defence during the Holocaust. As Holocaust scholar Havi Dreifuss argues, however, over the course of the 1950s, 'although there were several institutions in Israel that proclaimed the Jewish triumph over the Holocaust, including the Ghetto Fighters' House and Yad Vashem itself, research was not high on their list of their priorities', and academic research on the Holocaust was still quite limited in Israel before the Eichmann trial.[31] Nonetheless, those publications that dealt with the Holocaust tended to focus on Jewish involvement in armed resistance to the Germans.

A number of memoirs and historical volumes had been published in the 1950s, including *The Book of the Ghetto Wars* (1954), edited by Yitzhak Zuckerman and Moshe Basok and published by the Ghetto Fighters House. *The Book of the Ghetto Wars* contained more than 150 testimonies and parts of original sources from the Ghetto Fighters House archives, although more than 40 per cent of the book was devoted to the Warsaw ghetto, especially its underground activity and rebellion. Nonetheless, the political context in Israel led each movement to emphasize the role of its own members in the struggle against German oppression, while critiquing what was still seen as the collaboration of the Judenrate.

In 1963, despite the prominence accorded to members of the underground affiliated with Zionist youth movements who testified at the Eichmann trial (most notably Yitzhak Zuckerman, Zivia Lubetkin and Abba Kovner), Hashomer Hatzair still felt that their members (Kovner and Mordecai Anielewicz notwithstanding) had not received their due in the historiography. The movement felt that both the Ghetto Fighters House and Yad Vashem marginalized Hashomer Hatzair and its members as participants and members of the underground. Therefore, in 1963, Abba Kovner and other members established Moreshet (the Heritage Circle), which sought to transcend the politicization of Holocaust research.[32] Moreshet would end up playing an instrumental role in developing projects that explored Jewish experiences beyond armed resistance, in particular through the work of Yehuda Bauer, who would go on to become the leading Holocaust scholar at the Hebrew University, and Yisrael Gutman, himself a survivor who fought in Warsaw and began his academic career after the Eichmann trial; his *Revolt of the Besieged: Mordecai Anielewicz and the Uprising of the Warsaw Ghetto* (Hebrew, 1963) can be seen in the context of restoring Hashomer Hatzair to a more prominent role in leading the revolt. Although, as Dreifuss suggests, this early work 'is based almost exclusively on Jewish sources, lacks certain historical contexts, and inserts reconstructed excerpts of Gutman's own diary along with other testimonies', Gutman's 'focus on the lives of Jews in the Holocaust on the basis of their own sources and the ability to reconstruct and explain personal dilemmas as well as complex social interactions' would become a defining feature of his research and writing and make a major contribution to the historiography of the Holocaust in general, and of the Warsaw Ghetto in particular.[33]

While Israeli cinema had not focused on the Holocaust (aside from indirect references to the experiences of survivors in Israel), Haim Gouri's *The 81st Blow* (1974) predated many later mainstream Holocaust films. Gouri, who as noted, had been profoundly influenced by the Eichmann trial, was moved to create the film based largely on witness testimony from the trial. The film, produced by the Ghetto Fighters House, was nominated for the Academy Award and received positive reviews noting, in *Ma'ariv*: 'this is an authentic testimony of the Holocaust, of barbarism and the degradation of humanity, a shattering document that cannot be expressed in words, a metaphysical experience, an apocalyptic nightmare that leaves the spectator numb and speechless.'[34]

After Eichmann: 1967–77

Even after the execution of Eichmann, the shadow of Jewish vulnerability and powerlessness hung over Israel. First in May 1967, when Gamel Abdel Nasser threatened to 'drive the Jews into the sea' and then again after the triumph of the Six-Day War, when the miraculous reversal of Israeli fortune seemed to be divinely ordained (indeed, as shall be seen, some in Gush Emunim interpreted the Holocaust and the Six-Day War in messianic terms). In the crisis that preceded the Six-Day War, when Egyptian leader Gamel Abdel Nasser threatened Israel with annihilation, promising the 'destruction of Israel', 'the eradication of Israel' and 'to wipe Israel off the map' many Israelis clearly heard echoes of the Holocaust and comparisons of Nasser to Hitler were commonplace. As far back as 1958, after the second war with Egypt in 1956, Ben-Gurion had compared Nasser with Hitler.[35] In the leadup to the pre-emptive strike against Egypt (and Syria and Jordan), the memory of the Holocaust formed a critical frame of reference that guided public and political rhetoric. An editorial in *Ha'aretz* by Eliezer Livneh warned the 'danger of Hitler' was returning in the form of Nasser.[36]

And even in the aftermath of the war and Israel's unprecedented military victory, the lessons of the Holocaust continued to resonate. The aftermath of the war with its miraculous redemption from near annihilation seemed to confirm the necessity of a powerful Jewish military that could save Israel from destruction. As noted by Tom Segev, in the words of one young soldier interviewed after the war and published in the volume, *The Seventh Day*:

> People believed we would be exterminated if we lost the war. We got this idea – or inherited it – from the concentration camps. It's a concrete idea for anyone who has grown up in Israel, even if he personally didn't experience Hitler's persecution. Genocide – it is a real possibility. There are the means to do it. That's the lesson of the gas chambers.[37]

These lessons also seemed to guide Israeli foreign policy after the war, as questions of what to do with the conquered land (and by extension the millions of Palestinians now living under military occupation) began to dominate diplomatic discussions.

In his role as Israeli foreign minister after the 1967 war, Abba Eban defended Israel's reputation after the war while asserting its right to defend itself against aggression. Although a proponent of a peace agreement that would involve some exchange of territory, Eban also invoked the memory of the Holocaust in resisting a return to the 4 June 1967 boundaries. In a November 1969 interview with Der Spiegel, Eban explained:

> 'We have openly said that the map will never again be the same as on June 4, 1967', he said. 'For us, this is a matter of security and of principles. The June map is for us equivalent to insecurity and danger. I do not exaggerate when I say that it has for us something of a memory of Auschwitz. We shudder when we think of what would have awaited us in the circumstances of June, 1967, if we had been defeated; with Syrians on the mountain and we in the valley, with the Jordanian army in sight of the sea, with the Egyptians who hold our throat in their hands in Gaza. This is a situation which will never be repeated in history.'[38]

Among religious Zionist adherents of the newly formed Gush Emunim, or the bloc of the Faithful, the conquest of the West Bank and the Old City of Jerusalem, the return of Western Wall, the Temple Mount and numerous biblical sites to the Jewish state seemed to be playing out on a meta-historical, theological level that had post-Holocaust implications. Some even suggested that perhaps the Holocaust, the creation of the state and then the triumph in 1967 were signs of the Messiah, of a divine redemption from destruction. As explained by Eliezer Don-Yehiya in his analysis of the thought of Rabbi Zvi Yehuda Kook, the ideological inspiration for Gush Emunim:

> The establishment of Jewish independence in the Jewish homeland in the wake of the most tragic event in Jewish history signaled for Rav Zvi Yehuda the actual beginning of the messianic era, and with it, the divine obligation incumbent on all Jews to take part in the continuing process of redemption by defending and extending Jewish presence and sovereignty in the land of Israel.[39]

Even so, on the political and educational level, Yad Vashem as an institution struggled with how to incorporate the history and meaning of the Shoah into Israel's national narrative.[40] Despite increasing evidence of a broad range of Jewish responses to persecution during the war, however, most published historical literature on Jewish resistance during the Holocaust, and the Warsaw Ghetto Uprising in particular, continued to reinforce the view that only the revolt in Warsaw served as the counterpoint to a history of Jewish passivity. Speaking at a conference at Yad Vashem dedicated to the subject of 'Jewish Resistance during the Holocaust' convened in 1968 on the twenty-fifth anniversary of the revolt in Warsaw to present a much broader array of resistance activities (including Jewish education, underground political work, the role of youth movements, Jewish partisans, documentation projects in ghettos, the struggle for daily life, Jewish involvement in allied resistance movements, rescue work and more), Dr Yosef Burg (minister of social welfare for the state of Israel) brought greetings on behalf of the state, less than a year after the momentous turning point in Israel's history, the Six-Day War. Burg, one of the founders of the National Religious Party in Israel and an Orthodox Jew, presented the choice to engage in resistance as a major transformation in Jewish self-understanding.

> I am certain that this conference will show how large a role the individual, isolated Jew, as well as the Jews organized in group frameworks, played in the struggle against the demonic oppressor. We must remember that this struggle marked a departure from the traditional passive martyrdom and Kiddush Hashem to a new active 'sanctification of the name' – a process which involved a difficult spiritual revolution. It was a departure from the historical passivity of the believing Jew, but only a Jew who believed profoundly in the future of the Jewish people could make the

transition in our generation from self-sacrificing Kiddush Hashem to the Kiddush Hashem of armed resistance. Thus our generation is a direct continuation of all the previous generations who believed in, and suffered for, the eternity of the Jewish people.[35]

The Six-Day War also inspired the first monument to be erected at Yad Vashem, *The Pillar of Heroism* dedicated in March 1970. In the aftermath of the Six-Day War, in which Israel had triumphed over its foes and demonstrated its ability to control its destiny, the 'pillar of heroism' would continue to fulfil the mandate of Yad Vashem to honour the bravery of the ghetto fighters who had fought back against the Nazis. Arieh Elhanani, who had designed the Hall of Remembrance at Yad Vashem which opened in 1961, approached the artist Buki Schwartz to design a monument commemorating Jewish heroism on the Mount of Remembrance at the highest location on the site, to be the last and final point of any visit to Yad Vashem. Dedicated in March 1970 during the first international conference of Concentration Camp Prisoners and Jewish Fighters against the Nazis, the 21-metre-tall pillar was designed to be seen from a great distance by all who visited the site. It bears an inscription composed by Yehuda Leib Bialer, then member of the Yad Vashem Board. The pillar is three-sided and made of concave panels of shining stainless steel; the front panels bears the inscription:

<blockquote>
To the martyrs
To the ghetto fighters
To the partisans in the forests
To those who rebelled in the camps
To the fighters of the underground
To the soldiers in the armies
To those who saved their brethren
To the courageous people who took part in the clandestine immigration
The heroes of valour and revolt
For everlasting life
</blockquote>

Noteworthy is the fact that the inscription emphasizes the concept of heroism, while contrasting the martyrs (named first) with all other forms of armed resistance, including those who took part in the rescue of Jews during and after the war, along with the movement for clandestine migration to pre-state Palestine that would be so crucial in the struggle for statehood.

Nonetheless, scholars in Israel in the 1970s and 1980s still sought to refute what was seen as the tendency to dismiss Jewish resistance in the general historical literature as insignificant, not only by emphasizing lesser-known cases of armed resistance that took place beyond Warsaw, but also by expanding the definition of the term 'resistance' to encompass a much broader spectrum of Jewish responses to persecution. Along with Yehuda Bauer, Israel Gutman's work helped broaden the scope of research on Jewish

FIGURE 3.6 *The pillar of heroism, Yad Vashem, Jerusalem, dedicated March 1970 (photo by author, July 2021).*

responses to persecution among Holocaust historians in Israel, who began to broaden the definition of 'resistance' beyond armed combat. Students of Bauer and Gutman and this newer school of historical writing on the Holocaust would continue to expand research on the nature of Jewish life and death under Nazi occupation in the decades that followed.

Despite an expanded understanding of the nature of Jewish experiences during the Shoah, none of this research or broader identification with the suffering of the six million or the survivors undermined the one central conclusion that had been in place since 1945: the one – and perhaps, only – appropriate response to the Shoah would be represented through the rebirth of the Jewish people in the Land of Israel. Such was the message embedded in the annual calendar with the week of commemoration and celebration from Yom HaShoah to Yom HaZikaron to Yom Ha'atzma'ut. And with the continued development of Yad Vashem as the Jewish people's Holocaust memorial, located right next to Mount Herzl, the site of Israel's military cemetery and the location of the tombs of Israel's great leaders, memorial architecture continued to reinforce this reading of history, from destruction to rebirth, both at Yad Vashem and beyond. Nathan Rapoport, whose Monument to the Ghetto Fighters was dedicated in Warsaw in 1948 on the fifth anniversary of the Warsaw Ghetto Uprising (and a replica at Yad Vashem in 1976), began work on his *Scroll of Fire* in the early 1960s, an idea for a memorial scroll first proposed to Yad Vashem in 1963.[41]

Ultimately the monument would be dedicated at the Martyrs' Forest on the outskirts of Jerusalem in 1972 rather than at Yad Vashem. The monument's plaque noted that the towering 8-meter-high sculpture was a 'sign that points to the Jews' Eleventh Commandment' Thou Shalt Not Forget.

Nathan Rapoport, the inspiring monument's creator, lost his family in the Holocaust. At first he wanted to erect six poles in memory of the six million. Afterwards he tried to connect them three by three. Thus two cylinders shaped like a scroll were made, a symbol representing the people of the Book. The Scroll of Fire, an eight meter high bronze monument, has been standing here since 1972. The scroll's first cylinder describes the destruction caused by the Holocaust and the second describes that nation's revival between the time of its struggle for independence and the Six Day War.

Around the monument a view of the Jerusalem hills can be seen – long peeks (sic) with deep valleys between them, covered with natural woodlands as well as forests planted by the JNF. This was the historical heart of the ancient kingdom of Judaea. Here, atop the solitary mountain, stands the Scroll of Fire, a symbol of a people who were bound on the altar and from there came to life. In this place the JNF conducts a ceremony of its own every year on Holocaust Rememberance (*sic*) Day. Please respect the place and what it represents.

Carved in the sculpture are numerous symbols embedded by Rapoport in the two cylinders that symbolize destruction: Janusz Korczak with 'his' children; people marching to camps; helmets and daggers of faceless Germans; tanks driving over the ghettos; ghetto fighters with knives, stones and Molotov cocktails and a Menorah that accompanies the Jewish people. And on the second scroll are symbols of the Jewish people's revival: survivors breaking through barbed wire fences, *ma'apilim* sailing to Israel; a kibbutz with a water tower and grapevines; a mother says goodbye to a son who goes to fight in 1948; June 1967 soldiers in front of the wall after the conquest of Jerusalem and the blowing of a shofar. Inside the monument are carved the thoughts of Rapoport: 'My words have been made of bronze and stone. They are silent, heavy and longlasting.' Completed after Israel's 1967 Six-Day War, the monument etches into bronze a reading of Jewish history that links together the history of the Jewish people and Israel's destruction: from the abyss of the churban in Europe to the triumphant return of the Jewish people to the last remaining wall of the Temple in Jerusalem. Inscribed inside the monument is a verse from Ezek. 37.12-14 that evokes the prophetic vision of Ezekiel's resurrection of the dead:

> [12]Thus says the Lord GOD; Behold, O my people, I will open your graves, and cause you to come up out of your graves, and bring you into the land of Israel.
>
> [13]And ye shall know that I am the LORD, when I have opened your graves, O my people, and brought you up out of your graves,
>
> [14]And shall put my spirit in you, and ye shall live, and I shall place you in your own land.

In the aftermath of the Six-Day War, the continued hostilities of the 'War of Attrition' (1969–70) and the terrorist campaign against Israeli and Jewish targets around the world seemed to only reinforce the sense that the Jewish people continued to 'dwell alone' and must rely on a strong Israel to defend itself. The September 1972 Munich Massacre at the Olympic Games, which resulted in the deaths of eleven Israeli Olympians and one German police officer in a botched raid heightened such continued parallels. As the first Olympics held in Germany since the 1936 Berlin Olympics, the Munich Massacre contained so many obvious parallels to the Holocaust. As a terrorist attack orchestrated by the Black September group (affiliated with the PLO and Fatah), the deadly debacle seemed to demonstrate that a straight line could be drawn from the time of the Nazis to the contemporary enemies of Israel.

On 4 September 1972 eight Palestinian terrorists, members of the Black September terrorist group, had stealthily penetrated two out of three apartments on 31 Connollystrasse in the Olympic Village in Munich, which housed the Israeli delegation to the Olympics. Two of the athletes, Moshe Weinberg and Yossef Romano, were murdered on the spot, and nine others were gathered in one room as hostages. The terrorists demanded the release of 232 terrorists held in Israel and another 2 imprisoned in Germany. After the failed rescue attempt by West German police on the night of 5–6 September 1972, the affair ended with the death of all the hostages and

FIGURE 3.7A *Nathan Rapoport, Scroll of Fire memorial, Forest of the Martyrs, Moshav Kisalon, Israel (photo by author, July 2021).*

FIGURE 3.7B *Nathan Rapoport, Scroll of Fire memorial, Forest of the Martyrs, Moshav Kisalon, Israel (photo by author, July 2021).*

five out of the eight terrorists. At a subsequent meeting in October 1972 to discuss how to respond to the tragedy and how to fight this new form of terrorism, MK Ya'acov Hazan, of the Mapam party, argued that this was a difficult war like all wars and therefore: 'we must not only defend ourselves, but also attack. We must search for the terrorists and kill them. We must change them from hunters to prey.' Golda Meir hinted that Israel was not inactive in the war on terror abroad, and that 'there are thoughts and there are plans' and added: 'there are friendly countries that say: You can't do that here, here we're in charge. All this is not simple. That isn't our country.'[42] Ultimately, the Mossad would reportedly hunt down every single terrorist responsible for the Munich massacre.[43] Nonetheless, throughout the 1970s, the PLO and the Popular Front for the Liberation of Palestine employed the tactic of airline hijackings to terrorize Jewish targets (especially El Al) as civilian extensions of the Jewish state.[44]

In October 1973, Egypt and Syria surprised Israeli defences unprepared for invasion on Yom Kippur, the holiest day of the Jewish year. The war exposed both political, defence and intelligence lapses, and led to heavy losses for Israel in the first week of fighting. Although Israel emerged victorious from the Yom Kippur War, the heavy losses at the start of the war, the surprise nature of the attack and the dependence on the American patron for military support reinforced a sense of Jewish victimhood that had come to occupy a more central place in Israeli collective identity. As noted by political scientist Charles Liebman:

> The fact remains that the Yom Kippur War demonstrated that the state of Israel is not a secure haven for Jews. Its security is precarious, its survival dependent upon the support of a great power. This contradicts the central message of Zionism, a message reinforced by the Holocaust myth, that there is no secure place for Jews except in their own land where, unlike everywhere else, they are an independent self-sufficient people. In other words, the Yom Kippur War threatened this central message and myth of Israeli society.[45]

The Yom Kippur War forced Israelis to acknowledge that they had not triumphed over Jewish history, piercing the very brief aura of invincibility after the Six-Day War, while also coinciding with a new interpretation of heroism, which in the aftermath of the Eichmann trial emphasized individual stories of struggle and survival over and above the value of collective sacrifice that had prevailed in the 1948 war.[46] Israel's relationships with its neighbours came to be increasingly understood through this prism of Holocaust memory. According to Rabbi Yehuda Amital, the founding rabbi of Har Etzion Yeshiva in the West Bank and a native of Romania whose entire family had been killed in Auschwitz,

> The dreams of normalization have been exposed as hollow. The State of Israel is the only state in the world which faces destruction … The

vision of the prophet – 'a people that dwells alone and that shall not be reckoned among the nations' – is fulfilled in front of our eyes in the most physical sense.[47]

The losses suffered during the Yom Kippur War re-traumatized Israeli society and, along with a shift from a collectivist to a more individualistic ethos, a Labor Zionist corruption scandal and the empowerment of the Sephardic electorate against the Ashkenazi Labor Zionist elite, helped lead to the political victory of Menachem Begin and the Likud in 1977. Unlike his Labor Zionist predecessors, Begin invoked the Holocaust repeatedly as a justification for the need for Israel's existence and the need for a strong armed defence.

After the collapse of the Labor governments that had dominated Israeli politics since its founding, the election of Menachem Begin in 1977 solidified the memory of the Holocaust, which as we have seen had already come to occupy a much more prominent place in Israeli collective memory and society, as a central cornerstone of Israeli political life and foreign policy. Begin, whose entire political career, according to Tom Segev, had in some way been shaped by the Holocaust, from the battle against reparations to the anxious period before the Six-Day War became 'the great popularizer of the Holocaust' who did 'more than anyone else to politicize it'.[48]

Begin, who received the 1978 Nobel Peace Prize for his efforts to achieve peace with Egypt together with Anwar Sadat, even invoked the memory of the Holocaust at the White House peace treaty signing ceremony in March 1979: 'I have come from the land of Israel, the land of Zion and Jerusalem, and here I am in humility and with pride as a son of the Jewish people, as one of the generation of the Holocaust and redemption.' Noting that this was the third greatest day of his life (after the creation of the state of Israel, whose 'independence in our ancestors' land was proclaimed after 1,878 years of dispersion, persecution, humiliation and, ultimately, physical destruction' and the unification of Jerusalem),

> This is the third day in my life. I have signed a treaty of peace with our great neighbor, with Egypt. The heart is full and overflowing. God gave me the strength to persevere, to survive the horrors of Nazism and of the Stalinite concentration camp and some other dangers, to endure, not to waver in nor flinch from my duty, to accept abuse from foreigners and, what is more painful, from my own people, and even from my close friends. This effort, too, bore some fruit.
>
> Therefore, it is the proper place and the appropriate time to bring back to memory the song and prayer of thanksgiving I learned as a child, in the home of father and mother that doesn't exist anymore, because they were among the 6 million people – men, women, and children – who sanctified the Lord's name with the sacred blood which reddened the rivers of Europe from the Rhine to the Danube, from the Bug to the Volga, because, only because they were born Jews, and because they didn't have a country of

their own, and neither a valiant Jewish army to defend them, and because nobody, nobody came to their rescue, although they cried out, 'Save us, save us' – de profundis- – 'from the depths of the pits and agony.' That is the Song of Degrees, written 2 millennia and 500 years ago, when our forefathers returned from their first exile to Jerusalem and Zion.[49]

And not just in times of peace, but especially in times of conflict, Begin invoked the memory of the Holocaust. In June 1981, Begin justified destroying the Iraqi nuclear facility with the words,

> There won't be another Holocaust in history. Never again, never again. We shall defend our people with all the means at our disposal. We shall not allow any enemy to develop weapons of mass destruction against us.

After the invasion of Lebanon and the subsequent siege of Beirut in August 1982, Begin defended Israel's actions arguing, 'no one anywhere in the world can preach morality to our people'.[50] According to Begin, after the Holocaust the international community had lost its right to demand that Israel answer for its actions. While in the early years of the state, the Labor Zionist establishment sought to maintain distance from the equation that the Holocaust was the reason and justification for the existence of the Jewish state, based first and foremost in historical Jewish claims to their ancestral homeland, Menachem Begin did not hesitate to invoke the memory of the Holocaust at every turn, both when politically expedient and not. His more frequent referencing of the memory of the Holocaust coincided with a deepening identification by the Israeli public with this memory in the educational, cultural and political spheres.

Israeli Holocaust Literature

The works of survivors such as Aharon Applefeld, Uri Orlev, Shamai Golan, Dan Pagis, Avrom Sutzkever and Tuvia Ruebner joined the texts of veteran Israelis like Avraham Shlonsky, Nathan Alterman and Haim Gouri to become a central component of *Yom Hashoah* commemorations since the 1960s and attain a paramount position in classroom literature.

As noted previously, while the 1948 generation of writers tended to focus on the mythological sabra and the struggles involved with the creation of the state of Israel, literature created by both survivors and their children in the decades after the Eichmann trial introduced Israeli audiences to stories of death and survival, along with the lingering effects of intergenerational trauma that continued to hover over Israeli society. Over the course of his career, Aharon Appelfeld (1932–2018) would author more than forty books including novels, essays, short stories and plays and eventually garner such literary honours as the Israel Prize, the Bialik Prize and the National Jewish

Book Award (in the United States); he has been described as Israel's 'most celebrated Shoah-author.'[51] Born in 1932 in a village near Czernowitz (at the time part of Romania, present-day Ukraine), Appelfeld's childhood would be violently disrupted in 1941 when his mother was killed (shot by Romanian troops) and he and his father were deported to forced labour camps in Transnistria, where they were separated before he managed to escape. Over the next few years, Appelfeld roamed the Ukrainian countryside and hid in the forests, occasionally finding lodging among peasant farmers and villagers. After three years surviving in this way, he joined the Red Army which had advanced from the East.[52]

After a few months in a DP camp in Italy, Appelfeld arrived in pre-state Palestine in 1946. Only fifteen years later did he discover that his father had in fact survived, the two assuming that the other had died. Deprived of his childhood, his family and an education, Appelfeld sought to rebuild his identity in his new homeland. In an interview with Philip Roth published in the *New York Times Book Review* in 1988, Appelfeld recalled his early years in Israel:

> I came here in 1946, still a boy, but burdened with life and suffering. In the daytime I worked on kibbutz farms, and at night I studied Hebrew. For many years I wandered about this feverish country, lost and lacking any orientation. I was looking for myself and for the faces of my parents, who had been lost in the Holocaust. During the 1940's one had a feeling that one was being reborn here as a Jew, and one would therefore turn out to be quite a wonder. Every utopian view produces that kind of atmosphere. Let's not forget that this was after the Holocaust. To be strong was not merely a matter of ideology. 'Never again like sheep to the slaughter' thundered from loudspeakers at every corner. I very much wished to fit into that great activity and take part in the adventure of the birth of a new nation. Naively I believed that action would silence my memories, and I would flourish like the natives, free of the Jewish nightmare, but what could I do? The need, you might say the necessity, to be faithful to myself and to my childhood memories made me a distant, contemplative person. My contemplation brought me back to the region where I was born and where my parents' home stood. That is my spiritual history, and it is from there that I spin the threads.[53]

Among his first stories to be published in Hebrew was 'Bertha', a story about a young woman around twelve or thirteen, who seems to suffer from a developmental disorder, living with Max, a middle-aged man, a refugee from the Holocaust, who is a travelling salesman. As Appelfeld would recall in an interview, he brought the story to a newspaper editor who admonished him: 'We came to Israel to forget Bertha … . What are you going to learn from such a story?'.[54] Appelfeld would go on to write dozens of works imagining Jewish experiences during the Holocaust in a fictional sense, attempting to recover his own memories while constructing a Kafka-esque alternate world. *Badenheim 1939*, published in 1975, was perhaps his best-known book (translated for a broad international audience) and presented pre-war European Jews living in an Austrian spa village, enjoying music, pastries and a life of luxury, all while blissfully ignoring their impending doom before finally boarding a train to take them to Poland. As noted by literary scholar Dvir Abramovich:

> While readers may be startled by the strange silences of *Badenheim 1939* and the orderly unfolding of the monstrosity that lures Jews into accepting and collaborating in their own extermination, they are also likely to be stunned by the victims' blindness to the cruel reality that the trains taking them for 'resettlement' are, in fact, transporting them to the killing centers.[55]

Other writers, both survivors and Israeli-born writers, also began to reflect on the ways in which the encounter with the Holocaust challenged the Zionist world view and the belief in the 'new Jew's' ability to conquer it. In his semi-autobiographical account of his service in the Jewish Brigade after the Second World War, Hanoch Bartov described the dilemmas of Jewish behaviour for Palestine-born 'sabras' finally faced with the opportunity to exact revenge against Nazis and their families after the war. For soldiers who had waited the entire war to confront the enemy, entering Tyrol with truck emblazoned with the slogans 'Die Juden Kommen' (The Jews Are Coming), Bartov's stories of the encounter presented a profound wrestling with the tension between the desire for revenge and the need to maintain one's humanity in the face of evil. In 'Enemy Territory' (*The Brigade*, 1968) the narrator, Elisha Krook, finds himself unable to abide his fellow Jewish soldiers perpetrating sexual violence against the daughter of an SS officer as an act of revenge, finally lifting his gun to engage his own comrades, ordering them to run before he 'shoots them like dogs'.

> At long last I had done something of my own free will, and what had I done – rushed to save my own purity. In a moment all the hymns of hate had been wiped out and I was my father's son again. Rotten with purity. A *mensch*. A lousy human being. Now I knew: We were what we were, condemned to walk the face of the earth with the image of God printed on our foreheads like the mark of Cain. Incapable of seeing a little girl raped. Incapable – lily-white Jewish soul … and already I could hear the sound of the shell growing on my back like a hump, the armor that would protect our hearts like the shield of a medieval knight. How would we vanquish them if we became like them?[56]

Bartov (who had been moved by the Eichmann trial to write his account) reflected on the inability of the sabra, born and raised in Jerusalem, to vanquish his diaspora past and his diaspora mentality, while also holding the encounter with Nazism and the Holocaust as a barometer with which to judge Jewish behaviour. References to the Holocaust in literature and poetry would come to be more commonplace through the 1970s as writers like Yoram Kaniuk (*Adam Ben Kelev* or *Adam Resurrected*) and the poet Dan Pagis wrestled with questions of human and Jewish behaviour, or of the universal and the particular aspects of the meaning of the Holocaust in their works.

Like Appelfeld, Dan Pagis was also a survivor originally from pre-war Romania (Radauti, Bukovina) where he was born in 1930. Deported with his family at the age of eleven to a forced labour camp in Ukraine (from which he escaped), Pagis reached Israel in 1946. For nearly twenty-five years he did not write about his experiences until he began to publish poetry in Hebrew, which in its very spare form would become profound reflections on the nature of evil and the Jewish (poetic) response in Hebrew, rather than Yiddish, as Avraham Sutzkever had been doing continuously since the war. Pagis received his PhD from Hebrew University and became a professor of medieval Hebrew literature publishing scholarly works on medieval poetry, along with his own poetry.

Gilgul was his first volume of poetry to address the Holocaust, published in Israel in 1970 twenty-five years after the end of the war. Born a German-speaking child in Romania, the title '*Gilgul*' symbolized his reincarnation as a Hebrew-speaking poet in his new homeland. In the poem 'Testimony', Pagis reflects (in his characteristically sparing style) on the question of whether even the Nazis were created in the same divine image, and whether he as a shadow was made by the same creator. If the Nazis were created in God's image and he was just a shadow [here Pagis plays on the Hebrew *Tzelem* (image) and *Tzel* (shade)] made by a different creator, why is he the one fleeing to God, perhaps even apologizing for his survival? And against whom is Pagis actually offering his 'testimony'?

Also published in the collection of poems titled *Gilgul* (1970) was what would become perhaps his most famous poem, 'Written in Pencil in the Sealed Train Car'.

Here in this carload
I, Eve,
With my son Abel.
If you see my older boy,
Cain, the son of man,
Tell him that I

Only nineteen words long (in the original Hebrew), the poem itself does not address the Holocaust directly (aside from the freight car in the title) and yet it marks such a profound reflection on the Holocaust that it has become commonly used in Holocaust education and even reproduced as part of memorial displays at Yad Vashem (installed in 1995) and Belzec.

As noted by literary scholar John Felstiner, even the title of the poem poses a challenge to speech and translation in the aftermath of the Holocaust, while also suggesting the potential for the Hebrew language to represent in words what other languages cannot. 'Twelve syllables balance 6–6 at midpoint, their phonic pattern making a chiasmus where testimony crosses with genocide: *katuv b'iparon bakaron hechatum*, literally, "written in pencil in the [box] car sealed"'.[57] Echoing the High Holiday liturgy of Rosh Hashanah and Yom Kippur when the fate of the Jewish people is first *written* and finally *sealed*, the poem plays upon the expectation of the reader and the duality of fragility/finality of a life *written* and a life *sealed* (in the boxcar). In the body of the poem there are nineteen words (in Hebrew) that appear in six short lines and except for one word – transport (*mishloach*) – there is no mention of the Holocaust. The Hebrew used in the poem juxtaposes the modern euphemisms for the Nazi genocide (transport, boxcar, perhaps even the pencil used to write the lists) with the biblical Hebrew references that root the dilemma of good versus evil in a much more ancient context. The metaphor that Pagis uses to present the encounter between good and evil, between the shared humanity of Jews, Germans and the descendants of Adam and Eve is the first murder on earth, Abel slain by his brother Cain. Genesis 4 serves as the required context for the twentieth-century tragedy. The poem also captures the duality of how to understand the Holocaust: is this a specifically Jewish story or one with universal implications for all humanity? If Eve and Abel in the boxcar represent the Jewish people, but Cain who has murdered his brother represents Nazism and the fratricidal nature of humanity, then what is the shared responsibility of all humans to one another? Adam, who is in fact absent in the scene (only represented as the father of Cain), may also symbolize the absence of humanity, as the world stood idly by. Pagis leaves the poem unfinished, suggesting it may be read as an endless loop or the readers may fill in the blanks, drawing their own conclusions from a trauma that can never be completed, never rendered with a definitive conclusion. As Abramovich argues, too,

> Through his searing deployment of allusion, Pagis conveys the unexpressed terrors and grief of loss through what is unsaid, through a weeping character who chokes midway, unable to utter and articulate the ungraspable enormity of her situation. ... the poem's effective power derives from its direct call to the modern hearer to act, rousing us to resist the more easily assumable posture of the bystander, and to transform the mythic message relayed by Eve into the actual.[58]

In the period after the Eichmann trial, and especially after the Yom Kippur War, Israeli society began to undergo a transition from its founding collectivist socialist Zionist ethos to one that recognized the importance of the individual and the experiences of the 'I' rather than the 'we'. In this

FIGURE 3.8 *The Memorial to the Deportees, Yad Vashem, Jerusalem, with the Dan Pagis poem, 'Written in Pencil in the Sealed Train Car' (Hebrew) in the foreground (photo by author, July 2021).*

context, perhaps coincidental, perhaps not, the use of the 'I' by Pagis is indeed noteworthy: every human life, every individual experience must be learned from and appreciated, regardless of the moral or political lesson associated with it. At the same time, every individual must wrestle with the implications of these unanswerable questions by him or herself.

4

The centrality of the Shoah: 1979–2000

When Menachem Begin invoked the memory of the Holocaust at the Egypt peace treaty signing ceremony at White House in March 1979, this followed the creation of the US president's commission on the Holocaust just four months earlier, established by President Jimmy Carter to be chaired by noted Holocaust survivor and author, Elie Wiesel. (In September 1979, the commission would recommend the establishment of a memorial museum in Washington, which would eventually open in April 1993 as the United States Holocaust Memorial Museum.) The *NBC* mini-series, *Holocaust*, which aired on US television from 16 to 19 April 1978 on the thirty-fifth anniversary of the Warsaw Ghetto Uprising, would be broadcast on Israeli television in September 1978, with some 50 per cent of the country's entire population of three million tuned in to the broadcast.[1] The hugely influential TV mini-series, starring Meryl Streep, James Woods and Tovah Feldshuh (among others), had profound implications on increasing public discussion and awareness of the Holocaust in America, West Germany and even Israel, where, as we have seen, the TV event tapped into a growing interest in confronting the memory of the Shoah. Thirty-five years after the end of the war, a new generation seemed more eager to engage with this difficult history than their parents had been.

Beginning in 1979, Holocaust education became a mandatory component of the high-school curriculum and the first high-school textbook, *The Holocaust and Its Meaning* by Israel Gutman and Chaim Schatzker, came into use. Scholar Dan Porat suggests it is possible to trace stark changes in Israel's evolving relationship to the memory of the Shoah as 'representation of the Holocaust in the educational system shift(ed) from a marginal event better forgotten in the 1950s and 1960s to an event that from the late 1970s on defines Israeli identity'. In Israel's first decades, the treatment of the Holocaust in the Ministry of Education's curricula was still peripheral, with an emphasis on armed resistance (specifically the Warsaw Ghetto Uprising, the Jewish partisans and the Jewish Brigade) while, according to Porat, 'the annihilation of the Jews was marginalized'.[2] Even after the Eichmann trial, as discussion of the Holocaust entered public discourse more prominently, the educational system lagged behind. While additional lessons on Jewish experiences during the Holocaust were added to curricula, it was only after 1977 (and the election of Menachem Begin) that the Holocaust would become a core part of the government-sanctioned educational framework. As we have seen, the trauma of the Yom Kippur War also added to a greater willingness to consider Jewish vulnerability within Jewish history. In March 1980 the Knesset passed a Holocaust memory law which would obligate the Ministry of Education to find new ways to teach the Holocaust. In mandating Holocaust history as a required subject in 1979, the Ministry of Education added the subject to the history of the Jewish diaspora and teaching on Zionism/Israeli-Arab conflict as the three mandatory topics (out of a total of twenty-six) in the high-school history curriculum. This meant that at a minimum students would learn about the Holocaust in at least thirty separate lessons.[3]

Changes in curricula were not merely the result of political developments, however. On a very personal level, the new political leadership believed it essential to add education about the Holocaust to the curriculum. For the minister of education, Zevulun Hammer, a member of the National Religious Party (NRP) whose own grandparents were killed by the Nazis, teaching Israeli students about the Holocaust could also help resolve an array of social problems and even discourage emigration out of the state:

> How to bring the Jewish nation to immigrate to [the Land of Israel], and how to convince Israeli students, those born here, raised here, and educated here, not to emigrate from here. I see this as a central topic of Israeli education ... . [The Holocaust] has an important part in our physical struggle, and no less significant, in our spiritual struggle, the desire to live in the State of Israel.[4]

For Hammer, the commandment to remember the Holocaust was invoked not only out of a sacred obligation to those who perished, but as a political invocation to preserve the Zionist future.

Yitzhak Shamir, a long-time member of the Revisionist movement and a Likud stalwart who would become prime minister in 1986, also invoked the Holocaust as tribute to the lives lost and as driven by contemporary political realities. Shamir was born in Ruzhany (in present-day Belarus) and immigrated to Palestine in 1935. In his 1984 Yom HaShoah speech, Shamir (nee Yezernitsky), who had lost his parents and two sisters in the Holocaust, noted the degree to which this visceral loss was not only felt on a personal level, but became the loss felt by the entire nation:

The wounds are still open, the severed organs have not yet regenerated. Day in and day out we feel the absence of the six million, our brethren and sisters, who were not fortunate enough to come with us to the homeland. Our brothers and sisters, fathers and mothers, massacred and burnt, accompanied and accompany us in our daily existence in all fields of life and development. They were with us in all our wars, in all our struggles from the past to this very day. Only in the unseen presence of the six million can one explain the establishment of the state and its continuous existence in face of the world nations and warmongers who spit venom and hatred towards us.[5]

Unlike their Labor Zionist predecessors, Likud politicians seemed more comfortable invoking the Holocaust as confirmation of a Zionist world view that saw Israel's battle with its enemies as a continuous chain in the Jewish struggle with antisemitism, which had not been vanquished by the creation of the state of Israel. Memory of the Holocaust was proof that Israel needed to remain strong in the face of all its enemies, past, present and future.

This ideology also seemed to be present in the settlement movement in the West Bank or Judea and Samaria, the biblical names associated with the Greater Land of Israel movement, which grew rapidly under the Likud governments following 1977. The Religious Zionist settlers of the West Bank saw themselves as the new vanguard of Jewish pioneers tasked with a divine mission to settle the Holy Land. Initially animated by Rabbi Zvi Yehuda Kook's prophecies of a divine meta-historical process at play that saw Israel's miraculous victory in the Six-Day War as a response to the catastrophe of the Holocaust, some in the movement believed that the apocalyptic destruction of European Jewry was necessary to usher in a pre-messianic age that would be accompanied by a return to the biblical lands of Judea and Samaria. With additional support from Likud governments under Begin and Shamir after 1977 (despite the withdrawal from Sinai and accompanying dismantling of settlements there in 1982), some in the settlement movement came to be convinced that the task of settling the land was not only part of the expansion of the boundaries of the state, but in fact a needed response to an eternal truth that had been revealed to the Jewish people by the Holocaust. Thus, for example, Harold Fisch, who was born in England but immigrated to Israel in 1957, where he became a professor of English Literature at Bar-Ilan University and one of the founders of the Movement for Greater Israel after the Six-Day War, believed that the Holocaust demonstrated that any belief in emancipation and acceptance of Jews by the nations of the world had failed; contrary to the classical Zionist ideas of Herzl, Zionism would never solve the problem of antisemitism.[6] For Fisch, the Arab-Israeli conflict, and the conflict with the Palestinians, was a continuation of this antisemitism and the response to it amounted to an existential defence of Judaism and the Jewish people. Building on Gush Emunim's official slogan 'The Land of Israel, for the People of Israel, according to the Torah of Israel',

God's covenant with the Jewish people meant that the Jewish claim to the Land superseded all other mundane earthly considerations. Settlement of the Land was not only divinely ordained, it would continue to protect the Jewish people against its eternal enemies. As explained by Fisch, 'to recognize the Arab hostility to Israel as diabolical, as a continuation of Hitler's war against the Jews, involves a recognition of the essential abnormality of the Jewish condition, and a recognition, also, that this abnormality has not ended with the establishment of a Jewish state'.[7] Even though the settlement movement would come to be composed of diverse strands – with Israelis moving to the West Bank and Gaza (until 2005) for many reasons: some political, some economic and some theological – the underlying implications of such non-negotiable components of the movement, especially in the West Bank, would be profound, as the movement grew to nearly 500,000 Israelis by 2022.

For broad sections of the modern Orthodox world, the linkage between the memory of the Shoah and the creation of the state of Israel indeed seemed divinely ordained. Rabbi Joseph Ber Soloveitchik, head of the Yeshiva University's Isaac Elchanan Theological Seminary in New York after 1941 (he was born in Poland in 1903, received his doctorate in Berlin in 1931 and arrived in Boston in 1932), epitomized the viewpoint as he expressed it in a sermon delivered on Israel's eighth Independence Day in 1956, entitled '*Kol Dodi Dofek, (Listen! My Beloved Knocks!)*',

> Eight years ago, amid a night of terror filled with the horrors of Majdanek, Treblinka, and Buchenwald; in a night of gas chambers and crematoria; a night of absolute divine self-concealment; a night ruled by the devil of doubt and destruction which sought to sweep the maiden from her house into the Christian church; a night of continuous searching, of yearning for the Beloved – that very night the Beloved appeared. 'God who conceals Himself in his Dazzling hiddenness' suddenly manifested Himself and began knocking at the tent of His despondent and disconsolate love, twisting convulsively on her bed, suffering the agonies of hell. Following the knocks on the door of the maiden, enveloped in mourning, the State of Israel was born!
>
> ...
>
> Let us not forget that the venom of Hitlerian antisemitism, which made the Jews like the fish of the sea to be preyed upon by all, still infects many in our generation who viewed the horrific spectacle of the gassing of millions with indifference, as an ordinary event barely requiring notice. The antidote to this deadly venom that poisoned minds and numbed hearts is the State of Israel's readiness to defend the lives of its children, its builders. Listen! My Beloved Knocks![8]

Theologically, Soloveitchik's articulation of the clear manifestation of the divine presence through the creation of the state, after 'God had concealed himself' in the time of Majdanek, Treblinka and Buchenwald, could be extended to the next stage of Israel's divinely inspired expansion.

Beyond Modern Orthodoxy and the National Religious camp, the 1980s also saw increasing engagement with the memory of the Holocaust in the Haredi (ultra-Orthodox) sphere, among both the Lithuanian Mithnagdic Yeshivot and the prominent Hasidic dynasties. On the theological level, Haredi thinkers expressed a range of explanations for the destruction of European Jewry, with some opponents of Zionism, like the Satmar Rebbe Joel Teitelbaum (based in New York) believing that the murder of six million Jews in Europe was punishment for the sins of the Zionists who had attempted to hasten the arrival of the messianic age. Others believed that no new explanatory framework needed to be created and that what has been called the Holocaust was simply another in a long chain of catastrophes in Jewish history. Likewise, for this reason, Rabbi Abraham I. Karelitz, the 'Hazon Ish' (1878–1953), perhaps the most important and influential Haredi rabbi and leader in the Yishuv/Israel from the early 1930s until his death in 1953, argued that the creation of special memorial days for the Holocaust's victims was unnecessary as Judaism already possessed fast days like the 10th of Tevet and the 9th of Av to mourn past tragedies. Rabbi Eliezer Menachem Shakh (1898–2001), head of the Ponevezh Yeshivah in Bene Berak, founder of the Degel HaTorah political party, and the leading authority in the Israeli 'Lithuanian' Haredi camp until his death in 2001, likewise expressed his belief that no new ritual or ceremonial observances needed to be added in the wake of the Holocaust, although for different reasons. As noted by scholar Kimmy Caplan, Rabbi Shakh explained the Holocaust as the ultimate reckoning for sins committed by generations of Jews, exacted at a single moment. In a talk at the Ponevezh Yeshivah in 1990, he commented:

I ask how and what a Jew should think in view of such a terrible Holocaust. Surely there is a reckoning for all of this; after all, nothing comparable to this horrific Holocaust has occurred in centuries. Obviously the answer is very clear. God exacted a one-on-one reckoning, a lengthy reckoning that spanned centuries until it added up to six million Jews, and that is how the Holocaust happened. This is what a Jew should believe, and if a Jew is not at peace with this belief, he is a heretic.[9]

On a theological level, the Holocaust must be understood as divine punishment for the sins of previous generations of Jews; at the same time, no other explanatory framework was necessary: God's punishment had been exacted and Jews were commanded to continue to obey the divine law as they always had. Kaplan argues that Shakh likely aimed his remarks at Rabbi Menachem Mendel Schneerson (1902–1994), the seventh Lubavitcher *Rebbe*, whom he regarded as a highly dangerous enemy of Jewry and Judaism, partly for his contrary belief that the Holocaust must not be understood in terms of reward and punishment. According to Schneerson:

> The destruction of six million Jews with incomparable cruelty – a terrible holocaust, the likes of which had never occurred before (and may it never recur, please God) – cannot be a punishment for sins since even Satan himself could not do a reckoning of that generation's iniquities that would suffice, heaven forefend, to justify so grave a punishment.[10]

Despite such debates over the meaning of the Shoah and how it should impact continued Jewish life in the aftermath, it is clear that beginning in the 1980s a serious attempt was made within Haredi society to begin addressing the Holocaust in the educational sphere. New textbooks were developed within Haredi educational frameworks in the 1980s, and new generations of university-trained scholars like Esther Farbstein, who studied at the Hebrew University of Jerusalem under the supervision of Yehuda Bauer, began to conduct academic research on Haredi responses to Nazi persecution during the Holocaust, while also coordinating Holocaust education at the *Michlalah* College in Jerusalem and developing Holocaust studies within the Beys Yakov educational framework. As a descendant of the Gerrer Rebbe whose husband directed the Mithnagdic Yeshiva in Hebron, Farbstein's impact on Holocaust studies in the Haredi world has been particularly noteworthy.

In 1986, the release of Claude Lanzmann's documentary, *Shoah*, would be greeted as a major cinematic event in Israel. The film premiered at Jerusalem's Cinematheque in June 1986, fourteen months after the film's world premiere in France. An audience that included Prime Minister Shimon Peres, along with President Chaim Herzog, and Chief Rabbi Avraham Shapira sat in the theatre to view the 566-minute film, along with the film's director Claude Lanzmann. The film, which did not utilize any archival footage, relied on survivor testimony and in many cases situated Holocaust survivors in Israel, retelling their experiences against an Israeli backdrop. Thus, Motke Zaidel recounted his escape from the Ponar forest near Vilna in the Ben Shemen forests of Israel; Avraham Bomba described the killing process at Treblinka and his work as a barber first in Jaffa overlooking the shores of Tel Aviv and then in a barbershop in Holon (near Tel Aviv); Simcha Rotem and Antek Zuckerman described the Warsaw Ghetto Uprising and the escape from the burning ghetto at the Ghetto Fighters House near Acre.[11]

In one of the 9-hour film's most memorable sequences, Lanzmann interviewed Avraham Bomba in a barbershop in Holon, where he cut the hair of an unidentified customer, evoking his job at Treblinka where he had to cut the hair of Jews before they were executed in the gas chambers. As he recounted the day that a transport arrived from his hometown of Częstochowa, Bomba explained, 'I knew a lot of them. I knew them; I lived with them in my town. I lived with them in my street, and some of them were my close friends. And when they saw me, they started asking me …

"What's going to happen to us?" What could you tell them? What could you tell them?' Bomba began to recall that a fellow barber suddenly saw his own wife and sister enter the gas chamber. At that moment, Bomba stopped: 'I can't', he says. 'It's too horrible. Please'. After a pause of nearly 90 seconds, as Lanzmann's camera remained on Bomba's face, the tough, sabra-like exterior of the survivor who had rebuilt his life in Israel seemed to break.

'I won't be able to do it', he pleads.
'You have to do it', Lanzmann tells him.
'Don't make me go on. Please'.
Lanzmann replies: 'You have to do it. I know it is very hard. I know
    and I apologize'.

Bomba is overwhelmed and struggles to regain composure, and yet, as he wipes his faces and continues to cut the hair of the man in the chair, viewers observe the struggle between past and present, the reckoning between deep and traumatic personal memories shared in the very mundane present. As noted by Michael Renov, in this difficult barbershop testimony, 'the kernel of trauma, buried and of the Real, erupts less as language, more as signs of bodily distress – [the] grimacing, [the] tears, the cessation of activity'.[12] By lingering on Bomba's silent struggle to regain composure, to fight against traumatic memory that will reduce him to tears, viewers become witnesses to the ways in which the past can burst forth into the present.[13]

FIGURE 4.1 *Abraham Bomba cuts the hair of an unidentified customer in* Shoah.

Source: https://www.youtube.com/watch?v=C-XyfftYSP0 (screenshot).

Jonathan Freedland, creator of a documentary about the reception of *Shoah* in Israel, notes:

> This gets close to the heart of what was singular about Lanzmann's film. If it had a message, it was that the Holocaust was not in the past: it had a presence in the present. It was all around. It did not exist only in archival monochrome, but in colour, in the here and now. The places where it happened were not in some distant galaxy, on the mythical Planet Auschwitz. They happened in this world: in this forest, in this field, in this village. And its pain lives on in this world too, in the places where the victims are remembered and the places where the survivors fled. The Holocaust runs deep in the soil of Poland and Germany and Lithuania and Belarus and every place Jews were killed, of course. But the Bomba sequence, like the shots of Motke Zaidel in the Ben Shemen forest, told that Israeli audience watching in Jerusalem that the Shoah was alive in their country too. They could not escape it. Too many people, and too many of their children, had been shaped – or broken – by it.[14]

Beyond convincing his audience, and perhaps specifically an Israeli audience, of the very presence of the past, Lanzmann also seemed to want to disrupt the heroic constructions of Jewish behaviour that had been at the centre of Israeli memory of the Shoah. The film focused on the Jewish encounter with the machinery of destruction: the trains, the camps, the gas chambers, the mass killings, but heroism and resistance are not entirely absent from the film; in fact, Lanzmann's placement of two ghetto fighters (his interview with Abba Kovner is entirely excluded from the final cut of the film) Simcha Rotem (Kazik) and Yitzhak (Antek) Zuckerman is quite intentional.

Rotem, who had been seen in the film interviewed at the Ghetto Fighters House, recounts his attempt to rescue the remaining fighters trapped in the Warsaw Ghetto as the camera reveals a scene of the Warsaw Ghetto memorial plaza at Yad Vashem in Jerusalem. Interspersed with the French translation for Lanzmann, Rotem recalls his last hours in the ghetto, searching for his comrades in the ruins of the burnt-out ghetto.

> Yes, I was all the time alone, except for the voice of the woman that I spoke of, and a man that I had met at the moment that I came out of the sewer; I was completely alone the length of my travels across the ghetto. There was still Richek and the two sewer guides inside the tunnels, but otherwise I did not meet a single living soul. I remember a moment in which I experienced a moment of tranquility, of serenity, in which I said to myself, I am the last living Jew here. I am going to wait until morning, I am going to wait for the Germans. And that would be the end.

Lanzmann cuts the interview with Rotem here; Yitzhak Zuckerman, also interviewed at the Ghetto Fighters House and included in the film, is presented as a broken man able to share his memories only when he drinks: 'if you could lick my heart you would be poisoned', he tells Lanzmann. As Alterman had suggested in his poem in 1954, the ghetto fighters have stepped down from their pedestal to blend in with the masses, their experiences have become more relatable, merged with those experiences of all Jews who encountered the machinery of destruction. Such representations paralleled a general transition from the earlier collective memory of the Shoah that privileged narratives of resistance to a broader range of experiences during the war which opened a space for a more comprehensive identification with the Holocaust among the broader Israeli public.

On 16 February 1987, the trial of John Demjanjuk commenced in Jerusalem. Twenty-five years after the execution of Adolf Eichmann, Demjanjuk was only the second person to be tried in Israel on charges of crimes against the Jewish people and crimes against humanity after he was extradited from the United States for having falsified immigration documents after the Second World War. The prosecution alleged that Demjanjuk had served in Treblinka after volunteering to join a special SS unit trained at the Trawniki camp. Based on the testimony of several Jewish survivors of Treblinka who identified Demjanjuk as the notorious 'Ivan the Terrible' who operated the diesel engine used to poison hundreds of thousands of Jews to death using carbon monoxide gas in the gas chambers, Demjanjuk was convicted and sentenced to death on 25 April 1988, only the second time an Israeli court had imposed the death penalty. In 1993, based on new evidence retrieved from newly opened Soviet archives, which suggested that another man, Ivan Marchenko, may have been 'Ivan the Terrible' and that Demjanjuk may have instead served as a guard at the Sobibor extermination camp, Israel's Supreme court overturned the previous conviction, while leaving the door open for the prosecution to try Demjanjuk again, based on the new Sobibor evidence. He would be released and eventually tried again in a German court from 2009 to 2011, where he was convicted and sentenced in 2011 (he died in a German nursing home in 2012, pending appeal of the conviction).[15]

As noted by Thomas Friedman in his contemporaneous coverage of the trial for *The New York Times*, 'to almost everyone's surprise, the Demjanjuk trial has taken Israel by storm and has become nothing less than an obsession for many Israelis'.[16] Responding to broad popular interest in the trial, proceedings were broadcast live on Israeli radio, while a closed-circuit TV stream broadcast proceedings to hundreds of people who gathered each day in a viewing hall adjacent to the courtroom. Prime Minister Yitzhak Shamir's spokesman, Avi Pazner, described the trial as 'the obsession of a generation which seemed to have no feeling about the Holocaust – the third generation of Israelis, people who not only did not know the Holocaust but their parents did not know it'. Many described the trial as perhaps the last chance to hear eyewitness testimony of survivors of the Holocaust, although it was in fact that testimony which would ultimately undermine the prosecution's attempts to prove beyond a reasonable doubt that Demjanjuk had in fact been 'Ivan the Terrible'. Still, the testimonies of survivors at the trial once again had a profound impact on the ways Israelis perceived the memory of the Holocaust. Friedman highlighted this aspect and impact of survivor testimony in his coverage, especially for a generation that seemed ready to understand their parents' experiences in a new light: 'for many Israeli survivors of the Nazis, the specificity of the violence that is discussed at the trial is being viewed as their answer both to those who say the Holocaust did not happen, and to their own children who could never understand why the Jews let it happen'. Itzhak Yaacovy, a survivor of Auschwitz living in Jerusalem, noted the impact the trial had on his children's understanding of his experiences:

My children, who were born in Israel, are also tied to the radio. It is bringing this whole thing to life for them. Ten years ago, when my son was 14 years old, he came to me one day and said, 'Father, I don't understand why you did not resist, why you just went like sheep to the slaughter'.

I told him: 'I was four years younger than you at that time. It was not so easy. How can you ask me such a question?'

It hurt me very much ... I felt terrible. After this trial started, my son, who is now in college, came to me and said: 'Father, I want to apologize. I never should have asked you what I did'. Actually, I had forgotten all about it, but he remembered.[17]

As a legal trial, however, the prosecution of Demjanjuk was flawed and differed in notable ways from the trial of Adolf Eichmann – not only in the approach the judges took to their task of pursuing justice, but quite specifically in the reliance on survivor testimony at the trial as eyewitnesses in a criminal sense (not just as witnesses in a historic sense).[18] While the court accepted survivor's identifications of Demjanjuk in photo spreads as the notorious 'Ivan the Terrible', it turned out this strategy only served to underline the unreliability of memory and the danger of including survivor testimony in a criminal prosecution forty years later. Even so, betraying to a certain extent a perception of its role that extended beyond the pursuit of justice and sought to vindicate the testimony of the witnesses and memorialize the murdered victims, the trial court that condemned Demjanjuk to death entitled a section of its judgment, 'A Monument': 'we shall erect in our judgment, according to the totality of the evidence before us, a monument to their [the victims'] souls, to the holy congregations that were lost and are no more.'[19] The Demjanjuk trial was evidence of an Israeli public increasingly fascinated by the most sordid aspects of the history of the Holocaust.

Some observers warned that Israel's approach to the memory of the Holocaust, shifting in tone from a focus on resistance to a collective identification with victimhood, could have lasting, unintended consequences. Survivor Yehuda Elkana warned that by becoming the eternal victim, Israel would see itself as always persecuted and always self-righteous in its actions, thereby enabling it to oppress others.[20] In an essay written in 1982, the

American-born Orthodox Rabbi David Hartman, who made Aliyah to Israel in 1971, warned that the Holocaust must not become the basis for the Jewish future.

> One of the fundamental issues facing the new spirit of maturity in Israel is: Should Auschwitz or Sinai be the orienting category shaping our understanding of the rebirth of the State of Israel? ... Israel is not only a response to modern antisemitism, but is above all a modern expression of the eternal Sinai covenant that has shaped Jewish consciousness throughout the millennia. It was not Hitler who brought us back to Zion, but rather belief in the eternal validity of the Sinai covenant ... . It is dangerous to our growth as a healthy people if the memory of Auschwitz becomes a substitute for Sinai.
>
>   The model of Sinai awakens the Jewish people to the awesome responsibility of becoming a holy people. At Sinai, we discover the absolute demand of God; we discover who we are by what we do. Sinai calls us to action, to moral awakening, to living constantly with challenges of building a moral and just society which mirrors the kingdom of God in history. Sinai creates humility and openness to the demands of self-transcendence. In this respect, it is the antithesis of the moral narcissism that can result from suffering and from viewing oneself as a victim ... .
>
>   We will mourn forever because of the memory of Auschwitz. We will build a healthy new society because of the memory of Sinai.[21]

The Israeli philosopher Adi Ophir warned that by 'sanctifying' the memory of the Holocaust, present generations might engage in a form of idolatry that would prevent them from truly wrestling with the memory of the Shoah and its implications for the future, while also allowing for it to be invoked for present political purposes. In a 1987 article in the magazine, *Tikkun*, his 'Anti-Theological Treatise' identified (satirically) four 'commandments' that ruled the new 'religious consciousness built around the Holocaust'.[22] They were: 'thou shalt have no other holocaust before the Holocaust of the Jews of Europe; Thou shalt not make unto thee any graven image or any likeness; Thou shalt not take the name of the Holocaust in vain; Remember'. Ophir warned against the danger of enforcing these commandments, through which historians and community leaders seek to 'establish the boundaries of Jewish legitimacy; they establish the Holocaust as a transcendent event which precedes and qualifies any attempt to fashion a modern Jewish identity'.[23] By sanctifying the Holocaust, Ophir suggested, the commandments prevented any comparison to the Holocaust, making it a uniquely Jewish event which would be fenced off as a specifically Jewish tragedy, and not be studied for the purpose of preventing genocide in the present or future. Furthermore, by fashioning a modern Jewish identity solely based on the sanctified memory of the Holocaust, the current generation would be engaged in a form of idolatry antithetical to the foundational components of Judaism.

Nonetheless, such warnings, which may have reflected a concern with the growing prevalence of references to the Shoah in both popular and political culture that paralleled the growth of a broader Holocaust memory culture in America, Israel, and elsewhere, did nothing to slow the deeper identification with the memory of the Shoah which proceeded apace. The fall of the Berlin Wall and the collapse of the Iron Curtain in Eastern Europe opened up new possibilities for connecting with that traumatic past, just at the time when even more survivors journeyed from the former Soviet Union to Israel beginning in 1991.

The March of the Living and state-sponsored programmes to bring thousands of Israeli teenagers to sites of concentration and death camps in Eastern Europe commenced in 1988, becoming an initiation ritual for high-school seniors before their service in the army and cementing a sense of existential threat and need for military strength as well as national pride.[24] Jackie Feldman, who has written extensively about the Israeli trips to Poland, estimates that between the mid-1980s and 2002, over 100,000 Israeli youth visited the death camps in Poland on trips organized either by schools under the auspices of the Ministry of Education, or by youth movements and private tour agents. Until trips were temporarily suspended in summer 2022 (following a dispute over Polish supervision of the tours after the passage of a Polish law criminalizing speech that alleged any form of Polish collaboration with German crimes during the war), the youth tours of Poland tended to follow a prescribed itinerary, which included visits to death camps like Treblinka and Auschwitz, tours of cemeteries, remains of former Jewish shtetls and abandoned synagogues, and ceremonial re-enactments of the 'March of the Living' at Auschwitz-Birkenau and in the Warsaw Ghetto. Tours include testimonies from survivors, helping the youth who participate to become 'witnesses of the witnesses' bestowed with the responsibility to pass the torch of memory from one generation to the next. As explained by Feldman:

> The sequence of ceremonies and the structure of each individual ceremony prescribes a sequence of redemption. Students leave Israel for Warsaw, where they are introduced to pre-Holocaust Jewish life in Poland. From there, they proceed to a series of death camps, performing ceremonies at each site, before returning to Warsaw to visit the sites of the Warsaw Ghetto Revolt. Students approach the Warsaw Ghetto Fighters' Memorial by walking the symbolic 'Memorial Route of Jewish Martyrdom and Struggle' in reverse, from the Umschlagplatz (deportation square) to the Memorial. The students' path, like the monument's iconography, moves from martyrdom and destruction to revolt. Immediately after the rousing chant of the national anthem, students will board the plane for the flight home. The Monument, symbolizing physical resistance and military heroism, serves as the portal of entry into the land of Israel. The student bodily re-enacts the path from exile to redemption (galut to ge'ulah) as a voyage in *space*.[25]

FIGURE 4.2 *March of the Living delegations at Auschwitz in 1992. Rabbi Israel Meir Lau, a native of Piotrkow Trybunalski, was liberated from Buchenwald at the age of eight and in 1992 was chief rabbi of Tel Aviv (and later, the chief rabbi of Israel). According to Lau, pictured in the top photo above, it was decided that the March would carry eighteen Israel flags to symbolize the Hebrew word 'Chai' or Life, the numeric equivalent of the number 18 in Hebrew.*

Source: Photo taken by Ivy Sara Patt, from the collection of the author.

The trips to Poland, which resumed in 2023 following a compromise between the Israeli and Polish governments, have become a *rite of passage* for most Israeli youth, where the encounter with the Jewish people's traumatic recent past concludes with a triumphant return to a strong, resilient and powerful Jewish state. (Likewise, it is not uncommon for American Jewish youth who participate in the *March of the Living* to also adorn themselves with Israeli flags as they participate on the march.) As the distance between the Jewish state and the Jewish diaspora past shrinks, the identification with the suffering of Jews in the Holocaust grows, as does the implicit linkage between the destruction of Jewish life in Europe and its rebirth in the state of Israel.

In her 2001 Yom HaShoah speech, Israel's minister of education, Limor Livnat, a member of Benjamin Netanyahu's Likud government, conveyed a sense that, in the words of Feldman, 'the Holocaust never really ended, and that, but for the State and its defense forces, the Jews in Israel would today be on their way to the gas chambers'.

> Primo Levi once wrote that an unbridgeable abyss yawns between one who was there and one who wasn't. Astoundingly, it seems today that this gap is narrowing. Many of us feel as though we might have been there; to a certain extent, it's as if we were there. Our young people, second and third generation offspring of native-born Israelis, gravitate towards Auschwitz. They want their own feet to tread that cursed earth, as though to assure themselves that the sun which rises there is the same one which rises in our world. I've watched them there clinging to one another, clutching the flag of Israel, weeping … . We shouldn't suppose that we differ from our grandfathers and grandparents who went to the gas chambers. What separates us from them is not that we are some sort of new Jew. The main difference is external: we have a state, and a flag and an army: caught in their tragedy, they lacked all three.[26]

No longer do Israelis feel that their triumph over Jewish persecution is a consequence of having been born in an Israel that removed itself from the cycle of Jewish history. Instead, their survival and their identity is no more than an accident of history, but for the grace of God, this line of thinking suggests, they too may have died in the gas chambers.

Israeli Holocaust literature

The 1980s also saw the growth of what has been termed 'second-generation' literature and film, which grew out of the increased literary productivity of survivor authors themselves.

The 'second-generation' or children of Holocaust survivors, building on the works of the previous generation, began to use art, literature and film-making as a means to reflect about their parents' historical trauma and the second-hand trauma that they had inherited as individuals, bearing witness to the witnesses of the Holocaust. Likewise, works created by writers who were not the children of survivors, such as Yehoshua Sobol's play *Ghetto* (1984), raised aspects of Holocaust history in the cultural sphere in a new way. Sobol was born in Israel in 1939 and studied philosophy at the Sorbonne. His 1984 masterpiece, *Ghetto*, examined the conflicting reactions to the theatre that flourished in the Vilna Ghetto. The play was performed in Germany soon after its initial staging in Haifa and would eventually be translated into twenty languages and performed in twenty-five countries, earning Sobol awards for best play of the year in Israel, Germany, England and Japan. *Ghetto* (the first play in a trilogy about the Vilna Ghetto that also included *Adam* and *Underground*) depicted daily life in the Vilna Ghetto in 1941 and 1943. As a fluent Yiddish speaker, Sobol was able to draw upon primary archival materials, basing parts of the show on Hermann Kruk's Vilna ghetto diary, the Bundist librarian (who is also one of the leading characters in the play). Sobol quoted Kruk's diary from 17 January 1941: 'one should not produce theatrical shows in a graveyard', while also examining the tension between resistance and survival. The show problematizes the moral dilemma of creating art in times of oppression and asking whether art that witnesses can overcome the moral hesitation of creating something frivolous in a murderous context. The controversial head of the Vilna Ghetto, Jacob Gens, who was accused of preventing the revolt in Vilna at the behest of the Gestapo, is also depicted in the play, although Sobol raises difficult questions about the ghetto fighters, their drive to fight and the question of whether their desire for resistance may have caused more damage. In his plays, Jewish leaders collaborated with the Germans in order to save more people, while the fighters led violent actions that only caused revenge on the innocent.[27] The fact a play like Sobol's could begin to raise such difficult and controversial questions in the cultural sphere and gain critical acclaim signalled a new willingness to both remove the ghetto fighters from their wartime and post-war pedestal and re-examine the wartime history in the 1980s.

Another work created by an Israel-born writer not descended from survivors, David Grossman's *See Under Love* (1986), focused on the effects of the Shoah on survivors and their children in Israel.[28] Hailed as a 'masterpiece' by contemporary critics, Grossman's novel incorporated both fantasy and post-modern techniques, while also attending to the ways in which memory and trauma passed from one generation to the next. Authors who were in fact children of survivors, like Savyon Liebrecht and Nava Semel, created literature that examined the lasting impact of the Shoah, crucially situating these stories within the Israeli landscape in the voice of those who had grown up in Israel. As noted by literary scholar Ephraim Sicher,

In the 1980s the 'second generation' acquired a legitimacy that had been denied their parents. Their telling of their parents' stories became a telling of their own, an unwilled voicing of what they had not known and had not lived through. It was an attempt to recover personal and collective memory from a politicized public discourse and to express something of the guilt for the stigmas attached to the survivor immigrants, perhaps for the Jewish leadership's inability to help the European Jews in their hour of need and the formal denial of the relevance of the of the Holocaust to national identity. In some cases guilt is expressed for somehow not being 'there', either as an expression of the desired but impossible rescue of the six million or as an expression of inferiority to those who had the strength to survive.[29]

Beginning in the 1980s, psychologists in Israel (and America) began to study the intergenerational transmission of trauma from survivors to their children, observing that children in these families confirmed that at home there was a psychological presence of the Holocaust, suggesting that they experienced the Holocaust 'through osmosis'. Yael Danieli's research also found that survivor parents may have also inadvertently transmitted their own wartime experience in their attempt to teach their children how to survive in the event of further persecution.[30] Dina Wardi has described this group as 'memorial candles', individuals who have taken the task of remembering their family's history despite the burden. It is important to note that not every member of the 'second generation' reacts to their parents' experiences in the same way and yet, certain members of this cohort assume this responsibility more than others. Each 'memorial candle' straddles what Wardi calls a 'double reality': they live in the present, while also being a part of the past as bearers of their parents' and grandparents' history. Traumatic memories may also be passed from one generation to the next, leading to nightmares, mental health issues or familial struggles that stem from the Holocaust. What Wardi terms 'borrowed memories' other scholars have described as 'post-memory' (see Marianne Hirsch). As Wardi also points out, the majority of the 'memorial candles' are females, which we can also be seen reflected in the trends of 'second-generation' Israeli Holocaust literature.[31]

Savyon Liebrecht, who was born in Munich in 1948 to Holocaust survivors and studied philosophy and literature at Tel Aviv University, began publishing her Hebrew short stories in 1986. Liebrecht's stories address multiple themes including relations between Arabs and Jews, the Orthodox and the secular, but are especially noteworthy for tackling women's experiences during the Shoah. Liebrecht's stories directly address the traumatic nature of sexual violence perpetrated against women, which, as we may recall, had been sensationalized in works like Katzetnik's *House of Dolls*, but not tackled head on in examining their impact not only on the women who were victims and survivors, but on subsequent generations of descendants.

'Morning in the Park with Nannies', published in the 1992 collection *It's All Greek to Me, He Said to Her*, introduces a narrator who witnessed sexual abuse in a brothel during the war, where she worked as a seamstress.

The unnamed narrator sits among a group of other nannies in a Tel Aviv park, when she recognizes a new nanny immediately, even though it has been decades since she last saw her in the brothel. Watching her care for the young child, the narrator is suddenly back in the war, asking the nanny if she remembers the scenes of sexual violence she observed and endured:

> Do you remember the three girls that were taken out one night for an orgy? The Germans were drunker than ever. At dawn two of them crawled back, their bodies bruised all over. The third girl had been rolled up in a carpet, her long hair hanging out of one end, dragged into the garden, and set on fire. The drunken Germans stood and watched the hair, flaring up readily, and the smell of burnt flesh filled the rooms until the wind blew. One of the girls told us, before she was taken to the doctor and never returned, that the Germans had strangled her friend while violating her body. In the morning the other girl began to spew blood. She came to my room for shelter and showed me the fist marks on her lower abdomen.[32]

Liebrecht's narrator raises themes of sexual violence that had long been silenced, not only in literature, but in testimony, in commemoration and in any public discussion of the Shoah: 'How did you guard your soul in that place?', she asks the woman (and perhaps herself).[33]

In the story, 'Excision', a seemingly mundane incident – a four-year-old girl is sent home from kindergarten with lice – becomes an echo of the Shoah, when her grandmother, Henya, an Auschwitz survivor, insists that the only solution is to cut the girl's hair off entirely. As she explains to her son, Zvika:

> Zvika, listen to me. I know what's good for my children. I've been through a lot and I know. When you've got lice, no chemical and no washing will do. The best thing is to crop the hair right at once, down to the roots. Every hour there are more and more eggs; every minute counts.

Ziva, Henya's daughter-in-law is furious, 'so what if that's what they used to do in the camps forty-five years ago. The world has advanced a little since then, and we're not in the camps now' and insists that her mother-in-law be kept far away from her daughter, 'tell her never to set foot in here again. I never want to see her face. Never again for the rest of my life!' She is apoplectic when she learns that her daughter has not only been exposed to her grandmother's extreme reaction, but to the rationale for this behaviour, rooted in the experience of Auschwitz and memories of lice crawling on the body of a boy shot at Auschwitz.

> Do you hear where your child is saying? She knows what the lice did when people died in the camps. Does a four-year old have to hear such things? Is such a story fit for her someone her age, I ask you? I want my child to hear stories about Cinderella, not about Auschwitz.[34]

And yet, in presenting Henya's traumatic reaction to the spectre of lice, Liebrecht wants the reader to understand not only how such trauma may be passed from one generation to the next, but to develop empathy for the experience of the survivor who still sees these memories before her eyes. The daughter-in-law who seeks to banish her mother-in-law and her memories of the Shoah from her house becomes the villain, emblematic of an approach to ignoring the Holocaust that Israelis seem ready to move on from. Liebrecht, born in post-war Germany and raised in Israel, becomes the ideal translator of Holocaust memories for an Israeli audience.

Nava Semel, born in Tel Aviv to Holocaust survivors, Yitzhak and Mimi Artzi (and the younger sister of acclaimed Israeli musician, Shlomo Artzi), was also a pioneer in creating Israeli Holocaust literature that examined the last effects of the Shoah on the second generation. Her first prose book, 'Hat of Glass' (1985), was a collection of short stories about the sons and daughters of Holocaust survivors, and recipient of the Massuah Prize from the Institute for Holocaust Studies. Her later novel, *And the Rat Laughed* (2001), recounts the abuse of a five-year-old Jewish girl at the hands of the peasant family paid to hide her, while also grappling with the complexities of translating and conveying brutal stories of survival from one generation to the next. Unfolding from multiple perspectives as a story told by a grandmother to her granddaughter, the novel at first omits much more than is told to the third generation, eventually revealing the horrific nature of the abuse the five-year-old girl was forced to endure at the hands of a Polish peasant boy in the lightless potato pit where she was supposedly 'rescued'.[35]

According to literary scholar Ranen Omer-Sherman, Semel challenges the notion that survivor testimony can be cathartic or redemptive.

> 'The storyteller is supposed to gain something from the very act of telling the story. Release, after all, according to the experts, is supposed to bring relief … . And yet, no gain seems to present itself in the case of her story. The natural act of returning to the past and rummaging through memories brings solace only to those with very different stories to tell.[36]

Historian Dalia Ofer argues that 'the main motifs in second generation literature are a profound identification with the survivor parents, the fear of disappointing them, the desire to protect them, and apprehension that the parents' experiences will carry them back to "there", from where they will not be able to return'.[37] This group also began to express feelings, memories and experiences that had remained largely private or within families until then, using their native voices to assert a place for survivor memories in broader Israeli society. Even so, there was nothing cathartic about retelling and sharing the memories; the trauma endured.

The late 1980s and early 1990s saw an outpouring of cultural creations that processed the trauma of the Holocaust, paralleling a more global interest in the subject (such as in *Escape from Sobibor*, 1987, *Europa,*

Europa, 1990 or *Schindler's List*, 1993). Gila Almagor created two films in the late 1980s and early 1990s, drawing on her personal memories as the daughter of a survivor family, which introduced the subject to a much wider Israeli audience through *The Summer of Aviya* (1988) and *Underneath the Domim Tree* (1995). Like 'Excision', *Summer of Aviya*, based on the autobiographical novel by acclaimed theatre actress Gila Almagor, includes a scene where a young Aviya is sent home from school with lice, only to also have her hair shorn by her mother Henya (played by Almagor herself), just as they did in the camps.

The documentary film *Because of That War* (1988) portrayed the experiences of rock musician Yehuda Poliker and his partner Yaakov Gil'ad, both children of survivors driven to write rock songs about the Shoah chronicling their parents' experiences. Film scholar Yosefa Loshitzky identifies *Because of That War* as part of an effort to 'take the Holocaust out of the Museum', to make it more accessible to a younger Israeli public, while also 'expropriat(ing) the Holocaust from the Israeli Right' (which she also links to the timing of the First Intifada). Through popular music that could be broadcast on the radio, 'the assimilation of Poliker and Gilead's Holocaust "hits" into Israeli mainstream culture signified a change in the perception of the Holocaust by the Israeli public. The Holocaust was no longer perceived as "another planet" requiring a "new language", but rather a human event that could be represented through terms and concepts borrowed from everyday life'.[38]

Yehuda Poliker, the son of Jacko, a Greek survivor from Salonika, had already risen to prominence as a rock star in Israel with his band, *Benzin*. After the breakup of *Benzin*, Poliker and Ya'akov Gilad felt compelled to work on *Ashes and Dust*, to musically document their experiences as children of survivors growing up in Israel; Gilad's mother, Halina Birnbaum, was a survivor of the Warsaw Ghetto, Majdanek, Auschwitz, and a death march to Ravensbrueck. Poliker and Gilad first composed the songs on *Ashes and Dust* for a radio programme that was aired on Yom Hashoah in Israel in 1986, dedicated to the experiences of Holocaust survivors' children.[39] The album they created is a unique blend of rock, folk, pop and Greek music, which mixes bouzoukis and accordions with heavy guitars and sampled synthesizer sounds creating a new genre of lachrymose rock memorializing the Holocaust.[40] In an interview Gilad noted their drive to persist in creating the album despite objections from DJs on Israeli radio that the subject was too depressing to play in the radio: 'We said, "You can't put it in the ghetto and shove it off." We said, "We live it every day, and so do our parents, and we believe there are many people who also live it every day".[41] The album quickly became a best-seller played far more frequently than just on Yom Hashoah. The lyrics engaged with the lasting legacy of the Holocaust on the next generation, the memorial candles who carried the burden of Treblinka and Auschwitz's ashes amidst the dust of Israel. The song 'Ashes and Dust' carried the lament passed from one generation to the next, 'if you're going, where are you going, forever is just ashes and dust' along with the anticipation of the upcoming transfer of the burden of memory to the next generation: 'Who will sweeten your nights, Who will listen to your crying, Who will stay by your side [while you are] on your way'.

Because of That War, first as an album and then as a documentary, cast a bright spotlight on the burdens of the war carried by the generation after who could not forget the past no matter how hard they tried. It was a past they carried with them every single day. Children like Ya'akov Gilad and Yehuda Poliker may have been intended as the substitute for the families lost during the war, named after two and even three relatives who died in the Holocaust, but they could not replace that past, literally carrying in their identity the obligation of commemoration.[42] 'Because of that war' they sang, because of the memories they now also carried, 'because of the memories, we are also victims'.

Shlomo Artzi, brother of Nava Semel, was also deeply influenced by his parents' experiences and would become one of Israel's most successful musicians. His folksy rock came to be synonymous with Israeli popular music of the 1980s, 1990s and beyond, making him one of Israel's best-selling musicians of all time. On his 1988 album *Hom Yuli August* (the heat of July August), Artzi also broached his father Yitzhak's wartime experiences on the song 'Romania'. Yitzhak Artzi, who had been the leader of the Romanian underground and helped rescue children from transit camps during the war, would also serve in the Knesset between 1984 and 1988. 'In Romania his parents are buried and even his grandfather, and the water rises from the ditch … . No he does not dare to look at me, if he looks it will be painful, this way he was always alone like an island, no it wasn't his fault'.

In 1989, Chava Alberstein, who had already established herself as one of Israel's most popular folk singers began to introduce Yiddish poetry and music into her repertoire. Born in Sczeczin in Poland in 1947, Alberstein moved to Israel at the age of four with her parents, both of whom were survivors.[43] Alberstein released the album *Chava Zingt Yiddish* (Chava Sings in Yiddish) in 1989, which included such Holocaust songs as Avrom Sutzkever's 'Under Your White Stars', about his longing for contact from God alone in the Vilna ghetto, and 'The Partisan's Song', '*Zog Nit Keyn Mol*', written by Hersh Glick, the anthem of the Jewish underground and partisans in occupied Europe. On a subsequent album, *The Well*, recorded with the New York-based Klezmer group, the Klezmatics in 1998, she would include even more Holocaust poetry set to music. The fact that renowned musicians, children of survivors, were introducing their parents' wartime experiences, along with the music and languages of the Jewish communities destroyed in the Shoah in music and poetry – and the fact that the Israeli public, as seen in popular reception and album sales – was ready for this music, reflected a greater openness to engage with the memory of the Shoah and a broader spectrum of wartime experiences.

Also in the 1980s and 1990s, non-European Jews, that is, Mizrahi, North African, and even Iraqi Jews, began to claim the Holocaust as part of their experience, even if they were removed from the places that the Nazis had reached during the war (except for Vichy regime camps in Algeria, Morocco and Tunisia, along with Italian camps in Libya). Collective memory of the Holocaust became a unifying principle for Jews from diverse backgrounds as second-generation, Israeli-born, Mizrachi Jews claimed in different ways that they could empathize with European Jews – mainly because they themselves understood what it meant to be victims of discrimination – at the same time that after Begin's rise to power the memory of the Holocaust became an integral part of the collective national identity.[44] Even if such claims were challenged by descendants of survivors, the push for additional research on Sephardic experiences during the Shoah (such as those of Greek Jews like Poliker or the impact of German, French and Italian occupation in North Africa) suggests that inclusion in the collective memory of the Holocaust serves as a way to facilitate greater inclusion in the national community.

Why did this movement begin to develop in Israel (or for that matter in the wider world) in the 1980s? Perhaps the children of survivors felt more empowered to express what their parents could not express, both their experiences during the war and their role in helping building the country just three years later. Or perhaps shifts in a society that had privileged individual self-sacrifice for the collective good began to open up more space for valuing individual experiences. Or, as we have noted, perhaps the combination of the Eichmann trial and the continuing struggle against neighbours bent on Israel's destruction meant that the Holocaust had never actually ended, and the ways in which Israelis processed continuing trauma had as much to do with the legacies of the Holocaust as it did other aspects of the Israeli experience. Israeli trauma of the 1980s – both the quagmire of the Lebanon War that began in 1982 and then the Intifada, or outbreak of the Palestinian Uprising in 1987 – may have also triggered a deeper identification with the Holocaust as a frame of reference.

In all respects, 'memories' of the Holocaust continued to serve as a frame of reference for any number of experiences that many children of survivors in Israel endured. After the quagmire that was the Lebanon War (1982–5) and the massacres in Palestinian refugee camps perpetrated by Phalangist militias as Israeli soldiers stood guard nearby, some Israelis questioned whether Israeli soldiers were capable of the same inhumanity as the Nazis. Ari Folman, creator of the 2008 film *Waltz with Bashir*, explained his repression of any memory of the massacre at the Sabra and Shatilla Palestinian refugee camps in Beirut by Phalangist militias as related to a deeper repression of his parents' experiences from the Holocaust. As he explained in an interview with Ethan Bronner of the *New York Times*: 'in Israel the Holocaust is in our DNA. We see mass murder, and what on earth could it remind us of but our past?'[45] Folman's parents were both survivors of Auschwitz and he explained that the Holocaust was a constant presence as he was growing

FIGURE 4.3 Waltz with Bashir *(2008) screengrab.*

up. The film recounts Folman's efforts to recover his repressed memories, including insightful scenes involving Folman's therapist, who notes that in his service in Lebanon, guarding the camps where the massacres took place, Folman 'unwillingly took on the role of the Nazi'. Perhaps, the therapist implies, Folman suppressed his memories to distance himself from this feeling of shame and guilt.

Even as the 1980s and the Lebanon War and the outbreak of the First Intifada in 1987 forced Israelis to grapple with whether the Zionist movement was always justified in its foreign policy or in its relations with the Arabs in general and the Palestinians specifically, the growth of a post-Zionist critique willing to question the founding mythologies of the state also had an impact on the nature of Israel's relationship to the history and memory of the Holocaust.

Tom Segev's 1991 *The Seventh Million*, part of a broader wave of post-Zionist critiques, triggered research on the place of the Shoah in Israeli collective memory and its influence on state, society, culture and national identity has emerged as a vast field, accompanied by intense historiographical debate.[46] As Israeli society began to question some of its founding myths, Segev's provocative research argued that Israel's early leaders had not only not done enough to rescue European Jews during the Holocaust, but had then treated them in a manner that was far from compassionate after their arrival, preferring silence and repression to active engagement with the traumatic recent past. 'After the war, a great silence surrounded the destruction of the Jews', Segev argued. 'Then came moral and political conflicts, including the painful debate over relations with Germany, which slowly brought the Israelis to recognize the deeper meaning of the Holocaust. The trial of Adolf Eichmann served as therapy for the nation, starting a process of identification with the tragedy of the victims and survivors, a process that continues to this day'.[47]

A new vein of post-Zionist historiography, comfortable in critiquing the historical development of the Zionist movement and the Yishuv leadership, has attempted to study the history from an 'objective', non-Zionist viewpoint capable of incorporating the viewpoints of other groups (namely Holocaust survivors themselves) who, they argue, had been largely co-opted by the state in previous historical treatments. These scholars have investigated the Yishuv's responses to the destruction of European Jewry and attitudes of Israeli society to Holocaust survivors in the first decades of the state, while also highlighting the roles that survivors played in building the state and shaping its society. Scholars have also studied the impact of certain critical events – such as the debate over reparations from Germany and Holocaust-related trials in Israeli courts – on Israelis' perceptions of the Holocaust; and the ways collective memory of the Holocaust has shaped Israel's politics, diplomacy and military activity.[48]

The post-Zionist critique found expression in historical research on the Holocaust, especially among political scientists and journalists who asked whether Israel had cynically manipulated the memory of the Holocaust for political purposes or taken advantage of the desperation of survivors after the war to make them part of the struggle to create the state (see in particular the work of Idith Zertal, *From Catastrophe to Power: The Holocaust Survivors and the Emergence of Israel* (1998) and *Israel's Holocaust and the Politics of Nationhood* (2005)).

Willingness to question the founding myths (post-Zionism) also opened a space for coming to terms with Israel's role in the continued plight of the Palestinian refugees who had been displaced first by the 1948 war and then again in the conquest of the West Bank and Gaza in 1967.

As a consequence of the First Intifada, the Iraq War and a belief that the continued settlement of the West Bank would undermine the Zionist project, Israel's new Labor government in 1992 entered into secret negotiations with the PLO to advance what came to be known as the 'Oslo Peace Process' to grant Palestinian sovereignty over negotiated portions of Gaza and the West Bank. In his September 1993 speech at the White House for the signing of the Israeli-Palestinian agreement, Prime Minister Yitzhak Rabin, who had served as chief of staff in the IDF for the 1967 war that saw the conquest of the West Bank, alluded to the long hoped-for peace by Israelis traumatized by generations of terror and violence. But unlike Menachem Begin, he did not mention the Holocaust.

> We have come from Jerusalem, the ancient and eternal capital of the Jewish people. We have come from an anguished and grieving land. We have come from a people, a home, a family, that has not known a single year not a single month in which mothers have not wept for their sons. We have come to try and put an end to the hostilities, so that our

children, our children's children, will no longer experience the painful
cost of war, violence and terror. We have come to secure their lives and to
ease the sorrow and the painful memories of the past to hope and pray
for peace.[49]

Nonetheless, this did not stop his political opponents from using the
memory of the Holocaust as a rhetorical tool to warn of the great dangers
they saw associated with pursuing peace with Israel's enemies, especially the
Palestinians. Thus, for example, opponents of the Oslo Peace Process like far-
right politician, Moshe Feiglin (founder of the 'This Is Our Land' movement
to protest the Oslo Accords), charged: 'Rabin is the Judenrat loading us
onto the trains' or 'leading us like lambs to the slaughter'. Likewise, Ariel
Sharon, a general in the IDF, former defence minister in the right-wing Likud
government, and later prime minister, asked: 'What is the difference between
the Jewish Council in the ghetto and the [Rabin] government? There, the
Jews were forced to collaborate; here the government is doing everything
of its own free will'.[50] Benjamin Netanyahu, then leader of the Likud party,
spoke at a 5 October 1995 rally in Zion Square in Jerusalem to protest the
peace process (the same square where Begin rallied the public against the
Reparations Agreement). In the crowd, protesters held posters which had
photo-shopped Rabin's head onto the body of SS General Heinrich Himmler,
while the crowd chanted 'In blood and fire, we will cast out Rabin', 'Rabin
is a traitor' and 'Rabin is a murderer'. Such incitement would inspire Yigal
Amir to assassinate Yitzhak Rabin one month later in November 1995; Amir
argued that according to Jewish law he was justified in assassinating Rabin
because he had prevented the death of others (who would be endangered
by the peace process). While the assassination of Rabin prompted great
soul-searching in Israel over incitement and the violent rhetoric that had
poisoned political discourse, a series of bus bombings by Hamas helped lead
to the election of Benjamin Netanyahu and his Likud government in 1996.
Nonetheless, the Oslo Accords continued as did the usage of Holocaust
analogies in the political sphere.

Many observers began to criticize not only the politicization of the
memory of the Holocaust, but the trivialization of this memory through its
coarse usage in the public sphere, removed from a sacred, commemorative
space. This critique came predominantly from the political left in opposition
to what had become the dominant narrative since Begin, namely that Jews
have been persecuted and will always be persecuted, and that this view has
triumphed over the classical Zionist belief in the ability to create the New
Jew who can conquer diaspora history and function in the modern world.
This critique of a cynical manipulation of the memory of the Holocaust
for political purposes (especially to justify exerting power over the
Palestinians) also found expression in the increasingly frequent references
to the memory of the Holocaust in Israeli humour, beginning in the 1980s.
Even so, as Liat Steir Livny argues, satirical skits about the Holocaust in

FIGURE 4.4 *Newspaper reproduction of posters branding Rabin a 'Nazi'.*

Israel did not minimize or trivialize the Shoah but instead simultaneously reinforced the centrality of the Shoah in Israeli society while also allowing for critiques of the instrumentalization and politicization of the Shoah in Israel.[51]

Since the 1990s, sketch comedy in Israel has often focused on satirizing the politicization and trivialization of the Shoah while simultaneously highlighting how the saturation of the Shoah in the public sphere minimizes the meaning of the Shoah and shapes the world view of Israelis. The 1990s Israeli sketch comedy show *HaHamishia HaKamerit* (The Camera Quintet for which the noted Israeli author Etgar Keret, a son of Holocaust survivors, also served as a writer) included sketches on all aspects of Israeli society, with occasional references to the Holocaust. Several of these addressed the nature of Israel's relationship with Germany, such as the skit 'Feldermaus at the Olympics', which included the bumbling Israeli diplomat Feldermaus interceding at a track and field event in Stuttgart in 1995. The sketch makes fun of Jewish athletic ability (or the lack thereof) while appealing to German guilt to allow a Jewish runner to gain some advantage in the race.[52] After asking the German track and field judge for a competitive advantage for the little Israeli runner 'with legs like popsicle sticks' but receiving no assistance, Feldermaus plays the 'Holocaust card'.

> Haven't you seen *Schindler*? Haven't the Jewish people suffered enough?
> His mother is in the stadium, after everything she has been through [implies she is a survivor] she has come back to see him compete.

Once the judge agrees to give the Israeli athlete a small head start to lessen the 'historical suffering', the two Israeli diplomats promise to honour the heroism of the judge: 'We will take your details and get you a place on the Righteous Persons Boulevard [at Yad Vashem]'. The skit does not make light of the Holocaust itself, although it does lampoon the Israeli tendency to make use of memory of the Holocaust, particularly in its relationship with Germany, to secure every competitive advantage. Likewise, the joke about the 'Righteous Persons Boulevard' also highlights the degree to which a Holocaust memorial and museum like Yad Vashem can be politicized.[53]

In another skit called 'Ghetto', which jokes about trivialization through street-naming practices in Tel Aviv, two friends talk about how to drive to a party in Tel Aviv.[54]

> Are you coming with a car?
> Here's what you have to do: drive on Warsaw Ghetto, make a U-turn on Concentration Camp Boulevard, and park in Dachau Square.
> Is it close?
> What? Dachau? It's here, just around the corner.

In making light of Israeli street-naming practices, the sketch also highlights how such practices might trivialize historical places and events and emphasizes the centrality of concentration camps and ghettos in the Israeli collective psyche.

Another *HaHamishia HaKamerit* short sketch called 'Schindler', which is modelled after Claude Lanzmann and *Shoah*, shows two men walking in a field in the distance, speaking French and a pigeon hybrid of Polish and Yiddish. A survivor (played by Rami Heuberger, who also acted in the film *Schindler's List* as Josef Bau) describes being lined up in formation on a cold night. Suddenly a big black car pulls up: 'Afterward they told us it was Schindler'. He describes a lot of shouting.

> What happened on that night?
> > [speaking as if in Polish] I remember it as if it was yesterday. It was a very cold night, they told everyone to stand in lines.
> > The ladies, too?
> > Men, women, all. All around guards, screams of the guards.
> > And then, what happened then?
> > Then, he arrived. We saw from far away a black car … and HE got out. A very handsome man. Very elegant. Very impressive.
> > Was that Oskar Schindler?
>
> [Long pause] Afterwards, they told us it was Schindler.
> > But that night? That night we didn't know. Didn't know anything.
> > Afterwards?
> > Afterwards? Lots of shouting. What is this? Like this.
> > Was it Schindler?
> > What Schindler? Spielberg. Screaming at us. This was no good.
> That was no good. Screaming at us to run faster. Do it again. And they returned us to the train cars and told us to start over. It was horrible. Really horrible.
> > And afterwards? [in French]
> > Afterwards? They paid us and we went home.
> > What?
> > We went home. It was really, really late. But they paid us very, very little.
> > Spielberg?
> > He received the Oscar.

The punch line is in fact a commentary on forms of representation and the ease with which the lines can be blurred between genres – documentary, feature film – and who the actual hero of this historical episode actually is – Schindler or Spielberg – with an ironic pun at the end: He won the Oscar![55] Like the scene in *Seinfeld* where Jerry gets in trouble for 'making out during *Schindler's List*', the comedians remind us that the representation of the

Holocaust is not sacred, but that in sanctifying cinematic representations of the *Shoah*, we distance ourselves from the actual meaning of the event. At the same time, the laugh lines in the jokes: using the Righteous Persons boulevard at Yad Vashem as political capital, lampooning Lanzmann's interview style in *Shoah*, the assumption that an Israeli audience would have seen *Schindler's List* or the tendency to name Tel Aviv streets after concentration camps and sites of Jewish heroism indicate that Israeli comedians could safely assume that an Israeli audience increasingly knowledgeable in the history of the Holocaust would get the jokes.

As the memory of the Shoah became an even more central component of Israel's collective national identity, it is unsurprising that we would see the Holocaust invoked for political (or comic) purposes with increased frequency. While such comedy may have been a reflection of the increasingly common place the Shoah occupied in the collective national identity – as seen in politics, literature, film, foreign policy and culture – this would only preview an even deeper identification with the memory of the Shoah as Israelis confronted the twenty-first century, the failure of Oslo Accords, the prospect of a nuclear armed Iran and the passing of the last generation of living eyewitnesses to the Holocaust. As the children of survivors in Israel inherited the mantle of Holocaust memory in Israel, that memory broadened from a family heirloom passed from one generation to the next, to a broader collective social identification.

Israel's relationships with its neighbours have come to be increasingly understood through the prism of Holocaust memory. From the Yom Kippur War, the destruction of the Iraqi nuclear reactor, the invasion of Lebanon, the First Intifada, the failure of Oslo, the Second Intifada and even with the present threat posed by a nuclear Iran, the memory of the Holocaust, understood within memory of threats of annihilation and inability to separate from diaspora Jewish past, continues to play a central role in Israeli politics and foreign policy. This has also paralleled a deepening identification with the memory of the Holocaust on the part of the broader Jewish Israeli public, not just among survivors and their descendants.

5

'We are all survivors': Israel and the Holocaust in the twenty-first century

Since 1977 (and even more so in the twenty-first century) Israeli Jews have internalized a much closer relationship to the Shoah, with references to the Holocaust in politics, culture and education commonplace in public discussion. The centrality of the collective memory of the Shoah in Israeli national identity has coincided with the transition from the founding collectivist socialist ethos to a more individualistic, free-market, capitalist system and at the same time especially after the failure of the Oslo Accords and the continuing threat posed by an Iran with nuclear aspirations, the sense of victimization and trauma of the Second Intifada seems to have led to an even greater identification with and politicization of the memory of the Holocaust. Regardless of what the historical record suggests about the challenges of drawing a straight line from the liberation of the concentration camps to the establishment of the state, in collective memory, the two events, Shoah and Tekumah, have become inextricably linked in broad public understanding of that history.

Speaking at the annual Yom HaShoah commemoration in 2015, Israeli president Reuven Rivlin declared: 'all of us, each and every one of us, has a number tattooed on his arm.' Why and how have Israelis come to a place and time when the Israeli president can make such a statement? Why and how has the Shoah become a central component of Israel's educational curriculum, with trips to Poland a seemingly necessary rite of passage for many students, and Yad Vashem a required visit for all politics leaders? This chapter will examine the ways in which the Holocaust has become an increasingly central part of Israeli collective memory and national identity and the reasons for this transformation. In a highly divided society, 'remembering the Holocaust' becomes the central unifying principle that, according to a 2016 survey by the Pew Foundation, two-thirds of Israelis can agree is an essential part of their Jewish identities.[1] 'Remembering the Holocaust' and the ways in which Israelis remember the Holocaust becomes especially significant as the visions of the Zionist future and past have become increasingly polarized, debates over the possibilities of peace with the Palestinians continue to divide, and religion and religious identity no longer functions as a unifying force. The central place of 'remembering the Holocaust' in Israeli collective identity tells us a lot about the ways in which Israelis view themselves and their relationships with the rest of the world.

2000 and the end of Oslo

Ehud Barak served as prime minister of Israel from July 1999 to March 2001. One of the most decorated soldiers in Israel's history, Barak transitioned to politics in 1995 after presiding over the implementation of the first Oslo Accords and the peace agreement signed with Jordan in 1994 as IDF chief of staff. Born on Kibbutz Mishmar HaSharon in 1942, Barak's maternal grandparents, Elka and Shmuel Godin, were murdered at Treblinka during the Holocaust. On a visit to Poland in 1992, when he was then serving as the chief of the IDF General Staff, Barak noted, 'we came 50 years too late'.[2]

As prime minister in March 2000, Ehud Barak welcomed Pope John Paul to Israel for a historic five-day visit to the Holy Land, in which the Polish-born pope visited the holy sites of the three major religions. In his remarks at Yad Vashem, where the pope met Holocaust survivors including Israel's Chief Rabbi Israel Meir Lau and noted Holocaust historian, Israel Gutman, the Pope John Paul recalled his childhood in Wadowice, which had a sizable Jewish community that was almost entirely exterminated during the war.

> My own personal memories are of all that happened when the Nazis occupied Poland during the war. I remember my Jewish friends and neighbors, some of whom perished, while others survived. I have come to Yad Vashem to pay homage to the millions of Jewish people who, stripped of everything, especially of human dignity, were murdered in the Holocaust. More than half a century has passed, but the memories remain.
>
> Here, as at Auschwitz and many other places in Europe, we are overcome by the echo of the heart-rending laments of so many. Men, women and children, cry out to us from the depths of the horror that they knew. How can we fail to heed their cry? No one can forget or ignore what happened. No one can diminish its scale.
>
> We wish to remember. But we wish to remember for a purpose, namely to ensure that never again will evil prevail, as it did for the millions of innocent victims of Nazism.[3]

FIGURE 5.1 *Pope John Paul II visiting Yad Vashem on 23 March 2000. During this historic visit, the pope participated in a memorial ceremony in Yad Vashem's Hall of Remembrance.*

Source: YouTube screengrab: https://www.youtube.com/watch?v=qXA5BztXaA8.

For the pope, who had spent much of his career trying to improve relations between Jews and the Catholic Church, including a key role at the Second Vatican Council in 1965, the Yad Vashem speech was viewed as the climax of John Paul's efforts to reconcile Christians and Jews.

His visit to Israel also presaged even closer diplomatic ties between Israel and Poland under President Aleksander Kwaśniewski, president of Poland from 1995 to 2005. Kwaśniewski's visit to Israel in May 2000 followed the publication of a controversial new book by Historian Jan Gross, *Neighbors*, on the murder of the Jewish community of Jedwabne in 1941 by their Polish neighbours. Kwaśniewski emphasized the importance of coming to terms with Poland's Second World War history, even those parts of the history his fellow Poles would prefer to forget:

We are aware in Poland of the deadweight which our domestic antisemites have put on the present-day and the future of relationships between Poles and Jews. And that's why we forcefully emphasize: One must not falsify history! One must not conceal the truth! Every crime and every roguery should be named and castigated, and circumstances examined and revealed. The changes which have taken place in the consciousness of Poles towards history and other nations are one of the important accomplishments of the past few years. Great merits for these changes are due to our compatriot, Pope John Paul II, a great advocate of peace, understanding and dialogue between people, peoples and religions. His ideas, his trips, take for instance his recent trip to the Holy Land of three great monotheistic religions of the present-day world, are exerting big influence upon the transformations in Poland, including, naturally, the climate of international relations. I have come from a land which experienced history harshly. We are proud of our history and state, which regained independence twice in the 20th century. We know that similar pride in their state and history is taken by the Israelis. So, let history be a warning and encouragement to us in an equal measure. A warning against evil, but also against one-sidedness. Encouragement to overcome the adverse bygones and build up good relations between Poland and Israel and Poles and Jews all over the world.[4]

Poland, which had become a full member of NATO in 1999, recognized that confronting antisemitism and Holocaust denial was an important part of joining the West, but, as Kwaśniewski also implied, a country could not let history dictate its entire orientation to the present and the future.

By 2000, the annual trips to Poland for Israeli high schoolers at the end of their eleventh grade year had become a regular event, as nearly 40,000 students travelled to Poland each year. As pilgrimages for high-school students and IDF soldiers and commanders, the trips functioned as pilgrimages from the Holy Land in reverse: participants partook in the shared experience of the sacred journey to the sites of mass death in Poland before returning to the Holy Land, reinforcing the need for Jewish life in the 'new Jewish home'. Regardless of background, ethnic origin or upbringing, these trips become a unifying experience for diverse Israelis and a common target for shared jokes and satirical references. All the same, the cost of such trips, which could range from approximately $1,500 to 2,000/per student, meant that for many lower-income families the cost of the experience had become prohibitive, leading some schools to advocate for educational tours within Israel stripped of some of the symbolic and nationalist expressions of the tours to Poland.[5]

Within twenty years, shifting political realities would fray the warming relations between Israel and Poland, specifically over the issue of Holocaust history, but this was not the case in the early 2000s. In 2003, Poland invited the Israeli Air Force to participate in its celebration of the eighty-fifth anniversary of the Polish Air Force along with fourteen other countries. Brigadier General Avi Maor, a descendant of Holocaust survivors who participated in the journey, recalled that

> as soon as the offer was on the table, Maj. Gen. (Res') Amir Eshel – then commander of Tel-Nof AFB, decided that if we were flying to Poland, we would hold a flyby over the extermination camps … The idea wasn't

approved immediately by the Polish authorities. We talked to them and managed to reach a settlement which allowed us to perform the flyby.[6]

Major General Eshel specifically chose pilots with a 'deep connection to the Holocaust', and the pilots brought the photos of twenty-one Holocaust survivors with them, read their names out loud in Auschwitz and took them 'home'. As recalled by Brigadier General Maor, 'I felt that I was in the skies with the strength of the IAF, the IDF and the entire state of Israel, and that down there were the relics of the people of Israel'.

One of Barak's first steps as prime minister was to fulfil a campaign promise to withdraw from southern Lebanon, which was completed in May 2000. In the summer of 2000, Barak announced a willingness to negotiate a final status agreement with the Palestinians, to conclude the Oslo Peace Process which had commenced with the signing agreement in 1993. In July 2000, Barak negotiated with Palestinian leader Yasser Arafat at the Camp David Summit presided over by US president Bill Clinton, in an attempt to conclude the Israel-Palestinian conflict once and for all. The negotiations failed as both sides were unable to reach agreement on the final status issues which had been delayed at the beginning of the process: final borders, the status of Jerusalem and the Temple Mount, the right of return for Palestinian refugees and the question of Israeli settlements. Barak's political opponents criticized him for his willingness to negotiate with the Palestinians, including Rabbi Ovadia Yosef, the spiritual leader of Shas, which sat (at the time) in

FIGURE 5.2 *Israeli Air Force jets fly over Auschwitz concentration camp, 2003.*

the same government as Barak. Rabbi Ovadia Yosef, the former Sephardi chief rabbi of Israel, compared the Palestinians to 'snakes'. 'What kind of peace is this?' Yosef said. 'Will you put them beside us? You are bringing snakes beside us. ... Will we make peace with a snake?' At the same time, while calling the Nazis 'evil' and the victims 'poor people', Yosef said the six million 'were reincarnations of the souls of sinners, people who transgressed and did all sorts of things which should not be done. They had been reincarnated in order to atone'. Barak derided the comments as unworthy of a rabbi who had been the Sephardi chief rabbi of Israel: 'His words could harm the memory of those who perished in the Holocaust and could hurt the feelings of their families and the feelings of the entire nation.' Yosef (Tommy) Lapid, himself a Holocaust survivor, head of the secularist Shinui party and father of the future interim PM, Yair Lapid, called Rabbi Yosef 'an old fool' who was aiding neo-Nazis and Holocaust deniers: 'In the world it will be said that a distinguished rabbi in Israel is in effect confirming what Hitler said, that the Jews are sinners.' The chief rabbi of Israel at the time, Rabbi Israel Meir Lau, also a Holocaust survivor, who had survived the Buchenwald concentration camp as a young child and been orphaned during the war, lamented the politicization of the memory of the Holocaust, calling on Israelis to 'stop probing into it in such a blatant, painful, hurtful manner'.[7]

In September 2000, opposition leader Ariel Sharon visited the Temple Mount in Jerusalem. Soon thereafter, the Second Intifada erupted, proving to be far more deadly and violent than the first had been, leading to the death of approximately 1,000 Israelis and 3,000 Palestinians. Barak's government would be the last Labor government to lead Israel, as Sharon would go on to become Israel's prime minister following direct elections for prime minister in February 2001. Under Ariel Sharon, who had been willing to compare Yitzhak Rabin to Jewish council leaders during the Second World War for his willingness to negotiate with the enemy, Israel would in fact withdraw from the Gaza Strip in response to continuing attacks by Palestinian militants as part of the Second Intifada. This time, it was Sharon and his policies that would become the target of Holocaust analogies.

The Second Intifada and the outbreak of Palestinian violence and terrorism proved especially disheartening for Israelis, particularly for those who had supported the 'peace process' and advocated negotiations with the Palestinians to reach a final status agreement. While the uprising had a popular character in its early stages, the involvement of armed Palestinian gunmen, affiliated with Palestinian Authority (PA) militia groups like Fatah and the Al-Aqsa Martyrs Brigade, gave this intifada a different character from the first one in the 1980s. In addition to protests in the West Bank, Gaza and within Israel, Palestinian groups also directly attacked Israeli cities and towns, military installations, vehicles and civilians through suicide bombings, shootings and rocket launchings, which killed over 1,000 Israelis, and left thousands severely injured. The Palestinian Authority leadership, including Yasser Arafat, were directly linked to arms shipments intercepted by Israel en route to the Gaza coast, most notably a large cache found in January 2002 aboard the Karine A ship which was on its way from Iran to the Palestinian Authority.

The Israeli response to Palestinian violence included military operations in the West Bank and Gaza Strip designed to destroy the terrorist infrastructure. The IDF launched a major incursion into the West Bank in March–April 2002, following the March 2002 Hamas suicide bombing of a Passover seder at a Netanya hotel in which 30 were killed and 140 were wounded. In 2003, the Israeli government also approved construction of a security fence or barrier, intended to prevent Palestinian terrorists from reaching their civilian targets inside Israel. After the 9/11 attacks (and subsequent attacks in London and Madrid) the global context for response to terror had shifted. In Israel, too, especially during the Second Intifada and in the aftermath of the 9/11 attacks in the United States and the global war on terror, including American-led invasions of Afghanistan and Iraq, identification with trauma and the lasting effects of trauma became a more prominent feature of popular culture both in Israel and around the world. At the same time, the Second World War and the Holocaust continued to function as a frame of reference – both for Americans and for Britons who compared the attacks to those their countries had endured during the Second World War – and for Israelis who associated the trauma of terrorism with reference to what their people had endured during the Holocaust.[8] Such comparisons could also employ humour that in effect suggested: things could *always* be worse. For example, a popular joke during the Second Intifada, when Israel was undergoing a spate of bombings in cafes and other public places, went like this:

> Sara in Jerusalem hears on the news about a bombing in a popular café near the home of relatives in Tel Aviv. She calls in a panic and reaches her cousin, who assures her that thankfully, the family is all safe. 'And Anat?' Sara asks after the teenager whose hangout it had been. 'Oh, Anat', says her mother, reassuringly. 'Anat's fine. She's at Auschwitz!'

The irony: what could be safer for an Israeli teen in those days than a trip to Auschwitz?

At the same time, Israel's critics would come to increasingly denounce what they saw as the harsh crackdown on Palestinian violence as extreme and illegal, comparing the security wall around the West Bank or the blockade of the Gaza Strip to the Warsaw Ghetto. Such parallels continued to deepen the association between Israel and Holocaust implying that Israeli Jews, as collective descendants of victims of the Shoah, should know better, while Israeli politicians could refer back to Abba Eban's invocation of 'Auschwitz borders' to push back against any withdrawal to Israel's pre-1967 boundaries. We can see this confluence of factors playing a role in an even deeper association with the memory of the Holocaust in Israel's collective national identity over the first two decades of the twenty-first century.

National traumas for Israelis were not just the product of terrorism and war. In 1997, IAF Colonel Ilan Ramon had been selected by NASA to serve as a payload specialist on the Space Shuttle *Columbia*; in July 1998, he began training for the mission to space at the Johnson Space Center in Houston, Texas. On 16 January 2003, the seven-member crew of STS 107, including Col. Ramon, successfully launched aboard the Space Shuttle *Columbia* from the Kennedy Space Center in Florida for a sixteen-day mission. Ramon conducted a number of experiments during the successful mission, which had tremendous symbolic value as a source of national pride for Israelis. 'Being the first Israeli astronaut – I feel I am representing all Jews and all Israelis', Ramon said. Referring to his mother and grandmother, who both survived Auschwitz, he explained the added significance he felt: 'I'm the son of a Holocaust survivor – I carry on the suffering of the Holocaust generation, and I'm kind of proof that despite all the horror they went through, we're going forward.'[9] Ramon carried several personal souvenirs with him into space, including a credit card-size microfiche copy of the Bible. As the son and grandson of Auschwitz survivors, Ramon had asked Yad Vashem to provide him with a relic from the Holocaust with him on his mission to space. He immediately connected to 'Moon Landscape', which Petr Ginz, an exceptionally bright and talented Jewish boy, had painted from his imagination while incarcerated in the Theresienstadt ghetto. Yad Vashem produced a facsimile copy of the drawing for him to take to space.

Tragically, just minutes before landing on 1 February 2003 the *Columbia* exploded after entering the Earth's atmosphere; Ramon and the six American astronauts aboard with him were killed.

In 2004, in response to the ongoing violence of the Second Intifada and the cost of protecting settlements in the Gaza Strip surrounded by a hostile Palestinian population, Ariel Sharon, often dubbed 'the father of the settlement movement', resolved to disengage from Gaza and dismantle the settlements in Gush Katif. Soon after Sharon's government announced its intentions to disengage from Gaza, the protest movement among settlers in Gaza and their supporters (many of whom identified with the national religious settler movement) announced they would affix orange stars to their clothing to indicate that they were like European Jews persecuted by the Israeli government and the army, with the effort to evict them from their homes turning the Israeli government into 'the Nazis'. As one resident of the Ganei Tal settlement in Gaza and the son of a Holocaust survivor explained, 'I want to raise my voice to show that this is illegitimate, to shake the people of Israel to their core', noting that Holocaust survivors who lived in the Gaza settlements supported the effort.[10]

The ploy failed to prevent the disengagement, but it did succeed in attracting a great deal of attention. Shevah Weiss, a Holocaust survivor

FIGURE 5.3 *Petr Ginz, Moon Landscape, drawn in Thersienstadt; Ginz was murdered in Auschwitz. Israeli astronaut Ilan Ramon brought a facsimile copy of the drawing with him to space in 2003.*

and former speaker of the Knesset, described it as a 'a very troubling comparison ... The Nazis put Jews into gas chambers, killing them, crushing their bones, spreading the remains in great piles all over Europe ... What is going on here?' Yad Vashem director Avner Shalev warned that the 'plan to wear orange stars perverts the historical facts and damages the memory of the Shoah'. Even so, in August 2005, when 1,500 Israeli soldiers surrounded the Gaza settlement of Kerem Atzmona to forcibly evict its residents, the settlers placed posters from the Nazi era on their doors suggesting that the Israeli government was making Gaza 'Judenrein'. Settlers and their children wore orange Stars of David marked with the word 'Jude', and when removed by Israeli soldiers, engaged in performance theatre, re-enacting scenes from the Holocaust (specifically the iconic image of the boy in the Warsaw Ghetto), emerging with their arms up, screaming in unison, all wearing an orange star. Performing scenes from the Holocaust as protest may not have succeeded in derailing the Gaza disengagement, but they have played a role in subsequent government's hesitation to dismantle settlements in the West Bank.[11]

FIGURE 5.4 *Jewish settlers from Gaza employ Nazi-era imagery – including stars of David on their T-shirts – in protest against their forced removal by Israeli troops from their home, as they walk out of their front door to a waiting bus, 17 August 2005 in the Kerem Atzmona settlement outpost in the Gaza Strip.*

Source: David Silverman/AFP via Getty Images.

Such invocations of the Holocaust in the context of Israel's policies vis-à-vis the Palestinians were a double-edged sword, however. For opponents of Israel who sought to protest the continued occupation of the West Bank even after the disengagement from Gaza, the implicit linkage between Israel and the Holocaust led to disturbing forms of Holocaust denial and distortion. If Israel had been granted statehood in response to the Holocaust, this line of thinking seemed to argue, perhaps the Jewish people had either invented the Holocaust or inflated the number of Jewish deaths to garner world sympathy and facilitate the creation the state? While offensive and grotesque, the association between the two events has been at the heart of rampant Holocaust denial in many parts of the Muslim world. After the death of Yasser Arafat, Mahmoud Abbas, who had previously served as prime minister of the Palestinian Authority, succeeded Arafat as president of the PA in January 2005 (a position he would continue to hold through 2023). In his 1984 book, *The Other Side: The Secret Relationship between Nazism and Zionism*, based on his PhD dissertation completed in Moscow in 1982, Abbas dismissed the Holocaust as a 'myth', arguing that

> it seems that the interest of the Zionist movement … is to inflate this figure so that their gains will be greater. This led them to emphasize this figure [six million] in order to gain the solidarity of international public opinion with Zionism. Many scholars have debated the figure of six million and reached stunning conclusions – fixing the number of Jewish victims at only a few hundred thousand.

Once he became a political leader within the Palestinian Authority, Abbas sought to moderate some of his previous positions, arguing that he had no desire to debate figures, while acknowledging the 'Holocaust was a terrible, unforgivable crime against the Jewish nation'.[12]

As sworn enemies of the so-called evil Zionist regime, the Iranian government has been at the forefront of Holocaust denial efforts since the 1990s. In April 2001, Ayatollah Ali Khamenei claimed at a conference on Palestine in Tehran that the Jewish people had 'exaggerated numbers' of Jews killed during the Holocaust as part of a plot 'to solicit the sympathy of world public opinion, lay the ground for the occupation of Palestine, and justify the atrocities of the Zionists'. In 2006 Iranian president Mahmoud Ahmadinejad sponsored a cartoon contest to solicit the 'best' and most creative cartoons denying or trivializing the memory of the Holocaust. Winners would receive gold and cash prizes; 1,200 submissions from over 60 countries poured in from around the world.[13] According to the US Holocaust Memorial Museum, the Palestine Museum in Tehran later opened an exhibition of 200 cartoons from this contest sponsored by President Ahmadinejad and in December 2006 the Iranian Foreign Ministry hosted a conference promoting Holocaust denial titled 'Review of the Holocaust: Global Vision'. Sixty-seven participants from thirty countries attended including former Ku Klux Klan leader and Holocaust denier David Duke, French Holocaust denier Robert Faurisson and officials of the neo-Nazi German National Democratic Party (NPD) among others.

As the enemies of Israel targeted the memory of the Holocaust in their war against the Jewish state, defending the historical veracity of the Shoah became part of the struggle to defend the state. At the same time, in 2005, Yad Vashem completed a lengthy process to redesign its core exhibition, with a grand opening in March 2005. In response to increased global competition from other Holocaust museums, including most notably the United States Holocaust Memorial Museum (USHMM) opened in 1993, Yad Vashem undertook an extensive redesign and construction project overseen

FIGURE 5.5 *Carlos Latuff – 'IsraHell's concentration camp'. This image shared the second prize in the International Holocaust Cartoon Competition 2006.*

by Safdie architects at an estimated cost of $90 million.[14] As described in the firm's project notes, the newly created core exhibition space was designed so as to not disrupt the layout of the existing memorial space on the Mount of Remembrance:

> To preserve the pastoral character of the delicate site and respond to the needs of Yad Vashem, the 'body' of the Museum is hidden within the earth, only allowing the elongated central spine to break through the earth and convey a sense of its true scale.
>
> Replacing the original building from 1957, the Holocaust History Museum includes a new reception building (Mevoah), a Hall of Names, a synagogue, galleries for Holocaust art, an exhibitions pavilion, and a learning and visual center. The main spine of the museum is a 650-foot-long triangular prism that cuts through the slope of Mount Herzl, penetrating from the south and emerging to the north, towards Jerusalem.[15]

Visitors to the new museum exhibition thus descend underground to enter the exhibition hall which is cut into 'angular trenches' guiding visitors back and forth through the central spine into specific exhibit spaces filled with artefacts, videos and documentary materials. The exhibit designers sought to make light a defining characteristic of the visitor experience so that museum-goers would transition from darkness to light, from the darkened Holocaust exhibit spaces to the sunlit main prism hall.

The exhibit was also intentionally designed for visitors to conclude their tour of the Museum with an 'expansive view out to Jerusalem ... As visitors complete their journey through the museum, the tunnel-like prism's walls open onto a panoramic view of sunlit Israel, metaphorically linking the Holocaust to the country's founding and spirit of optimism'.

As noted by scholar Amos Goldberg, the new Yad Vashem Holocaust historical museum was inaugurated in March 2005 with two days of ceremonies, which were 'among the biggest diplomatic and international events ever to take place in Israel, perhaps second only to Prime Minister Rabin's funeral'. Delegations from over thirty-five countries attended the inauguration, presided over by PM Ariel Sharon, President Moshe Katsav and Yad Vashem director Avner Shalev. Among the speakers were UN Secretary General Kofi Annan and Nobel Laureate Elie Wiesel. According to Goldberg, 'it seems that the whole world, or at least the "western world", in a unique expression of consensus, agreed in Yad Vashem on a contemporary categorical imperative – "thou shalt remember the Holocaust"'.[16]

Yad Vashem, with an annual budget of 45 million dollars and an impressive array of international donors, has become the second most popular tourist site in Israel, behind only the Western Wall. It is a required visit for IDF soldiers and also a frequent field trip destination for Israeli high-school students. But as Goldberg suggests,

FIGURE 5.6 *The exhibition hall at Yad Vashem cut as an angular trench into the ground, with visitors emerging from the exhibition with a view of the hills surrounding Jerusalem.*

Source: Photos by author.

Without losing its local and national (sacred) significance, it has transformed itself into a global memorial site, hosting millions of visitors from all over the world. It has become – together with the United States Holocaust Memorial Museum in Washington, DC (USHMM), the Memorial to the Murdered Jews of Europe in Berlin, and Auschwitz itself – an international Holocaust 'shrine' of pilgrimage. These four 'shrines' serve as anchoring sites for the new Holocaust ethical memory that has become a fundamental component in the current identity of the West. In a way, they also mark the geo-cultural map of this 'Holocaust consciousness': Western and Eastern Europe, North America and Israel. Hence, from its beginnings as a very local Israeli 'lieu de memoire' (site of memory), to use Pierre Nora's well-known term, Yad Vashem has become a very powerful and influential international and global cultural institution. In other words it is now a major agent in the global field of Holocaust memory.[17]

At the same time, as a player on the global field of Holocaust memory, the specific context of the Jewish narrative at Yad Vashem becomes even more significant. Just as the location of the United States Holocaust Memorial Museum in Washington, DC, or the Memorial to the Murdered European Jews or Auschwitz function in their specific geographic and political contexts, so too does Yad Vashem, emerging as it does into a re-nascent Jewish homeland, functioning within its particular Jewish national narrative of destruction and rebirth. This political context matters greatly for multiple reasons. Let us remember that in the early years of the state, it was by no means a foregone conclusion that Yad Vashem would be the primary site of Holocaust commemoration in the state. Alternative sites with a grassroots local character also emerged; religious shrines like the 'Chamber of the Holocaust' still exist, as do the community memorial gravestones at the Holon cemetery and other cemeteries around the country. Likewise, other memorial sites and museums can be found across the country from the Ghetto Fighters House in Akko to places like Moreshet, Massuah, Yad Mordechai and many, many more. And yet, the centrality of Yad Vashem as a required stop for all visiting political dignitaries and a sprawling memorial complex that functions as museum, research archive, educational institute and site for annual Yom HaShoah commemorations means that it has become the unquestioned central site of Holocaust memory in Israel. The question of who runs Yad Vashem becomes a political question, just as does every speech given at the site on Yom HaShoah. When an Israeli prime minister visits Yad Vashem or a visiting US president stops at the site (as did both Yair Lapid and Joe Biden in 2022) the symbolism of Holocaust commemoration is cast through a political lens.

But – the historical interpretation of the Holocaust also becomes political: how and why should the Holocaust be remembered? As a particular Jewish history that focuses on the Jewish narrative of the Holocaust or as a universal lesson for all humanity about the dangers of evil that might be perpetrated at any time in any place? In November 2005, the United Nations passed General Assembly Resolution 60/7 which 'resolves that the United Nations will designate 27 January as an annual International Day of Commemoration in memory of the victims of the Holocaust'. In contrast to Yom Hashoah, held annually on the 27th of Nisan to correspond with the timing of the Warsaw Ghetto Uprising and always scheduled one week before Israel's Memorial Day (Yom HaZikaron) and Independence Day (Yom HaAtzma'ut, reinforcing a specific Jewish national narrative), 27 January marks the date that Auschwitz was liberated by the Red Army; rather than marking a date where Jews, isolated, alone and abandoned by the rest of the world rose up in defence of the Jewish people, the UN resolution noted the need to mark a date that would recall 'the Convention on the Prevention and Punishment of the Crime of Genocide, which was adopted in order to avoid repetition of genocides such as those committed by the Nazi regime'. Furthermore, for the United Nations, the obligation to remember the Holocaust stemmed not only from an acknowledgement that 'the Holocaust … resulted in the murder of one third of the Jewish people, along with countless members of other minorities', but that it would 'forever be a warning to all people of the dangers of hatred, bigotry, racism and prejudice'.[18]

In April 2002, Yad Vashem held an international conference 'The Legacy of Holocaust Survivors: The Moral and Ethical Implications for Humanity'. Holocaust survivor Zvi Gil read *The Survivors' Declaration* at the closing ceremony of the conference in the Valley of the Communities at Yad Vashem. As he noted at the time, 'the Age of Holocaust Survivors is drawing to a close. Before long no one will be left to say, "I was there, I saw, I remember what happened." All that will be left will be books of literature and research, pictures and films, and multitudinous testimony. This will be a new era. The dark inheritance of the Shoah that was so indelibly stamped on the survivors' souls and hearts will become a sacred mission imposed upon humanity'. While emphasizing the deep connection to the state of Israel for survivors, which became for them 'an existential imperative' the declaration called 'on humankind to adopt principles of equality among men and nations'.

The Holocaust, which established the standard for absolute evil, is the universal heritage of all civilized people. The lessons of the Holocaust must form the cultural code for education toward humane values, democracy, human rights, tolerance and patience, and opposition to racism and totalitarian ideologies.[19]

FIGURE 5.7 *Yad Vashem Valley of the Communities.*

Source: Photo by author.

Nonetheless, it is debatable whether in the twenty years since then, the universalistic, humanistic, pluralistic lessons of the Holocaust emphasized by Gil have been adhered to, rather than a more particularistic, nationalist and specifically Jewish one. In this context, we can see Yad Vashem playing a very particular Jewish national goal in both its placement and its narrative of the Shoah. As argued by Amos Goldberg,

> This narrative also makes perfect sense in the Israeli context where remembering the Holocaust, as Idith Zertal so forcefully indicated, is perhaps the major pillar of current Israeli victimized identity, and where such identity has proven itself to be an extremely powerful and useful diplomatic tool in gaining international support in the context of the Israeli-Arab conflict and in maintaining the occupation in Palestine.[20]

Rather than serving as a warning to all humanity about the dangers of unchecked evil, the fragility and weakness of democracy and the need to protect the basic human rights of all threatened minorities, the particular Jewish narrative functions in an Israeli national context that justifies the need for the existence of a Jewish state, while also reinforcing a continued sense of Jewish victimization in the need to forcefully defend that state.

Yad Vashem also becomes the site for official state visits by foreign dignitaries and political pronouncements by Israel's presidents and prime ministers, often linking the obligation to remember the Shoah to current political events. Such pronouncements may in fact be justified – but what is clear is that the tendency to view Israel's national Holocaust memorial as a sacred and secular space that functions on the political sphere is generally unquestioned. Likewise, the question of who leads Yad Vashem has also become a political question, not only tied to the political coalitions that govern the state, but to the demands of the memorial site's growing dependence on philanthropic giving.

Avner Shalev served as director of Yad Vashem from 1993 to 2021, presiding over a period of remarkable growth at Yad Vashem that included the building of the new Holocaust History Museum, while founding the International School for Holocaust Studies, and enlarging Yad Vashem's archives and research facilities. Shalev had achieved a distinguished career in the IDF before taking the helm at Yad Vashem, rising to the rank of Brigadier General, then serving as director general of the Culture Authority in Israel's Ministry of Education and Culture for over a decade, and as chairman of the National Culture and Art Council. Under Shalev, Yad Vashem also came to be increasingly dependent on international philanthropy from a select group of donors, as the share of government support for the institution declined relative to philanthropic giving. According to a report published by the Israel State Comptroller's office in 2021, between 2007 and 2019, the Israeli government's share of Yad Vashem's income dropped from 42 to 31 per cent while in the same period, the share of total income received from private donors jumped from 16 per cent to 52 per cent. In 2019, this amounted to 101 million shekels ($31.4 million at 2021 exchange rates), equal to 53 per cent of the institution's operating budget. The report cited Yad Vashem documents showing that 'a significant share of the Yad Vashem budget relies on donations that have to be raised from scratch every year', and that 'a decline in donations could seriously impact Yad Vashem's income and consequently bring about a considerable reduction in operations and even the closure of departments'. According to the report, just 1 per cent of donors accounted for 79 per cent of all of the significant contributions between 2016 and 2019; in 2019 alone, 83 donors accounted for most of the funds contributed to Yad Vashem – a total of $30 million. State Comptroller Matanyahu Engelman warned that reliance on such a small group of super-donors made Yad Vashem especially vulnerable to any future economic crisis that could cause a sharp drop in contributions.[21] In 2022 the complexities of such connections came to the fore, when Yad Vashem was forced to suspend ties with Russian-Israeli billionaire Roman Abramovitch due to his ties with Vladimir Putin following the Russian invasion of Ukraine, despite the fact that Abramovitch had pledged at least $3 million to support Holocaust remembrance and education at Yad Vashem.[22]

At the same time, Vladimir Putin's attempt to justify the Russian invasion of Ukraine as part of a plan to de-Nazify the country led to an outcry among Israeli leaders, who rejected such false analogies as Holocaust distortion. In contrast, Ukrainian president Volodymyr Zelensky invoked the memory of the Holocaust repeatedly, drawing upon every weapon in his rhetorical arsenal to spur the nations of the world to action following the Russian invasion. In his speech to the German Bundestag on 17 March 2022, which happened to coincide with Purim when Jews around the world celebrated their victory over an attempted genocide, Zelensky asked his German audience whether the words 'Never Again' had become 'worthless'. And then three days later, on 20 March 2022 in remarks delivered over Zoom to members of Israel's Knesset, he appealed for military assistance and use of the Iron Dome missile defence system: 'when the Nazi party raided Europe and wanted to destroy everything. Destroy everyone. ... They called it "the final solution to the Jewish issue". You remember that. And I'm sure you will never forget!'[23] Responding to sharp criticism from Israeli politicians who rejected the parallel, Israel's prime minister at the time, Naftali Bennett, who had attempted to mediate negotiations between Russian and Ukraine, acknowledged the life and death struggle Zelensky and Ukraine face, while stating clearly, 'I personally believe that the Holocaust should not be compared to anything. It is a unique event in the history of nations, of the world – the systematic, industrial destruction of a people in gas chambers'.[24]

The notion of invoking the memory of the Holocaust as a core principle of Israel's need for strong military defence while rejecting comparisons to other genocides and historical events has become a core principle on the right wing of Israel's political spectrum. This had become especially clear in the ongoing enmity with Iran – and especially during the presidency of Mahmoud Ahmadinejad, who, as noted earlier, actively promoted Holocaust denial, while questioning why the Palestinian people should pay the price for the Holocaust if it actually did occur, and declared that he wanted to see Israel created on the territory of Germany while also saying that the current 'Zionist regime' should be 'wiped of the map'. For Prime Minister Benjamin Netanyahu (PM from 1996 to 1999 and 2009 to 2021 and 2023 to present) Holocaust references became a constant rhetorical tool when addressing Iran. For example, in his Yom HaShoah speech at Yad Vashem in April 2012, Netanyahu argued that the 'sacred obligation' to remember the Holocaust meant that the people of Israel:

'Must remember the past and secure the future by applying the lessons of the past. This is especially true for this generation – a generation that once again is faced with calls to annihilate the Jewish State. One day, I hope that the State of Israel will enjoy peace with all the countries and all the peoples in our region. One day, I hope that we will read about these calls to destroy the Jews only in history books and not in daily newspapers.

But that day has not yet come.

Today, the regime in Iran openly calls and determinedly works for our destruction. And it is feverishly working to develop atomic weapons to achieve that goal.

...

I will continue to speak the truth to the world, but first and foremost I must speak it to my own people. I know that my people is strong enough to hear the truth. The truth is that a nuclear-armed Iran is an existential threat of the State of Israel. The truth is that a nuclear-armed Iran is a political threat to other countries throughout the region and a grave threat to the world peace. The truth is that Iran must be stopped from obtaining nuclear weapons.

It is the duty of the whole world, but above and beyond, it is OUR duty.

The memory of the Holocaust goes beyond holding memorial services; it is not merely a historical recollection.

The memory of the Holocaust obligates us to apply the lessons of the past to ensure the basis of our future.

We will never bury our heads in the sand.

Am Yisrael Chai, veNetzach Yisrael Lo Yeshaker (The Nation of Israel Lives, and the Eternal Strength of Israel does not Lie)[25]

In his speech Netanyahu also invoked the warning of Ze'ev Jabotinsky the ideological forefather of Revisionist Zionism and Netanyahu's Likud party, who tried to warn the world of the impending catastrophe that faced Polish Jewry, before the Holocaust, warning Jewish audiences in Poland in 1938

FIGURE 5.8 *Benjamin Netanyahu at Yad Vashem, Yom HaShoah, 18 April 2012.*

that 'a catastrophe is coming closer … . the volcano which will soon begin to spit its all-consuming lava'.

Israel must of course take all threats to its security – and especially threats to annihilate it and wipe it off the map – as seriously as possible. But it is striking to see how Yom HaShoah and Yad Vashem become the place for such strategic threat assessments. The linkage between the memory of the Holocaust and calls for the defence of the state is unmistakable. The historical memory of the Holocaust drives the response to external threats and serves as a justification for not only Israel's foreign policy, but its very existence. Had the world and the Jewish people listened to Jabotinsky in 1938, Netanyahu suggests, had the British White Paper not prevented the creation of a Jewish refuge in Palestine, then the Holocaust, the volcanic eruption that consumed the Jewish people, might never have occurred. The memory of the Holocaust thus functions not only as an obligation to the Jewish victims of the past, it functions as an obligation to Jewish victims of the future.

This world view also led Netanyahu to form political alliances with other right-wing ethno-nationalist world leaders, which in the cases of Poland and Hungary would lead to a strange tolerance towards their revisionist politics of history; for example, the joint declaration in June 2018 with Polish prime minister Mateusz Morawiecki when Netanyahu essentially bought into the then Polish government's whitewashing of its complex past (following the February 2018 so-called Holocaust law in Poland signed by President Andrzej Duda). And similarly in July 2018, Netanyahu called Hungarian far-right president Viktor Orban a 'true friend of Israel,' not taking into account the revisionist politics of history of the Orban government. According to an ethno-nationalist reading of history based on the need to divide nation-states according to ethnic and pseudo-scientific understandings of racial origin, the antisemitism of extreme nationalists might be tolerated, as long as they support a strong Jewish national home for the Jewish people.

Netanyahu also commonly linked the Israeli-Palestinian conflict in terms of the Holocaust and the alleged collaboration of the Palestinian national leadership and other Arab states with the Nazi regime in the 1930s and 1940s; hence, in that reading of history the conflict with the Palestinians and Palestinian terror itself is an outgrowth, indeed a continuation of the Holocaust. For example, in October 2015, speaking before the Zionist Congress, Netanyahu claimed that Hitler got the idea to initiate the mass murder of European Jews from Hajj Amin Al-Husseini, the Mufti who visited Nazi Germany in November 1941. Palestinian Arab violence against the Jews had preceded the Second World War and the Nazi rise to power and Netanyahu argued that Jews living in what was then British Palestine faced many attacks in 1920, 1921 and 1929 – all instigated by the grand mufti of Jerusalem, Haj Amin al-Husseini, who allied himself with the Nazis during the Second World War. When the Mufti visited Hitler in Berlin, Netanyahu claimed, 'Hitler didn't want to exterminate the Jews at the time; he wanted to expel the Jews. And Hajj Amin al-Husseini went to Hitler and said, "If you expel them, they'll all come here." "So what should I do with them?" he asked. He said, "Burn them."'[26] According to Netanyahu, the Mufti had supposedly requested that Hitler kill the Jews to prevent them from coming to Palestine. In this case, much as we have seen with Begin before him, the Holocaust explains the need for a strong response to Israel's enemies and, even more so, the enemies of Israel today are the same enemies of the Jewish people who sought its destruction during the Holocaust; the Holocaust has not ended and the self-defence of the Jewish people continues.

On the other hand, such linkages between the Holocaust, the creation of the state of Israel and the Palestinians give rise to other historical questions: if the Holocaust serves as the prooftext and justification for the need for the creation of the state, what is the relationship between the Holocaust and the ongoing plight of the Palestinian people? This is a controversial debate – which reaches beyond academic circles – related to the historical connections between the Holocaust and the *Nakba* (Arabic for 'catastrophe', referring to the displacement of 750,000 Palestinians when Israel was founded). The 2015 volume *The Holocaust and the Nakba: A New Grammar of Trauma and History*, edited by a Palestinian, Bashir Bashir and a Jew, Amos Goldberg (English edition published in 2018, Hebrew version published in 2015 by the Van Leer Institute), raised these questions; when the Van Leer Institute in Jerusalem held a book event it faced angry demonstrators and had to step up security.

In the volume's introduction, Bashir and Goldberg note that one goal of the project was to put the two 'foundational catastrophes' of Jews and Palestinians into conversation with one another. Because Jews and Palestinians have been so focused on their own suffering and status as victims, they argue, both see their victim narratives as mutually exclusive and are unable to acknowledge – let alone empathize with – the suffering of the other group.[27] The volume seeks to 'transcend the binary, dichotomous confines that these national narratives impose on history, memory and identity' and propose a different 'register' which 'honors the uniqueness of each event ... but also offers a common historical and conceptual framework within which both narratives may be addressed'.[28] They seek to start a scholarly and broader public discourse about the conflicting memories of the Holocaust and the Nakba, raise awareness of their points of convergence and create empathy for the victimhood of the 'other' without blurring the boundaries or imposing identification. With this volume they aim to lay 'the groundwork for a language of historical reconciliation between the two peoples'.

Setting aside whether or not such an academic dialogue can serve as the basis for reconciliation and peace, it is noteworthy that the one premise of the project presumes that the Holocaust serves as the 'foundational catastrophe' for the Jewish state. Holocaust history and memory function therefore on a political level, as a tool to be used on both sides of the political spectrum. And it is equally noteworthy that most objections to placing the Holocaust/Nakba in the same sentence do not object to the notion of the Shoah as a foundational catastrophe; they object to comparisons of the two events, arguing that the Holocaust stands beyond any comparative framework.

Of course, by attempting to insulate the Holocaust from any framework, by suggesting that it is too sacred to be compared to anything else, the Shoah becomes the sole political property of the Jewish people. And once politicized, it may be trivialized. As argued by scholar Tuvia Friling in 2014, 'we should expect today's misuse and banalization of the Holocaust to continue in the foreseeable future'.

> Feats of trivialization and superficialization have been performed and are still being carried out by prime ministers, politicians across the political spectrum (from the Yishuv era onward), military commanders, and even scholars, intellectuals, and practitioners of culture and the arts. The Holocaust has been mobilized, and remains mobilized, for the sundry needs of people across the political spectrum from Ben-Gurion, who back in 1947 likened the Mufti to Hitler, via Menachem Begin, who likened Arafat to Hitler, to those during the Gulf War who likened Saddam Hussein to Hitler, and to Shulamit Aloni, who likened

the Israeli occupation of the territories to the German occupation in World War II, culminating with those who likened the disengagement and withdrawal from Gaza to the Holocaust, as in the photographs of children with their hands up, an orange Star of David on their shirts, at the time of the disengagement. Almost daily rhetoric in Israel equates today's powerful Jewish state to the situation of the Jews in World War II. Remarks by Itamar Ben-Gvir, an activist in the new Strong Israel party, at the Elections Committee meeting that discussed the expulsion of Haneen Zoabi from the Knesset – 'As I stand here today at the [...] podium, I do not stand alone: standing together with me are thousands of Jews murdered in terror attacks ...' – modeled after Gideon Hausner's opening remarks at the Eichmann trial, evoking a blood-curdling comparison of the two situations. Guy Pnini, captain of the Maccabi Tel-Aviv basketball team, calling his rival on the Hapoel team a 'Nazi' – they all carry the same stains of ignorance and crudity, as well as of the superficialization and cheapening of the Holocaust, those murdered in it, and those who survived it. Consequently, Israeli society is unlikely to stop 'remembering the Holocaust' in the coming decades.

As Frilling argues, the memory of the Holocaust functions as a powerful unifying feature in Israeli society where religion, the shared experience of military service and the absence of consensus on major domestic political issues, perhaps none more so than the two-state idea, fail to serve as unifiers (and functionally divide to a much greater extent).

> With most of these ideas – originally meant to be the bonds, the unifying forces, the leading ideas – lacking or attenuated, Holocaust Remembrance will become, almost strangely, despite its twisting, variegated, and patchwork nature, a kind of bond, an embrace, a cohesive force in Israeli society, even though every camp, great or small, will continue to flog and knead it as it wishes. If so, Israeli society, will not rush to embrace Yehuda Elkana's call, and the Holocaust will continue to resonate in the longue durée (long-term) process of forging and crystallizing Israelis' identity.[29]

As we have seen, such concerns of politicization, trivialization, banalization are quite justified, especially as we note the disconnect between the frequent invocation of the memory of the Holocaust and the simultaneous distancing from the *actual meaning* of the event. What does this mean in practice? As the tropes of Holocaust memory are repeated in all social, cultural and political spheres, the trauma of the event loses its meaning; yes, the event serves as a foundational trauma for Israelis, unifying Israelis from a broad swath of the social spectrum in a country divided in so many other ways. But the memory of the Shoah functions as a useful symbol not a traumatic historical event to be grappled with in any meaningful way.

Building on the critiques of Yehuda Elkana and Adi Ophir from the 1980s, who warned that obsessive remembering of the Shoah might cause Israel to always see itself as a victim, thereby facilitating the oppression of others, Avraham Burg has argued that an overemphasis on the memory of the Holocaust has prevented Israel from making peace with the Palestinians and turned memory into a pathology prompting political paralysis. As the son of Yosef Burg, a founder of the National Religious Party who came to Palestine as a refugee from Nazi Germany, and as former speaker of the Knesset himself and former head of the Jewish Agency, Burg's critique carries weight, both personally and politically. And yet, because it is perceived as a political critique, it perhaps has less resonance than it might have otherwise. In his 2008 book, *The Holocaust Is Over, We Must Rise from Its Ashes*, Burg argued that the obsessive focus on the traumatic memory of the Holocaust has caused Israelis to lose the ability to trust themselves, their neighbours or the world; this inability to trust, in turn, has paradoxically reinforced a diaspora mentality for Israelis, preventing them from functioning as a healthy, 'model nation' (to borrow Herzl's term). In Burg's analysis, the memory of the Shoah has also become a substitute religion, a foundational totem upon which to project the national identity.

When I study the components of my identity and the cause of my identity crisis, I recognize only one common thread that connects us all: the thick shadow, the unbearable heaviness of the Shoah and its horrors. It is the source of all and it absorbs all. So much so that sometimes I want to rewrite the Bible to begin: 'In the beginning there was the Shoah and the land had become chaos'.

The Shoah is more present in our lives than God. The Musaf prayer says of God that 'his glory fills the world' – here is no place in the world without the presence of God. Listening to the Israeli, Jewish, and even wider world's discourse today reveals that the Shoah is the founding experience not just of our national consciousness, but that of the western world as a whole. Army generals discuss Israel's security doctrine as 'Shoah proof'. Politicians use it as a central argument for their ethical manipulations. People on the street experience daily the return of the horrors, and newspapers are filled with an endless supply of stories, articles, references, and statements that emanate from the Shoah and reflect it back in our lives. The Shoah is so pervasive that a study conducted a few years ago in a Tel Aviv teaching school found that more than ninety percent of those questioned view the Shoah as the most important experience of Jewish history. This makes the Shoah more important than the creation of the world, the exodus from Egypt, the delivering of the Torah on Mount Sinai, the ruin of both the Holy Temples, the exile, Messianism, the stunning cultural achievements, the birth of Zionism, the founding of the state, or the Six-Day War.

In this analysis, then, the commandment *Zakhor*, to remember, has become secularized, but no less central to Jewish national identity. Trips to Poland indeed become reverse pilgrimages, where the return to the Holy Land makes the land holy not because it was given to the Jewish people by God, but because it is not the site of destruction, but the site of rebirth, the antithesis to the Shoah of European Jewry. The antithesis depends on the thesis, meaning Israel cannot exist without the Shoah; according to Burg, this has prevented Israel from functioning as a free and independent people, liberated from its past.

> I have no doubt that memory is essential to any nation's mental health. The Shoah must therefore have an important place in the nation's memorial mosaic. But the way things are done today – the absolute monopoly and dominance on every aspect of our lives – transforms this holy memory into a ridiculous sacrilege and converts piercing pain into hollowness and kitsch. As time passes, the deeper we are stuck in our Auschwitz past, the more difficult it becomes to be free of it. We retreat from independence to the inner depths of exile, its memories, and horrors. Israel today is much less independent than it was at her founding, more Holocaustic than it was three years after the gates of the Nazi death factories opened.[30]

Yishai Sarid's *The Memory Monster* (published in Hebrew in 2017 and English in 2020) explores these themes in a literary form, imagining a report by a promising young historian written for the chairman of Yad Vashem, based on the expert/guide's growing disenchantment with the experience of leading students on a pilgrimage to Poland. The young historian, whose dissertation was based on a comparative analysis of the killing techniques at the six extermination camps, begins to sense that his (and his students') obsession with power, murder and death may be influencing their world view, perhaps encouraging the victim to become the perpetrator. As a satire of the Holocaust memory industry, the book raises uncomfortable questions, asking its readers to consider how a nation can honour the memory of mass murder without becoming consumed by the memory monster.[31] In 2021 the book was adapted into a play, also called *The Memory Monster*, performed at the HaBimah theater (Israel's National Theater) in Tel Aviv. Adapted and performed by Ben Yosipovich, the play asks both rhetorically, and of the audience, whether the lessons of the memory monster reveal a bitter truth: 'that in order to survive in this world, everyone has to be something of a Nazi.'[32]

And yet, despite such expressions of concern about Holocaust saturation, obsessive remembering, and continued politicization it seems that as the twenty-first century continues and as distance from the Shoah grows, disentangling Holocaust memory from the political sphere in Israel becomes harder to do. The debate over who would replace Shalev at Yad Vashem after his lengthy tenure there can be seen in the context of the increasing political prominence of the site, which despite government funding tries to maintain scholarly and academic independence from the political sphere. Dani Dayan, who has served as the head of the *Yesha* (Judea and Samaria) settlement lobby and then Israel's consul general in New York, became the new head of Yad Vashem in 2021, despite almost no background in Holocaust education. As Eitan Nechin asked in an editorial published in *Ha'aretz*: 'how can former settler leader Dani Dayan, who doesn't believe Palestinians deserve equal rights, head an institution dedicated to documenting the most horrific consequences of the actions of a nationalistic, racist regime?'[33] From its founding Yad Vashem did not necessarily need to function as a political symbol or a political institution and yet, despite the dedicated efforts of scholars, researchers, archivists and educators at one of the world's leading institutions of Holocaust scholarship and memory, it becomes increasingly difficult to separate the memory of the Holocaust from the political sphere.

In 2018, the Polish government's passage of a controversial law, which criminalized any accusation alleging Polish complicity in Nazi crimes, tested Yad Vashem's delicate balance of this relationship. The original iteration of the law stated that 'whoever accuses … the Polish nation, or the Polish state, of being responsible or complicit in the Nazi crimes committed by the Third German Reich shall be subject to a fine or a penalty of imprisonment of up to three years'. The law, which was rightfully criticized as a form of Holocaust distortion, emanated in response to Polish nationalist attempts to counter nearly two decades of historical research in Poland by scholars like Jan Gross, Jan Grabowski and Barbara Engelking that had found copious evidence of Polish participation in both the murder of Jews in places such as Jedwabne, and extensive documentation of Polish collaboration in the capture and subsequent killing of Jews in Poland, where some 98 per cent of Jews who found themselves on German-occupied territory during the war were murdered. After months of negotiations between Israel and Polish government officials to soften the criminal aspects of the law, a joint statement still declared that the wartime Polish government-in-exile tried to stop the systematic murder of Polish Jews in Nazi death camps by trying to raise awareness among the Western allies, and that it 'created a mechanism of systematic help and support to Jewish people'. Furthermore, the revised law left historians open to civil lawsuits which hampered their ability to conduct research without fear of retribution, something which in fact has taken place in multiple instances since passage of the law. In an official statement by Yad Vashem historians David Silberklang, Dan Michman and Havi Dreifuss, they noted their deep concern over historical revisionism and factual inaccuracies, as well as the fear that 'the current wording still exposes researchers, students, teachers, journalists, politicians, tour guides, and employees of commemorative sites to harm'.

> Our principled position has been and remains that any attempt to limit academic and public discourse by means of legislation and punishment is

fundamentally improper and deals a serious blow to Holocaust research as well as Holocaust memory and commemoration.[34]

In addition to correcting the mistaken perception created by the statement that the Polish government-in-exile had done everything in its power to rescue Jews by raising awareness of the murder of European Jews, the historians also noted the misleading assertion in the statement which stated: 'we acknowledge and condemn every single case of cruelty against Jews perpetrated by Poles during World War II. We are honored to remember heroic acts of numerous Poles, particularly the Righteous Among the Nations, who risked their lives to save Jewish people'. As Silberklang, Michman and Dreifuss argued,

> While the joint statement does not note explicitly whether 'every **single case** of cruelty against Jews perpetrated by Poles' refers to many cases or few, it definitely stresses 'the heroic acts of **numerous** Poles'. In other words, assistance to Jews is presented as widespread, whereas – by implication – actions that were injurious to them were few. The past three decades of historical research tell a much different story: assistance to Jews by Poles during the Holocaust was relatively uncommon; assaults and even murder of Jews were widespread. (emphasis in original)

Furthermore, the scholars noted, the joint statement reads: 'some people – regardless of their origin, religion, or worldview, revealed their darkest side at that time'. By minimizing the role of Poles in acts of collaboration and murder while emphasizing heroic rescue and resistance, the statement became a form of distortion. Furthermore, statements that relativized evil by indicating that there were 'Polish criminals just as there were Jewish criminals and Russian and Ukrainian criminals, not only Germans' and alleging that Jews also *revealed* 'their darkest side at that time' likewise distorted the Holocaust by minimizing Polish complicity and reasserting charges of Jewish collaboration.[35]

The eminent Israeli historian of the Holocaust, Yehuda Bauer, also affiliated with Yad Vashem for decades, described the joint statement in a radio interview as a 'betrayal' that 'hurt the Jewish people and the memory of the Holocaust'. He repeated his criticism in an op-ed published in *Ha'aretz*, where he wrote, 'we accepted the mendacious official Polish narrative, and swallowed it'. He accused the Israeli government of sacrificing truth and justice 'for its current economic, security and political interests'.[36]

The negotiating team representing the government of Prime Minister Benjamin Netanyahu attempted to defend the joint statement by insisting that Yad Vashem's chief historian Dina Porat had reviewed the compromise to the law forcing Prof. Porat, an award-winning historian of the Holocaust in her own right, to insist that any input she may have had on revisions to the law was done on a 'voluntary, personal and confidential basis', and not as a representative of Yad Vashem; furthermore, she insisted, not all of her suggestions had been incorporated into the final draft in any event. This one example highlights the complexities of 'the politics of Holocaust memory' and the extreme difficulties of separating academic research from the political sphere, especially when politicians constantly make use of the memory of the past for present political purposes. The Polish Holocaust Law continued to reverberate into 2022 when the Israeli government of Yair Lapid suspended student trips to Poland over the fear that tour guides might be open to civil and criminal penalties for any assertions about Polish complicity that might be perceived to be in violation of the law.

In November 2022, the politics of Holocaust memory collided again, this time in a proposed 'Holocaust/Nakba conference' to be held at the Goethe Institute in Jerusalem, featuring the work of Amos Goldberg and Bashir Bashir. The proposed event, scheduled to be held on the anniversary of Kristallnacht, was to be called 'Grasping the Pain of the Others – Panel Discussion on the Holocaust, Nakba and German Remembrance Culture'. However, the event, scheduled to be held one week after an election that ushered in a new right-wing government in Israel, was cancelled following the objections from Israel's Foreign Ministry that protested 'the blatant cheapening of Holocaust and the cynical and manipulative attempt to create a linkage whose entire purpose is to defame Israel', by discussing the Shoah and the Nakba in the same programme. Yad Vashem director Dani Dayan called the event an 'intolerable distortion of the Holocaust'.[37]

In response to concerns about politicization and a 'cheapening' of Holocaust memory, we can see multiple grassroots initiatives that have attempted to overcome the sense that the memory of the Holocaust has been trivialized or manipulated for political purposes, to create a sense of authentic engagement with the actual meaning of the event. Such efforts may try to create alternative spaces for Holocaust commemoration that personalize the memory of the Shoah, allowing Israelis the opportunity to directly connect on an individual rather than collective level. Literature and film are two genres that do this powerfully by encouraging the intended audience to engage directly with the experiences depicted on a personal level. In the twenty-first century, representations of the Holocaust in Israeli literature and film have only continued to grow. Following the critical success of *Because of That War* in 1988, other documentaries created by children and grandchildren of survivors have continued to engage with the intergenerational transmission of memory and trauma while grappling with the question of what the role of subsequent generations will be once the last eyewitnesses to the Holocaust are no longer alive. In her study of Holocaust documentaries in Israel, *Remaking Holocaust Memory*, Liat Steir Livny argues that beginning in the 1980s, especially after the success of Lanzmann's Shoah and the advent of large-scale interview projects to record survivor testimonies, 'Holocaust documentaries focused on stories of survival as filtered through the perspectives of the second generation'.

The documentaries highlighted individual stories rather than a collective narrative, and addressed the impact of the Holocaust on survivors and their offspring....These testimonial films turned second-generation directors (not necessarily in a biological sense) into listeners, who were 'witnesses through imagination' or 'surrogate witnesses', whose gaze and voice defined a new form of empathy toward survivors.[38]

And, in turn, the 'second-generation filmmakers turned their audiences into witnesses to the witnesses'. However, in Israeli society, where identification and awareness of the Holocaust is so strong, sociological terms like 'second and third generation' must be modified and expanded, according to Steir-Livny. 'Therefore, in Israel, where Holocaust awareness is so intense, the terms second-generation and third generation can refer not only to the biological offspring of Holocaust survivors but can also, as a cultural term, define Jewish Israelis who grew up in an environment saturated with Holocaust awareness, anxiety, and stress'.[39] Films like *A Film Unfinished* (2010), *The Flat* (2011), *Hitler's Children* (2011), *Numbered* (2011) and *Pizza in Auschwitz* (2011) – just to name a few – not only examine the intergenerational issues noted earlier, they also play a role in deepening identification and awareness for Israelis more broadly, regardless of biological destiny. Israel has a remarkably robust cinematic production that is hugely disproportionate to a country of such a small size. At the same time, the small size of the country also means that the intense cinematic output is quite influential in shaping collective memory in the country. The degree to which Holocaust history and memory continues to deepen and grow through cinematic production corresponds to the survey data that shows 65 per cent of Israeli find 'Remembering the Holocaust' to be essential parts of their Jewish identities (as in the Pew's study cited earlier).

At the same time, such films can be provocative in exploring controversial aspects of Holocaust history or breaking taboos in revealing new forms of identification and commemoration. *The Flat* (2011) deals with untold family secrets, while interspersing director Arnon Goldfinger's family history (his grandparents, the Tuchlers, who had immigrated from Germany to Israel before the war, maintained a relationship with SS officer Leopold von Mildenstein, both before and after the war, despite the fact that he had been a key figure in the Nazis' Jewish Department responsible for working on emigration issues and recruiting Adolf Eichmann as a Jewish expert). What do such revelations mean for subsequent generations as they grapple with the nature of their personal relationship with the Shoah? As a genre, many such films explore the dynamics of family secrets and mysteries that transcend generations. In other cases, some families seek to cope with the constant, overwhelming presence of the memory of the Holocaust, as descendants of survivors engage with this legacy in different ways. *Pizza in Auschwitz* (2011) is a deeply poignant story that examines the responses of the second generation to their parents' trauma. Dani Hanoch, who describes himself as having 'earned a BA at Auschwitz', drags his two grown-up children, chain-smoking, feisty Miri and the more solemn, religious Sagi to Poland to retrace his steps during the Holocaust, and to spend one final night with him inside his old barracks in Auschwitz where they will share a box of takeout pizza. The film not only highlights the black humour that functions as an incredibly strong defence mechanism for some survivors (and their children), it also emphasizes the ways in which emotional trauma passes from one generation to the next, especially for the children who have survived growing up with a survivor.

As the Israeli film industry continues to grow, numerous feature films have also engaged with the history of the Holocaust, including adaptations of literary works such as Uri Orlev's *Run Boy Run* (2013) and Yoram Kaniuk's *Adam Resurrected* (2008), along with films like *Plan A* (2021), *Operation Finale* (2018), *June Zero* (2022), *Walk on Water* (2008), *The Matchmaker* (2010), *The Testament* (2017) and many more, all of which deal with various aspects of Israel's historical relationship to the Holocaust, from Abba Kovner's plot for mass revenge against Germany, to the Eichmann trial, and the continued legacies of Holocaust memory in Israel/German relations. In other spheres, filmmakers and content creators have sought to use film and new media to design new forms of Holocaust commemoration, to reach a younger generation less likely to consume old media. *Eva's Story* dubbed 'A Holocaust Story for the Social Media Generation' by the *New York Times* is the creation of an Israeli tech executive, Mati Kochavi, and his daughter, Maya, to engage 'screen-hooked post-millennials' in Holocaust education through a series of seventy short Instagram episodes that document Eva Heyman's experiences during the Holocaust, based on a diary she kept from 3 February 1944 until 30 May 1944. Eva was killed in Auschwitz on 17 October 1944, and her mother, Agnes Zsolt, survived the Holocaust and found the diary when she returned to their hometown of Nagyvarad in Hungary. She eventually committed suicide. The social media Holocaust education initiative was marketed aggressively in Israel and online, asking visitors: 'what if a girl in the Holocaust had Instagram?' and succeeded in attracting 1.1 million followers (as of November 2022).[40] But the attempt to dramatize a young girl's Holocaust diary with a smartphone transporting viewers back to 1944 was also panned by some critics as a dangerous trivialization of Holocaust memory. As noted by one Israeli teacher, 'the path from "Eva's Story" to selfie-taking at the gates of Auschwitz-Birkenau is short and steep, and in the end all those tut-tutters and head shakers will join in telling us about the lost and disconnected youth, devoid of values and shameless'.[41]

On the other hand, Israeli prime minister Benjamin Netanyahu endorsed the project and Yad Vashem, while distancing itself from the content of the project for which it had no input, stated

> that the use of social media platforms in order to commemorate the Holocaust is both legitimate and effective ... Yad Vashem is active and

FIGURE 5.9 *'Eva's story, If a Girl in the Holocaust Had Instagram' poster advertising Eva's story on a building in Israel.*

engages the public in a myriad social media channels including Instagram albeit in a different style and manner ... Not only do Yad Vashem's posts contain authentic material and historically based facts, we ensure that its content is both relevant to the public while being respectful to the topic.[42]

Other efforts to break through the formality and politicization of Holocaust education and commemoration have included more 'authentic' memorial ceremonies that encourage more intimate remembrances, like *zikaron ba-salon* (memory in the living room), bringing small groups of friends and family together to remember the Holocaust on a personal level, often with survivors or their descendants. As the organization (funded with the support of the Claims Conference) describes itself:

Zikaron BaSalon is a social initiative that takes place around the world on Yom Hashoah (Holocaust Remembrance Day) as well as on other dates throughout the year. Literally meaning 'remembrance in the living room' in Hebrew, the idea was born out of the understanding that modern society's connection with the memory of the Holocaust has significantly deteriorated.

Alongside formal events, Zikaron BaSalon offers a new, meaningful and intimate way to commemorate this day and address its implications through discussions at home among family, friends and guests. It is a unique and authentic tradition of people gathering together to open their hearts to the stories of the survivors, sing, think, read, talk, and most importantly – listen.

In its mission, *Zikaron BaSalon* seeks to create a more personal connection to the memory of the Holocaust for Israelis and participants worldwide. By remembering in the living room, the organization creates an alternative to the formal memorial ceremonies at Yad Vashem or the Ghetto Fighters House (the largest annual commemoration event often including up to 10,000 participants in the amphitheatre adjacent to the museum and the Kibbutz). Going beyond the formality of the public sphere, Zikaron BaSalon enables its 1.5 million participants to commemorate in the private sphere, to create a 'meaningful experience' in the intimate comfort of their own living room with friends and family.[43] The initiative cites the aforementioned 'Survivor Declaration' of 2002 and its statement that:

> In Jewish tradition, the command to remember is absolute. But its obligation does not end with the cognitive act of memory – it must be connected to both meaning and action. Today, we for whom the memory is burned in our hearts and on our flesh, gather to pass the torch of memory to the next generation. We pass to you as well, the fundamental lesson of Judaism, that memory must be accompanied by action of ethical and moral intent. This must be the foundation and the focus of your energies toward the creation of a better world.[44]

Zikaron BaSalon makes clear both the fear that the connection to the Holocaust has deteriorated and implicitly indicates a belief that the passing of the survivor generation will only accelerate such distancing. Thus we can see a paradoxical process: an affirmation of the central place Holocaust remembrance should have in contemporary Israeli (and Jewish) identity in both the public and private spheres, along with growing anxiety over its disappearance. Other groups have responded to anxiety over the passing of the survivor generation by asserting the central role that children of survivors should have in carrying on the legacy of their parents and grandparents. With the passing of the last survivor generation amidst rising anxiety about how to continue to tell the stories of survivors, self-identified 'second- and third-generation' descendants of survivors have created organizations in Israel and around the world determined to keep the stories of their loved ones alive.[45] Some children of survivors have sought to channel their parents' memories, offering testimony in the 'first person', instead of their parents.[46] Rather than retell their parents' stories from the perspective of their children, the children retell their parents' stories as if they were their parents. At the same time, other children of survivors, like the Israeli writer and professor, Michal Govrin, have wrestled with the challenge of how to remember the Shoah individually, collectively and in a format that can

FIGURE 5.10 *Zikaron BaSalon, c. 2019.*

transcend the paradigms of trauma and victimization through the creation of a Yom HaShoah *Hitkansut* Haggadah (more on this topic in this volume's Conclusion).

Furthermore, a broad array of organizations representing many different movements and sectors in Israel have organized Holocaust education initiatives that seek to connect with the next generation of students using both traditional and novel pedagogical techniques. These range from prominent organizations like Yad Vashem and the Ghetto Fighters House, to groups affiliated with youth movements and kibbutzim, like Moreshet, Yad Mordecai, Massuah and Givat Havivah, as well as smaller grassroots initiatives like Zikaron BaSalon and Edut Testimony Theater. Religious groups, like Ginzach Kiddush Hashem and education initiatives connected to Bar Ilan University, have also attempted to increase focus on topics like spiritual resistance or religious life before, during and after the Holocaust. And 2G/3G groups like Dorot Hemshech and Shem Olam have worked to organize training courses for children and grandchildren of survivors to educate about the Holocaust. Jews from the former Soviet Union have worked to include their wartime experiences in the Soviet Union, the Red Army and in Central Asia into the history of the Holocaust, as have Jews from North Africa and the Middle East.[47] More recently, other initiatives have worked to focus attention on the experiences of Sephardic Jews during the Holocaust, including works that document Sephardic victims across North Africa from Morocco to Libya, from Italy through the Balkans and the northern Mediterranean from Italy to Greece, Yugoslavia and Bulgaria.[48]

Furthermore, in the wake of the passage of the Polish 'Holocaust Law' in 2018 and subsequent debates over the effectiveness of sending Israeli youth to Poland on 'march of the living' trips, especially after the Covid-19 pandemic, many Israeli educational organizations have advocated for trips to sites of memory within Israel (or through the use of virtual reality tours of Auschwitz) that will maximize the resources of local initiatives while reaching students for whom trips to Poland are cost-prohibitive.

The Ghetto Fighter's House Center for Humanistic Education has focused on linking the lessons of the past to human rights education and the struggle against racism and xenophobia, while Givat Haviva, named after Haviva Reik, one of the paratroopers captured and killed in Slovakia and its Yad Ya'ari Research and Documentation Center, along with The Moreshet Mordechai Anielevich Memorial Holocaust Study and Research Center, educational initiatives work to implement 'educational programs for Jewish and Arab students that foster learning, understanding, and imparting of tools for a shared society in Israel'.[49] Their programmes include formal and informal educational offerings for all ages, which '(draw) on modern conflict resolution models and theories to encourage critical thinking and understanding of the other side'. Thus, in contrast to Holocaust commemoration that views the need to promote a strong defence of Israel against its enemies as a critical historical lesson, initiatives like those promoted by Givat Haviva (often as part of the education ministry's requirement that Holocaust education be offered in all sectors of Israeli society) frame Holocaust education through a prism of 'equality, mutual recognition, partnership ... and a shared society'. In many ways, therefore, we can see how Holocaust education and commemoration functions as a unifying feature that cuts across diverse segments of Israeli society, while also reflecting political divisions. One aspect bears repeating however: none of these initiatives question the central place that memory of the Shoah should have in Israeli national identity.

Even in the sphere of Israeli comedy and humour, the ubiquitous place of the Shoah seems to reinforce, rather than challenge, the centrality of the Shoah in Israeli national identity.

In her book *Is It OK to Laugh about It? Holocaust Humour, Satire and Parody in Israeli Culture*, Liat Steir Livny argues that in Israel, 'a unique post-traumatic society where the trauma of the Holocaust lives as an integral part of the present, Holocaust humour in Hebrew functions as an important defence mechanism that challenges and deconstructs the fear factors'. Steier Livny argues that satirical skits about the Holocaust in Israel do not minimize or trivialize the Shoah but instead simultaneously reinforce the centrality of the Shoah in Israeli society while also allowing for critiques of the instrumentalization and politicization of the Shoah in Israel. In Israel, where widespread Holocaust education has helped a younger generation of Israelis assimilate the Shoah as a central event in the formation of the state, a great familiarity with Holocaust history allows for a more nuanced engagement with aspects of the Jewish past through humour (as compared to the United States, where the humour deals with certain symbols of memory or Holocaust icons, but in a more superficial way). As Steir Livny argues:

In Israel, where there is a massive use of Holocaust rhetoric by politicians, journalists and educators ... the Holocaust has been assimilated as a central event, and young Jewish-Israelis perceive the Holocaust as the historical event that has had the greatest impact on them and their future, even more than the founding of the State. Other research has shown that the knowledge the second- and third-generation Holocaust survivors have about the Holocaust in Israel, and the way the Holocaust has shaped their identity is similar to those Israelis of the same age who are not biological offspring of Holocaust survivors. This phenomenon is very different from other places in the world.[50]

An analysis of the deployment of Israeli Holocaust humour as *insider humour*, that is, as jokes that only survivors and their descendants have licence to tell, suggests that President Reuven Rivlin's statement in 2015 that 'all of us, each and every one of us, have a number tattooed on their arm' means most Israelis view dark Holocaust humour as part of their cultural heritage. Does Holocaust humour in Israel indicate that all Israelis are now survivors or descendants of survivors of the Holocaust? Over the past twenty years (since the sketches of the Camera Quintet in the 1990s and references on Seinfeld in the United States) audiences in Israel and America have grown more comfortable with seeing representations of the Holocaust on film and on television. Even though such satirical representations of the Shoah may have been more biting in the 1990s, since 2000, audiences in Israel have grown more comfortable with seeing representations of the Holocaust on film and on television – and just as representations of the Holocaust have been more common, so have jokes and satire that use motifs of the Shoah in popular culture. More recent examples continue this trend, as in the late 2010 sketch 'Hope Kindergarten' from *Eretz Nehederet* (A Wonderful Country). That sketch imagines a right-wing kindergarten run by the ultranationalist Im Tirtzu organization, which educates (or indoctrinates) Israeli children with such games as 'Who Are They to Preach Us Morals?' reminding the children that European nations such as Italy 'helped the Nazis' and that the French had the 'Vichy Regime' while Turkey massacred the Armenians and the Kurds and Norway 'killed all the salmon'. 'What do we tell the world?', the kindergarten teacher asks her students: 'don't preach morals to us! There won't be another Auschwitz!' In this case both the politicization and the manipulation of the memory of the Holocaust for educational purposes are critiqued, as is the debate over whether or not to start Holocaust education for Israeli youth beginning in kindergarten.[51]

A 2012 *Eretz Nehederet* sketch makes fun of American Jewish youth on Birthright trips, stereotyping lazy, spoiled American Jews on their tour of Israel while making light of the cynical fundraising aimed at American Jews in a scene reminiscent of Sallah Shabbati planting trees for wealthy American Jewish donors.[52] Riding on the bus, the mostly American Jewish youths reflect on their visit to Masada, which was so emotional, so powerful, and just 'awesome!' The tour guide, Ze'ev, asks them to tell their parents that Israel is not what they thought; it is a progressive and developed place (not just camels in the desert). Then he asks for men to sit in the front, women in the back. With 'Heveinu Shalom Aleichem' playing in the background, the *madrich* (guide) Ze'ev informs the group:

> Here is the schedule for the rest of the day. At 12:00 we will arrive at the Haganah Museum [the tour groups screams and claps in joy; Josh shouts, 'Fucking awesome!'], from there we will continue to Hasmonean village to see the olive press [more cheers and applause], and at the end, only if there is time, only if we have time and all goes according to plan ['please, please, please', says Melissa, the New York Jewish princess], I intend to take you to ... Yad Vashem Museum [kids are beside themselves, 'Fucking awesome', screams Josh, while Melissa and her friend sing 'Yad Vashem, you so fine, you so fine you blow my mind!'].

Ze'ev continues with his explanation: 'Yad Vashem is a museum dedicated to the Holocaust [as he plays a recording of the theme from *Schindler's List*]. We will give you some time to yourselves to be sad and at the same time to SMS your parents to continue donating to the state of Israel so there won't be a second Holocaust, because the sequel is never as good as the original'. ('No problem', says one of the girls. 'My parents have lots of money; *abba sheli* has tons of *kesef rav* [my dad has tons of money]'.) Ze'ev passes around a blue JNF *pushke* (charity tin) equipped with a credit card swiper to collect donations.

The skit pokes fun at the degree to which the Holocaust has become a tourist attraction ('Yad Vashem, you so fine') and at the fact that, by some estimates, at least 95 per cent of Birthright trips make Yad Vashem a required stop on the standard 10-day itinerary. The commentary extends, however, to the willingness to make use of the Shoah as a philanthropic tool – please continue to support Israel 'so there won't be a second Holocaust, because the sequel is never as good as the original'. Playing the theme from *Schindler's List*, which absurdly accentuates the artificial sadness of such a limited visit within the framework of a tightly scheduled itinerary, the tour guide, Ze'ev, like Prime Minister Netanyahu, is willing to invoke the prospect of a second Holocaust to justify defence of Israel (where there are now more than six million Jews).

A more recent entry into the Israeli sketch comedy scene is *HaYehudim Ba'im* (The Jews Are Coming), a satirical TV show that completed its first broadcast season in January 2015 and completed five seasons by 2022. The show has been broadcast on Israel's historic Channel 1 (now called the KAN network) – for many years the only TV channel in the country – and it is devoted not to spoofs of contemporary Israeli politics but to sketches that target the entire history of the Jewish people since biblical times. Unlike *Eretz Nehederet*, which like the *Daily Show* tends to focus on politics and current events, *HaYehudim Ba'im* analyses central moments in Jewish history and culture through a comedic lens.[53] In addition to skits on Masada, the Dreyfus affair, the Kibbutz Movement, the Hebrew poetess Rachel and the Bible, the show offers satirical looks at the Second World War history and the Holocaust. The show's creators, Natalie Marcus and Asaf Beiser, are both descendants of Holocaust survivors (all four of Marcus's grandparents and Beiser's father).[54] To what extent does their frequent invocation of the Holocaust (in a humorous context on the show) constitute 'insider humour' created by descendants of survivors? Or does their humour reflect a deeper truth about the centrality of Holocaust memory (and the ability to laugh about it) in Israeli society? What can the frequent invocations of the Nazi symbols and Holocaust history on the show teach us about the place of the Holocaust in Israeli comedy and more broadly in Israeli society? As the show effectively returns the Shoah to the broader scope of Jewish history, the Holocaust is used as a prism for critiques of Israeli society, trivialization of the memory of the Holocaust and contemporary memorial practices. At the same time, through its classic satirical style the show asks difficult historical question behind the guise of comedy. *HaYehudim Ba'im* takes the state to task for trivializing the Shoah as part of a broader critique of the ways in which history and historical education have become politicized. Above all, it continues a tradition of self-deprecating Jewish humour that encourages Jews not to take themselves too seriously.

One episode includes a sceptical Hannah Szenes worrying about her fate before she is deployed as a parachutist; or in the same episode, 'Art Academy in Vienna', Adolf Schickelgruber's artwork is rejected and a committee member ridicules him, explaining his work must have some emotion, some anger in it. A young Hitler is encouraged by Jewish committee members to change his name 'to something more catchy', stop painting fanciful portraits of cats and channel his inner rage into something productive. In the sketch *Final Solution 2.0*, situated in 1956, the last surviving Nazis in Europe are meeting in a bunker to discuss the ultimate Final Solution. This time the final plan is to scatter Nazi sympathizers among all the media enterprises in Europe and guarantee that Israel does not receive one point in the Eurovision Song Contest. The plan is greeted with enthusiasm by all in the bunker, and one of the Nazis announces in German-accented Hebrew, 'Zeh yaharog otam [That will kill them]!' The sketch concludes with the Nazis gathered around the table singing the West German entry to the 1979 Eurovision song contest, 'Dschinghis Khan' (Genghis Khan).[55] The irony is that although the sketch parodies the Israeli tendency to perceive every slight against Israel as antisemitic, Israel in fact won Eurovision in back-to-back years in 1978 and 1979 for the songs 'A-Ba-Ni-Bi' and 'Hallelujah'. (Israel would triumph again in 1998, with Dana International's 'Diva' and in 2018 with Netta Barzilai's 'Toy'.)

In line with examining famous moments in Jewish and Israeli history, another *HaYehudim Ba'im* sketch imagines the execution of Adolf

Eichmann in Ramle prison in 1962, but the bumbling and inept guards are incapable of executing Eichmann, incapable of stooping to the depths of evil represented by Eichmann himself. In the end, Eichmann places the noose around his own neck, concluding that 'if you want something done right, you have to do it yourself'. Whereas the actual trial was meant by Israel's leaders to exhibit Jewish power, the sketch seems to highlight Jewish weakness, which, according to Zionist ideology, Jews in Israel had shed. By the same token, this sketch and others are also a subtle reflection of Israeli Jews' exercise of power and the ethical responsibility that comes along with it. Are Jews capable of 'acting like Nazis'? Is the state of Israel even capable of stooping to the same level as the Nazis? (Moni Moshonov, who plays Eichmann in the sketch and one of the Nazi officers in *Final Solution, 2.0*, is one of Israel's most recognizable comedic actors.) Although these questions are posed in a satirical manner, the answers are nonetheless uncomfortable, to say the least.

In *Don't Say Nazi* (Season 3), two friends sitting in an outdoor café in Berlin recognize Adolf Hitler sitting across the café. Hans recognizes him: 'I know him, he's that Nazi ... Hitler!' He is reprimanded by his friend, Fritz, 'stop saying that word! Nazi'. Hans retorts: 'But he is a Nazi. He is the head of the Nazi party. He's a Nazi'. Fritz explains, 'You cannot call every person who opposes your political viewpoint a Nazi ... . it demeans the level of discussion'. The word 'Nazi' is used at least twenty times in the three-minute sketch, as if reinforcing the casual manner in which the term has come to be thrown around in current political discourse. It has become so trivialized, the writers seem to suggest, that when an actual Nazi appears, it becomes impossible to actually label them a Nazi without questioning whether the appellation fits. The creators of the show, Natalie Marcus and Asaf Beiser, were themselves labelled 'Nazis' by opponents of the show who saw the satire of Jewish history as an attack on Jews and Judaism.

It would seem that Holocaust humour in Israel—where the Shoah is too central to Israeli national identity to be forgotten—can function in multiple ways: as a political tool to criticize the centrality of Holocaust memory in the culture and as a part of Jewish history that has become normalized in a way that its historical aspects, the heroic, the historical and the mythological, are no longer off limits for comedic reinterpretation. *The Jews Are Coming* still tends to use the Holocaust to critique the state for constructing national heroes, but as part of a broader critique of the ways in which history and historical education become politicized; it critiques trivialization and the slippage that occurs when terms like Nazi and fascist are overused, and above all, it continues a tradition of self-deprecating Jewish humour, that asks Jews not to take themselves too seriously. The *Jews Are Coming* makes the Holocaust part of Jewish history, equally subject to satire, fair game for critique and re-examination. At the same time, the show uses the backdrop of the Holocaust for contemporary critiques of Israeli society and politics, along with a foreign policy that allows for cosying up to genocidal dictators in Africa in the decades after the creation of the state. In other cases, the sketches satirize trends in Holocaust memorial culture and the Hollywoodization of memory, while also critiquing American responses to the Holocaust through assimilation and commercialization. What is clear is that the Holocaust humour on *The Jews Are Coming*, while certainly representing the 'insider humour' of descendants of survivors confirms Liat Steir Livny's thesis that the Shoah has become so central in Israeli culture and society that Holocaust humour stands right at the centre of Israeli society and culture. By making symbols of the Shoah fair game for Israel's best sketch comedy show, *The Jews Are Coming* returns the Holocaust to the broader scope of Jewish history, not only integrating Israeli humour into the best traditions of Jewish humour, but using humour to do what it does best: nothing is sacred or off limits. We can ask questions about every aspect of Jewish history, even the Holocaust. In order to really get the jokes, it helps to identify with that shared history.

Among the most keen observers of contemporary Israeli society, the creators of *The Jews Are Coming* and other humourists like them, use humour as a tool to examine and surface controversial, often taboo topics in Israeli society, including the wars in which the politicization of the memory of the Holocaust trivializes more than it memorializes. Nonetheless, in 2023, seventy-five years after the creation of the state, it would seem that Tuvia Frilling's prediction that the trivialization, superficialization and cheapening of the memory of the Holocaust continues to grow, as the Shoah and its symbols become an epithet to be hurled at one's political opponents. For example, placards at protests against the proposed judicial 'reform' blamed Prime Minister Benjamin Netanyahu and Justice Minister Yariv Levin for weakening democracy, comparing their government to Nazis. One poster, which started with an image of Theodor Herzl and ended with the symbols of the SS, read 'know from where you came, and where you are headed'. Another poster picturing Justice Minister Yariv Levin above a skull and crossbones, accused him of endangering democracy, comparing the SS of 1933 to 2023. By 2023, when opponents of the right-wing government's judicial reform warned that by weakening the judiciary the government was threatening democracy, comparisons to the rise of fascism and Nazism had already begun to lose some of their previous power.

Conclusion: Israel and the Holocaust, the future of the past

This book has traced the nature of Israel's evolving relationship to the memory of the Shoah. One of the core questions at the heart of this book asks why the Shoah has come to occupy an increasingly central role in the collective memory of Israel even as distance from the historical event continues to grow. This question points to the fluid nature of the relationship between history and memory – that while the study of history may involve a dispassionate record of events, memory is connected with the emotional negotiation that a society may have between available historical records from the past and the needs of the present. Collective memory tells us a great deal about how a nation sees itself. This also presumes that in its earliest years, the founders of the state, along with those who had already lived in the Yishuv during the Second World War, sought to maintain an emotional distance from what would be termed the Shoah, an emotional distance that has dissipated in the seventy-five years since the founding of the state.

It seems clear that in the past seventy-five years, the Shoah has become crucial to Israelis' self-understanding and collective memory; it is the frame of reference and primary association for most segments of society and for a new generation of political leaders descended from Holocaust survivors, such as Merav Michaeli, Yoav Gallant, Benny Gantz and Yair Lapid, it is central to their own identities. Since 1977 – and especially under Benjamin Netanyahu – Israelis have internalized a much closer relationship to the Shoah, with Holocaust education being a required part of the national educational system, and references to the extermination of European Jews commonplace in the political sphere, from protests over the Gaza disengagement to warnings over the Iranian nuclear threat. The frequent referencing of the memory of the Shoah in all spheres since the 1980s coincides with a transition from the founding collectivist socialist ethos to a more individualistic, free-market, capitalist system in which new narratives of national birth have replaced the legends of the 1948 generation. At the same time, especially after the failure of the Oslo Accords, the sense of victimization and trauma of the Second Intifada prods an even greater identification with and politicization of the memory of the Holocaust. Regardless of what the historical record suggests about the challenges of drawing a straight line from the liberation of the camps to the establishment of the state, in collective memory, the two events, Shoah and Tekumah ('resurrection'), become inextricably linked in broad public understanding of that history. As time grows from the event and the last living eyewitnesses pass from the earth, memory of the Shoah increasingly becomes the prism through which Israelis understand both their past and the nature of their present relationships with the wider world. 'Remembering the Shoah' also functions as one of the few points of consensus in an extremely divided society.

It may seem easy to explain this increased focus on the memory of the Shoah as the result of intense politicization of that memory. However, one prominent rebuttal to those who would allege that political manipulation has led Israelis to focus disproportionately on the memory of the Shoah is to compare the ways in which Holocaust memory functions for American Jews in the twenty-first century. According to the research of the Pew Foundation the percentage of American Jews who said that 'remembering the Holocaust is an essential part of what it means to be Jewish' was 73 per cent in the United States versus 65 per cent in Israel, even though the percentage of Holocaust survivors is smaller in the United States and the political and educational factors that lead to such an intense focus on Holocaust memory in Israel are not present to the same degree.[1] Is it possible then that in the natural course of events, it takes multiple generations for a society to come to terms with the consequences of a calamity as massive and catastrophic as the Holocaust? Even if that memory plays a central role in Jewish collective memory around the globe, it can mean different things in different places. What we have tried to examine is how that memory of the Shoah has evolved in Israel; what can this memory tell us about Israeli collective identity? What might that memory look like in the future? And just what is the nature of that memory? Is it historical memory of specific events? Is it political memory, in which the Shoah as symbol is invoked for contemporary needs? Is it social memory, focused more on the last living survivors, the carriers of memory, the last living connection to the event?

The intergenerational transmission of memory has been a central component of Judaism from its origins. In this sense, the focus on a shared memory of a catastrophic event, of the third *Khurbn* (the Yiddish version of the Hebrew word *Hurban*, or destruction, used to refer to the first and second destructions of the temple in Jerusalem), is by no means unusual. The destruction of the Second Temple in Jerusalem transformed Judaism, just as the expulsion from Spain did. What is different is that we now have a secular Jewish national identity that tries to make sense of this memory not in a theological way, but from the vantage point of a sovereign Jewish political entity that possesses power once again. 'Never again' does not only mean never again will the Jewish people become the victims of genocide, it also means, never again will the Jewish people be stateless and without the power to defend themselves. In this sense, statehood and the Shoah have indeed become inextricably linked. Memory of the Shoah in Israel is almost certainly not a memory that prescribes universal lessons meant for all humanity invoked to prevent all future genocides; because Israelis feel vulnerable and victimized, it remains a memory with particular meaning for the Jewish people that necessitates the defence of a strong Jewish state, always on guard against possible threats. Such is the reality that confronts Israel.

Has the memory of the Shoah become the *raison d'etre* of the Jewish state? Has the idea that the Jewish people are a nation like all other nations deserving of a homeland and that the return to their ancestral home will solve the problem of antisemitism once and for all been replaced by the notion that the Holocaust is prooftext for the existence of the Jewish state and that rather than solving the problem of antisemitism, the continued existence of antisemitism proves the need for the continued existence of the state?[2] While it may seem on the face of matters that the centrality of the memory of the Shoah would reflect a change in the national self-conception of Israelis from 1948 to 2023, has a deeper identification with the memory of the Shoah actually changed the relationship between Zionism and the wider world? Does the memory of the Shoah lead to deeper identification with Jewish experiences in the wider world? Or serve to confirm the need for a Jewish state?

What is at stake in the answer to this question has bearing on the fundamental meaning of Zionism: is the Jewish state the manifestation of the Jewish people's ancient longing for a return to the Land of Israel or is the Jewish state the only way to safeguard continued Jewish existence in the aftermath of the Holocaust and continuing antisemitism? In this sense, the memory of the Shoah functions as a symbol to reinforce the continued need for the existence of the Jewish state but that memory does not imply a deeper identification with the actual horror of the event itself; distance from the actual event still remains. As the event becomes more central has the intellectual distance from knowledge of the event actually lessened?

It also seems clear that the survivors – and the memories of the survivors – have assumed a centrality in Israeli society that reflects a dramatic shift from the 1950s to today. In 1954, the Israeli poet Natan Alterman gave voice to the notion that the ghetto fighters should not be 'set on a bright pedestal to be differentiated from the diaspora.' Whereas in 1954 it was the heroic deeds of the partisans and ghetto fighters that would be set on a bright pedestal, by the twenty-first century, all the Shoah survivors would be placed on such a pedestal. For years, those who had not fought with the underground were made to feel 'less than' and a small cohort of heroic mythologized figures were the focal point of memorialization. However, if we consider the demographic reality that between the years 1946 and 1956, approximately two-thirds of all Holocaust survivors leaving Europe (between 400,000 and 500,000 survivors reached Israel, or one-third of the total population of the country at the time) and then we factor the generational growth of the offspring of those survivors, it should not surprise us just how central that familial memory has become to the collective memory of the nation. And while that familial memory may have existed in tension with the dominant Zionist ethos of the founders of the state in 1948, who sought to shape and control the narrative of destruction and bravery (*Shoah ve-Gevurah*) today the tension is not between an ideology that negates the diaspora and exists in uneasy ambivalence with the destruction of European Jewry. There is widespread consensus over how important it is to remember the Shoah; the political divides around Holocaust memory in Israel centre on how to remember, why to remember and what to remember.

From the period of the war and its aftermath, the Shoah (and its survivors) represented a challenge to the state, a challenge to the idea that Zionism could ever effectively 'negate the diaspora.' Classical Zionist ideology once argued that it would be possible to transcend 2,000 years of exile through a return to the Land of Israel, to effect a revolution in Jewish history. But the dichotomy between home and exile was a false one; the deeper identification with the Shoah has returned Israelis to the broader scope of Jewish history. They do not stand outside it, they are bound with the fate of global Jewish history. In the early years of the state, the founders of the state sought to shape the memory of the Shoah through the creation of new Jewish national holidays and new national institutions, which often stood in tension with traditional memorial practices and sites of memory that leaned on existing dates of memory and existing modes of memorialization. A newer memorial practice, which seeks to adapt traditional forms of Jewish memory free from the political sphere, has attempted to reclaim what we have termed bottom-up social memory throughout this book, a memorial practice that has already been developed by the Jewish people that enables every generation to imagine themselves as if they too emerged from slavery. Beginning in 2012, the Israeli writer and daughter of Holocaust survivors, Michal Govrin, aware of the impact that the passing of the survivor generation would have on the modes of memorialization of the Shoah that had become prominent in Israeli society, convened a group of creative minds to develop a new ritual that would combine traditional forms of Jewish practice in a new liturgy of remembrance. Termed *Hitkansut* or Gathering, the ritual is intended as a form of active remembering that like the Passover Haggadah engages the participants in a process of convening, remembering, lamenting, confronting, honouring and reflecting. Participants transition from the responsibility to remember, to remembering responsibly. Organized around an arc that progresses from *kinah* (lament) to *kimah* (rising up), the Hitkansut

Haggadah includes both ancient and modern liturgy, from the *eleh ezkerah* (the 'these I shall remember' martyrology of Yom Kippur), biblical citations, to Primo Levi's *Shema*, excerpts from diaries of Eva Heyman and Etty Hillesum, poetry by Dan Pagis, symbols of resistance and the sanctification of life, and humour used by Jews during the war as a form of resistance and revenge. As noted by the American Jewish writer Dara Horn, who worked with a team of translators to prepare an English language version of the Haggadah sponsored by the Shalom Hartman Institute in Jerusalem:

> Like a Passover Seder, the Hitkansut includes fixed steps, from an invitation (in Hebrew, a *zimun*, echoing the invitation to traditional post-meal blessings) to an exploration of prewar Jewish life in diverse communities through memoir and music, to a full lament (an homage to biblical Lamentations and other traditional Jewish martyrologies, with an emphasis on individual and collective acts of witness), to discussion-prompting texts in sections about confronting evil and standing in opposition. It concludes with the interwoven Jewish concepts of *zakhor* and *shamor* – remembering and preserving – and with traditional calls to the sacredness of life, both individual and collective; the last line is the traditional blessing for the divine creation of the human being. Its many components, replete with the words of Zionists and humanists, religious and secular sources, traditional texts and unexpected ones, are designed to be flexible in the same way that a Passover Haggadah is; different communities will find different resonances in it and emphasize different things. Quotations from the Tanakh, the Talmud and the siddur, along with traditional prayers like *El Maleh Rachamim*, *Yizkor*, and *Kaddish*, are part of the core ritual and are also woven throughout.

Govrin, whose literary works have wrestled with the obligations of memories not passed from her mother to her, has described the *Hitkansut* as part of an effort to transcend the politics of memory that not only trivializes that memory, but also serves as a wedge that will divide Jews in Israel and around the world. As she has explained:

> The victimhood that increasingly pervades Shoah remembrance contributes to a deepening rift within Israel society. It leads people to struggle over who is 'more of a victim', over who does or does not 'belong'. Shoah remembrance has begun to divide Jews rather than unite them. Yet the Shoah threatened to annihilate communities from both east and west – to destroy any Jew simply because they were a Jew – including the Jewish yishuv in the Land of Israel, the Jews of the Arab world who were displaced in the Shoah's wake, as well as Jews living in the countries of the Allied powers and in the Soviet Union. This struggle over who is 'more of a victim' has catalyzed the shift of value from the victorious to

the oppressed. The various borrowings of the Shoah narrative for other calamities still inform today's identity and victimhood politics.[3]

In this sense, the creation of an old/new Jewish liturgical practice, to be commemorated on Yom HaShoah vehaGevurah – but in a format that encourages engagement, participation, reflection and active remembering is part of a project of reclaiming memory – not to be utilized as a political object lesson, but to be engaged with on an individual and simultaneously collective level.

Of course, this is but one model for commemorating the Shoah in Israeli society. For others, commemorations at Yad Vashem, the Chamber of the Holocaust, the Ghetto Fighters House, through Torah study in a yeshiva, in dialogue with Palestinian neighbours or in one's living room with descendants of survivors may seem more meaningful or appropriate. In many ways, these differences point to the manner in which the memory of the Shoah continues to function as a prism for how Israelis view themselves. And yet – that tension we have traced from the outset – between the state and its citizens over how to shape the memory of the Shoah persists – as it is likely to do for generations to come.

* * *

I hasten to add these lines to the final page proofs just days after 7 October 2023, when the Hamas terrorist organization launched a full-scale surprise attack and invasion of Israel – infiltrating communities in Israel's south, massacring civilians, taking hostages and indiscriminately firing thousands of rockets and missiles at population centres throughout the country. Thus far we know over 1,200 Israelis have been murdered, nearly 3,000 have been wounded, and up to 240 people, including women, children and the elderly have reportedly been kidnapped and taken as hostages into Gaza. This is the deadliest attack against the Jewish people in a single day since the murderous onslaughts perpetrated by Nazis during the Second World War. For many Israelis and Jews around the world, this has immediately brought to mind the horrific massacres perpetrated by the Einsatzgruppen. In remarks just days after the murderous rampage, reiterated in a historic wartime solidarity visit to Tel Aviv, US President Joe Biden noted, 'This is terrorism. But sadly, for the Jewish people, it's not new. This attack has brought to the surface painful memories and the scars left by a millennia of antisemitism and genocide of the Jewish people.' In a phone call with Biden, Israeli PM Benjamin Netanyahu explained, 'We've never seen such savagery in the history of the state' nor 'since the Holocaust … They took dozens of children, bound them up, burned them and executed them. They beheaded soldiers, they mowed down these youngsters who came to a nature festival, you know, put five jeeps around this depression in the soil and like Babyn Yar, they mowed them down, making sure that they killed everybody.' It is clear that in the aftermath of this catastrophic day and the war that follows, Israel will never be the same. The notion that Israel exists to protect innocent Jews from the murderous rampages of evil perpetrators has been shattered. And yet, it seems clear, that for Israelis and many Jews and non-Jews around the world, the memory of the Holocaust serves as the strongest reminder for why Israel must defend itself against all its enemies. For many Israelis, the tragedy of 7 October will likely cause a deeper identification with the history of Jewish suffering during the Shoah. We do not know what the future will bring, but it seems clear that the relationship traced in the pages of this book, between Israel and the Holocaust, will be bound ever closer in the collective memory of the nation.

NOTES

Introduction: Between history and memory

1 According to Pew, 65 per cent of Israeli Jews say 'Remembering the Holocaust' is an essential part of what being Jewish means to them (vs 35 per cent observing Jewish Law) https://www.pewresearch.org/religion/2016/03/08/ident ity/ and https://www.pewresearch.org/fact-tank/2016/03/16/a-closer-look-at-jew ish-identity-in-israel-and-the-u-s/.

2 See 'Bennett: Israel is ours because it's the Jewish homeland, not because of the Holocaust', *Times of Israel*, 22 January 2022, https://www.timesofisrael.com/ bennett-israel-not-ours-because-of-holocaust-its-the-jewish-homeland/ (accessed 26 May 2022).

3 Yissachar Teichtal, *Em Habanim Semeha: Restoration of Zion as a Response during the Holocaust*, trans. Pesach Schindler (Hoboken, NJ: Ktav Publishers, 1999).

4 Benzion Dinur, 'Galuyot ve-hurbanan', in Dinur, *Dorot u-reshumot: Mehkarim ve-iyunim ba-historyografyah ha-yisraelit* (Jerusalem: Mosad Bialik, 1978), p. 192.

5 See Koppel S. Pinson, 'Jewish Life in Liberated Germany: A Study of the Jewish DPs', *Jewish Social Science*, vol. 9, no. 2 (April 1947), p. 117.

6 Zeev W. Mankowitz, *Life between Memory and Hope: The Survivors of the Holocaust in Occupied Germany* (New York: Cambridge University Press, 2002), p. 69.

7 The Declaration of the Establishment of Israel, in N. Greenwood, ed., *Israel Yearbook and Almanac 1991/92* (Jerusalem: IBRT Translation/Documentation, 1992), pp. 298–9.

8 See Israel Declaration of Independence, Knesset, https://m.knesset.gov.il/en/ about/pages/declaration.aspx.

9 As former president of Iran Mahmoud Ahmadinejad asked in 2006: 'let's assume certain things did happen [in World War II]. Why should the people of the Middle East, for over 60 years, be paying for it under this pretext?' (24 April 2006) or Mahmoud Abbas, *The Other Face: The Secret Connection between the Nazis and the Zionist Movement* (Amman, Jordan: Dar Ibn Rushd, 1984):

> It seems that the interest of the Zionist movement, however, is to inflate this figure [of Holocaust deaths] so that their gains will be greater. This led them to emphasize this figure [six million] in order to gain the solidarity of international public opinion with Zionism. Many scholars have debated the figure of six million and reached stunning conclusions – fixing the number of Jewish victims at only a few hundred thousand.

10 Yehuda Bauer, 'The Impact of the Holocaust on the Establishment of the State of Israel', in *Major Changes within the Jewish People in the Wake of the Holocaust*, ed. Yisrael Gutman (Jerusalem: Yad Vashem, 1996), pp. 545–52. See also Evyatar Friesel, 'The Holocaust: Factor in the Birth of Israel', in *Major Changes within the Jewish People in the Wake of the Holocaust* (Jerusalem: Yad Vashem, 1996), pp. 519–44, who argues 'the destruction of European Jewry almost rendered the birth of Israel impossible'.
11 Tom Segev, *The Seventh Million: The Israelis and the Holocaust*, prologue (New York: Hill and Wang, 1993; Hebrew original 1991).
12 Dalia Ofer, 'The Yishuv, Zionism, and the Holocaust', in *Major Changes in the Jewish People in the Wake of the Holocaust*, ed. Israel Gutman (Jerusalem: Yad Vashem 1996), p. 471.
13 Segev, *The Seventh Million*, 1993; Hebrew original 1991. See also Idith Zertal, *Israel's Holocaust and the Politics of Nationhood* (Cambridge: Cambridge University Press, 2005).
14 Ofer, 'The Yishuv, Zionism, and the Holocaust'. A number of experts in the field have attempted to analyse the changing nature of Israel's relationship to the Holocaust since 1948. See, for example, Tuvia Friling, 'Remember? Forget? What to Remember? What to Forget?' *Israel Studies*, vol. 19, no. 2 (Summer 2014), pp. 51–69; Idit Gil, 'The Shoah in Israeli Collective Memory: Changes in Meaning and Protagonists', *Modern Judaism*, vol. 32, no. 1 (2012), pp. 76–101; Dalia Ofer, 'We Israelis Remember, But How? The Memory of the Holocaust and the Israeli Experience', *Israel Studies*, vol. 18, no. 2 (2013), pp. 70–85; Dina Porat, *Israeli Society, the Holocaust and Its Survivors* (London: Vallentine Mitchell, 2008); see also Tuvia Friling and Hanna Yablonka, eds., 'Special Issue: Israel and the Holocaust', *Israel Studies*, vol. 8, no. 3 (2003), pp. v–xi.
15 Yael Zerubavel, *Recovered Roots: Collective Memory and the Making of Israeli National Tradition* (Chicago: University of Chicago Press, 1995), p. 5.

1 Nazism, the Holocaust and the creation of the state of Israel

1 'Balfour Declaration, 1917', https://avalon.law.yale.edu/20th_century/balfour. asp (accessed 7 October 2022).
2 Ramsay MacDonald's letter to Chaim Weizmann, 13 February 1931, printed in *Current History*, vol. 34, no. 1 (April 1931), pp. 49–52. For more on British policy in Palestine in this period, see Anita Shapira, *Israel: A History*, chapter 3, 'Palestine Under British Rule' (Waltham, MA: Brandeis University Press, 2012).
3 See Hava Eshkoli, 'Yishuv Zionism: Its Attitude to Nazism and the Third Reich Reconsidered', *Modern Judaism*, vol. 19, no. 1 (February 1999), pp. 21–40 for an overview of the historiographical debates. See Avinoam Patt, 'Review of Nicosia, Francis R.', in *Zionism and Anti-Semitism in Nazi Germany* (H-Judaic, H-Net Reviews, April 2010), http://www.h-net.org/reviews/show rev.php?id=23871 (accessed 11 August 2023)).

4   Tom Segev, *The Seventh Million*, p. 20. Edwin Black, in *The Transfer Agreement: The Untold Story of the Secret Pact between the Third Reich and Jewish Palestine*, alleged that German Zionists were responsible for the survival of the Nazi regime because of their naïve and partisan cooperation with the Nazis in the *Ha'avara* (Transfer) Agreement, in defiance of the international Jewish boycott of Nazi Germany.

5   Eshkoli, 'Yishuv Zionism', p. 24.

6   On Arlosoroff, see the biography by Shlomo Avineri, *Arlosoroff* (London: Peter Halban Publishers, 1989).

7   See 'British White Paper of 1939', https://avalon.law.yale.edu/20th_century/brwh1939.asp (accessed 24 August 2022).

8   See as quoted in Dalia Ofer, '*Illegal immigration to Palestine during the Second World War 1939–1942*'; *Escaping the Holocaust: Illegal Immigration to the Land of Israel, 1939–1944* (New York: Oxford University Press, 1990), p. 23.

9   See Walter Laqueur, *A History of Zionism: From the French Revolution to the Establishment of the State of Israel* (New York: Schocken Books, 2003).

10 See Alexandra Garbarini, Emil Kerenji, Jan Lambertz, and Avinoam Patt, *Jewish Responses to Persecution, 1938–1940*, volume 2 (Lanham, MD: Alta Mira Press, 2011). Weizmann quoted in Norman Rose, *Chaim Weizmann: A Biography* (New York: Penguin, 1986), p. 354. On Zionist reactions to the Holocaust, see Dina Porat, *The Blue and the Yellow Stars of David: The Zionist Leadership in Palestine and the Holocaust, 1939–1945* (Cambridge: Harvard University Press, 1990).

11 Shabtai Teveth, *Ben Gurion and the Holocaust* (New York: Harcourt, 1996), preface, p. xix.

12 See, for example, the work of Tuvia Friling on this topic: *Arrows in the Dark: David Ben-Gurion, the Yishuv Leadership, and Rescue Attempts during the Holocaust* (published in English by the University of Wisconsin Press).

13 Official German record of the meeting between Adolf Hitler and the Grand Mufti of Jerusalem, Hajj Amin al-Husseini, on 28 November 1941 at the Reich Chancellory in Berlin (Source: *Documents on German Foreign Policy 1918–1945*, Series D, vol. XIII, London, 1964.)

14 See Ofer, *Escaping the Holocaust*, p. 35.

15 USHMM Holocaust Encyclopedia, 'Voyage of the Struma', https://encyclopedia.ushmm.org/content/en/article/voyage-of-the-struma (accessed 17 June 2023). For Stoliar's testimony, see also https://www.yadvashem.org/exhibitions/struma/david-stoliar.html.

16 See Corry Guttstadt, *Turkey, the Jews and the Holocaust* (Cambridge: Cambridge University Press, 2013).

17 USHMM Holocaust Encyclopedia, 'Jewish Aid and Rescue', https://encyclopedia.ushmm.org/content/en/article/jewish-aid-and-rescue.

18 USHMM Holocaust Encyclopedia, 'Tehran Children', https://encyclopedia.ushmm.org/content/en/article/tehran-children. See also Mikhal Dekel, *Tehran Children: A Holocaust Refugee Odyssey* (New York: W.W. Norton, 2019).

19 'Biltmore Declaration', 11 May 1942. https://www.un.org/unispal/document/auto-insert-206268/ (accessed 24 August 2022).

20 See 'Riegner Telegram', Samuel Sidney Silverman to Stephen S. Wise, 29 August 1942. Jacob Rader Marcus Center of the American Jewish Archives.

https://www.loc.gov/exhibits/haventohome/images/hh0171as.jpg (accessed 17 June 2023).

21 See, for example, Saul Friedlander, *The Years of Extermination: Nazi Germany and the Jews, 1939–1945* (New York: HarperCollins, 2007), p. 461; David Wyman, *The Abandonment of the Jews: America and the Holocaust, 1941–1945* (New York: Pantheon Books, 1984), p. 42. Both the Jewish Agency and the WJC offices were housed in the Wilson Palace in Geneva, not far from League headquarters. Nachum Goldmann and his secretary, Gerhart Riegner, thus found themselves at close quarters with Richard Lichtheim, representative of the Jewish Agency and Abraham Silberschein, a Zionist leader from Poland who had decided to remain in Geneva at the end of 21st Zionist Congress and who headed RELICO, another Jewish relief organization. Cohen, *Ben 'sham' le-'khan'*, 128.

22 'Nikmat Dam Yeled Katan Od Lo Bara Ha-Satan', *Davar*, 26 November 1942; 'Days of Prayer', *Davar*, 29 November 1942; 'Cries of Anger and Mourning', *Davar*, 3 December 1942; for more on press coverage of the Final Solution, see Laurel Leff, *Buried by the Times: The Holocaust and America's Most Important Newspaper* (Cambridge: Cambridge University Press, 2005), p. 156. See also Jacob J. Schacter, 'Holocaust Commemoration Tisha Be-Av: The Debate over Yom Ha-Shoa', *Tradition*, vol. 41, no. 2 (2008), pp. 164–97.

23 Mooli Brog on Shenhavi, 'In Blessed Memory of a Dream', *Yad Vashem Studies*, vol. 30 (2002), pp. 279–336.

24 David Roskies and Naomi Diamant, *Holocaust Literature: A History and Guide* (Waltham, MA: Brandeis University Press, 2013), p. 38. On Habas, see Encyclopedia of Jewish Women, Jewish Women's Archive, https://jwa.org/encyclopedia/article/habas-bracha (accessed 21 August 2018).

25 See Ziva Shalev, *Tosyah: Tosyah Altman, meha-hanhagah ha-rashit shel ha-Shomer ha-tsair le-mifkedet ha-Irgun ha-Yehudi ha-lochem* (Tel Aviv: Moreshet, 1992), chapter 5; Bracha Habas, *Michtavim Min Ha-Getaot* (Tel Aviv: Am Oved, 1943), pp. 41–3.

26 See as quoted in Hannan Hever, *Suddenly the Sight of War: Violence and Nationalism in Hebrew Poetry* (Stanford, CA: Stanford University Press, 2016), p. 36.

27 'Two Joans of Arc', 7 June 1943. Reuters called them the 'heroines' of the ghetto.

28 See Orly Lubin, 'Holocaust Testimony, National Memory', in *Extremities: Trauma, Testimony and Community*, ed. Nancy K. Miller and Jason Tougaw (Champaign: University of Illinois Press, 2002), pp. 131–42.

29 'Day of Protest Against Allies' Indifference to Jewish Tragedy Proclaimed in Palestine', Jewish Telegraphic Agency, http://www.jta.org/1943/06/07/archive/day-of-protest-against-allies-indifference-to-jewish-tragedy-proclaimed-in-palestine (accessed 21 August 2018).

30 'Mass Protest in Yishuv', *Davar*, 15–16 June 1943.

31 'Report on Hundreds of Thousands in the Yishuv Who Signed', *Davar*, 16 June 1943.

32 Tuvia Friling, 'Organizing Jewish Resistance: The Decision-Making and Executive Array in Yishuv Rescue Operations during the Holocaust', in *Jewish Resistance Against the Nazis*, ed. Patrick Henry (Washington, DC: Catholic University Press, 2014), pp. 245–76.

33 See Porat, *The Blue and the Yellow Stars of David*, pp. 239–62.

34 Porat, *The Blue and the Yellow Stars of David*, pp. 29–30, 75.

35 See Dalia Ofer, 'The Rescue Activities of the Jewish Agency Delegation in Istanbul in 1943', in *Rescue Attempts during the Holocaust. Proceedings of the Second Yad Vashem International Historical Conference*, ed. Y. Gutman and E. Zuroff (Jerusalem: Yad Vashem, 1977), pp. 435–50.

36 See Yehuda Bauer, *Jews for Sale? Nazi-Jewish Negotiations, 1933–1945* (New Haven, CT: Yale University Press, 1994); Leora Bilsky, 'Judging Evil in the Trial of Kasztner', *Law and History Review*, vol. 19, no. 1 (Spring 2001), pp. 117–60; Randolph Braham, *The Politics of Genocide: The Holocaust in Hungary* (New York: Columbia University Press, 1981); Anna Porter, *Kasztner's Train: The True Story of Rezso Kasztner, Unknown Hero of the Holocaust* (Vancouver: Douglas & McIntyre, 2007).

37 USHMM Holocaust Encyclopedia, 'Jewish Parachutists from Palestine', https://encyclopedia.ushmm.org/content/en/article/jewish-parachutists-from-palestine (accessed 11 August 2023). For a detailed account of the history and subsequent memory of the parachutists in Israel, see Judith Tydor-Baumel, *Perfect Heroes: The World War II Parachutists and the Making of Israeli Collective Memory* (Madison: University of Wisconsin Press, 2010).

38 See USHMM Holocaust Encyclopedia, 'Jewish Parachutists from Palestine', https://encyclopedia.ushmm.org/content/en/article/jewish-parachutists-from-palestine and https://www.nli.org.il/en/discover/history/figures/hannah-szenes.

39 Rebecca Erbelding, *Rescue Board: The Untold Story of America's Efforts to Save the Jews of Europe* (New York: Doubleday, 2018).

40 Ghetto Fighters House Archives, Adolf Berman Collection, #5973, 'A Voice from the Depths', underground leaflet, Warsaw, 1944.

41 Levi Arieh Sarid, *Be-Mivchan he-Anut veha-Pdut: Ha-Tnuot Ha-Halutziot bePolin Ba-Shoah ve-Achareha, 1939–1949* (Tel Aviv: Moreshet, 1997), pp. 198–9; David Engel, *Ben Shikhrur Li-Verihah: Nitsolei ha-Shoah be-Polin veha-ma'avak 'al Hanhagatam, 1944–1946* (Tel Aviv: Am Oved, 1996), p. 69; Yehuda Bauer, *Flight and Rescue: Brichah* (New York: Random House, 1970), pp. 25–9.

42 Abba Kovner, 'Reshita shel Ha-Bricha ke-tnuah Hamonit be-eduyotav shel Abba Kovner', *Yalkut Moreshet*, vol. 38 (1984), pp. 133–46; see discussion in Shalom Cholawski, 'Partisans and Ghetto Fighters – an Active Element among She'erit Hapletah', in *She'erit Hapletah, 1944–1948: Rehabilitation and Political Struggle*, ed. Israel Gutman (Jerusalem: Yad Vashem 1990), p. 250.

43 See in Dina Porat, *Nakam: The Holocaust Survivors Who Sought Full Scale Revenge* (Stanford: Stanford University Press), pp. 89–90.

44 Porat, *Nakam*, pp. 205–6.

45 For more on the Jewish Brigade's first encounters with survivors, see Yoav Gelber, 'The Meeting between the Jewish Soldiers from Palestine Serving in the British Army and She'erit Hapletah', in *She'erit Hapletah, 1944–1948, Rehabilitation and Political Struggle; Proceedings of the 6th Yad Vashem International Historical Conference, Jerusalem, October 1985*, ed. Yisrael Gutman and Avital Saf (Jerusalem: Vad Vashem 1990), pp. 60–80.

46 Yehuda Bauer, *American Jewry and the Holocaust* (Detroit: Wayne State University Press, 2017), p. 291. On the rescue work of Joseph Schwartz, see

Ruth Baki Kolodny, *Ani Yosef Achichem* (I Am Joseph Your Brother: The Life and Work of Joe Schwartz) (Israel: Modan, 2010).

47 The term *she'erit hapletah* is biblical in origin and had been used during the war in the Yishuv to refer abstractly to the population of Jews who would survive the war; in the immediate aftermath of the war, the term would also be used in very concrete terms by the American Jewish chaplain Rabbi Abraham Klausner, who began to compile detailed lists of survivors he met in the camps he surveyed in the US Zone of Germany, publishing them under the series title *She'erit Hapletah*, a reference to the writings of the prophets, that there would be a 'saving remnant' after the destruction. For a more detailed discussion of Klausner's role in the DP camps, see Avinoam Patt, 'The People Must Be Forced to Go to Palestine: Rabbi Abraham Klausner and the Surviving Remnant in Postwar Germany', *Holocaust and Genocide Studies*, vol. 28, no. 2 (Fall 2014), pp. 240–76.

48 24 June 1945 report of Chaplain Abraham Klausner, 'A Detailed Report on the Liberated Jew as He Now Suffers His Period of Liberation Under the Discipline of the Armed Forces of the United States', CJH, AJHS, Abraham Klausner papers, Box 3, Folder 11.

49 See Zalman Grinberg and Puczyc to OMGUS and UNRRA, 10 July 1945, YIVO, DP Germany, MK 483, #340. Noting that many Ukrainians who had collaborated with the SS continued to be well fed, the Jewish prisoners, who had always received the worst nourishment, continued to be malnourished and were still without proper clothing.

50 Mankowitz, *Life between Memory and Hope*, p. 31. For a transcript of the speech given by Zalman Grinberg at St. Ottilien on 27 May 1945, see YIVO, LS, MK 488, Roll 13, Folder 104, #10–14.

51 YIVO, DP Germany, MK 483, Reel 21. Dr. Zalman Grinberg, 'Appel an den judischen Weltkongress', St Ottilien, 31 May 1945. Klausner's requests for medical supplies for the newly formed hospital organized by Grinberg were met with replies of 'materials unavailable' from the JDC, leading Klausner to secure supplies on his own through individual contacts in New Haven, CT. See Abraham J. Klausner, *A Letter to My Children: From the Edge of the Holocaust* (San Francisco: Holocaust Center of Northern California, 2002), p. 26.

52 The first CCLJ meeting took place in Feldafing DP camp, near Dachau. For more on the early and extensive involvement of American Jewish chaplains in the relief efforts and organization of DP institutions, see Alexander Grobman, *Rekindling the Flame: American Jewish Chaplains and the Survivors of European Jewry, 1944–1948* (Detroit: Wayne State University Press, 1993).

53 See Avinoam Patt, *Finding Home and Homeland: Jewish Youth and Zionism in the Aftermath of the Holocaust* (Detroit: Wayne State University Press, 2009), chapter 1.

54 On the experiences of survivors in the British zone, see Hagit Lavsky, *New Beginnings: Holocaust Survivors in Bergen-Belsen and the British Zone in Germany, 1945–1950* (Detroit: Wayne State University Press, 2002).

55 Mankowitz, *Life between Memory and Hope*, p. 69. 'For many, their almost intuitive Zionism stood for the warmth, unquestioning acceptance and security of home; for the more politically minded it signified the only real hope for the

rescue and rehabilitation of the little that remained of European Jewry and, in the longer term, the promise of the Jewish future.'

56 See Mankowitz, *Life between Memory and Hope*, p. 36 and Mankowitz, 'The Formation of She'erit Hapletah: November 1944–July 1945', *Yad Vashem Studies*, vol. 20 (1990), pp. 336–70. (A number of early leaders of the Jewish DPs in Germany, including Samuel Gringauz, Zalman Grinberg, Leib Garfunkel (head of the organization of Holocaust Survivors in Italy), as well as the founders of the early DP Zionist youth group, *Nocham*, the United Pioneer Youth Movement, emerged from an early group of survivors from Kovno concentrated in Dachau. See Mankowitz, *Life between Memory and Hope*, p. 347.)

57 Judah Nadich, *Eisenhower and the Jews* (New York: Twayne Publishers, 1953), p. 231. The episode is also described by Heymont.

58 Heymont, letter 19, 22 October 1945, in Irving Heymont, *Among the Survivors of the Holocaust* (Cincinnati: Hebrew Union College Press, 1982) , p. 65 (my emphasis). See also description of Ben-Gurion's visit to Landsberg in the *Landsberger Lager Cajtung*.

59 Arieh J. Kochavi, *Post Holocaust Politics: Britain, The United States, and Jewish Refugees, 1945–1948* (Chapel Hill: University of North Carolina Press, 2001), p. 134.

60 See Meir Avizohar, 'Bikkur Ben-Gurion Be-makhanot Ha'akurim Ve-tefisato Ha-leumit Be-tom Milkhemet Ha'olam Ha-sheniah (Ben-Gurion's visit to the DP Camps)', in *Yahadut Mizrach Eiropah Bein Shoah Le-tekuma 1944–1948*, ed. Benjamin Pinkus (Sde Boker: Ben Gurion University, 1987), p. 260; Kochavi, *Post Holocaust Politics*, p. 94; Nadich, *Eisenhower and the Jews*, p. 238; based on Ben-Gurion's report of his visit to the DP camps, 6 November 1945. The Jewish DPs were granted the right to self-governance by the US Army in September 1946.

61 For more on the Bricha, see David Engel, *Ben shikhrur li-verihah: Nitsolei ha-Shoah be-Polin veha-ma'avak al hanhagatam, 1944–1946* (Tel Aviv: Am Oved, 1996).

62 From an early point following liberation it was evident that as much as half of the surviving population was under the age of twenty-five, and some 80 per cent were under age forty. For example, a survey of Jewish DPs in Bavaria taken in February 1946 found that 83.1 per cent of their number was between the ages of fifteen and forty, with over 40 per cent between fifteen and twenty-four, and 61.3 per cent between nineteen and thirty-four. Jewish Population in Bavaria, February 1946 (YIVO, MK 488, Leo Schwartz Papers, Roll 9, Folder 57, #581). A study by the AJDC of Jews in the US Occupation Zone in Germany over one year after liberation found 83.1 per cent between the ages of six and forty-four (YIVO, MK 488, LS 9, 57, #682; Jewish Population, US Zone Germany, 30 November 1946).

63 For a map depicting the DP camps, see 'Major Camps for Jewish Displaced Persons, 1945–1946', USHMM Holocaust Encyclopedia, https://encyclopedia.ushmm.org/content/en/map/major-camps-for-jewish-displaced-pers ons-1945-1946 (accessed 11 August 2023). For an overview on the history of Jewish DPs, see, for example, Mankowitz, *Life between Memory and Hope*; Margarete Myers Feinstein, *Holocaust Survivors in Postwar Germany, 1945–1957* (New York: Cambridge University Press, 2010); Avinoam J. Patt and

Michael Berkowitz, eds, '*We Are Here*': *New Approaches to Jewish Displaced Persons in Postwar Germany* (Detroit: Wayne State University Press, 2010).

64 On the rebirth of religious life in the DP camps, see Judith Baumel, 'The Politics of Spiritual Rehabilitation in the DP Camps', see in http://motlc.wie senthal.com/site/pp.asp?c=gvKVLcMVIuG&b=395149.

65 Anglo-American Committee of Inquiry, *Report to the United States Government and His Majesty's Government in the United Kingdom*, Lausanne, Switzerland, 20 April 1946 (Washington, DC: US Government Printing Office, 1946); see Lillian Goldman Law Library, Yale Law School, http://avalon.law.yale.edu/subject_menus/angtoc.asp (accessed 21 July 2019).

66 Aviva Halamish, *The Exodus Affair: Holocaust Survivors and the Struggle for Palestine* (Syracuse, NY: Syracuse University Press, 1998), p. 72

67 *Jidisce Cajtung*, 2 December 1947, reel 1, Jewish DP Periodicals Collection, YIVO.

68 See Bauer, 'The Impact of the Holocaust on the Establishment of the State of Israel', p. 551.

69 See the debate between Hagit Lavsky and Yechiam Weitz, 'The Survivors of the Holocaust and the Establishment of the State of Israel', (Hebrew), *Cathedra*, vol. 55 (March 1990), pp. 162–81. While Weitz seeks to argue that the establishment of the state took place despite the tragedy of the Holocaust, Lavsky argues quite convincingly that the Yishuv shrewdly took advantage of the post-Holocaust reality to advance the cause of the establishment of Israel. For the broader context around partition, see Penny Sinanoglu, *Partitioning Palestine: British Policymaking at the End of Empire* (Chicago: University of Chicago Press, 2019).

2 The state of Israel and the memory of the Holocaust, 1948–61

1 See Avihu Ronen, *Condemned to Life: The Diaries and Life of Chajka Klinger* (Haifa: Haifa University Press, 2011); Avinoam Patt, *The Jewish Heroes of Warsaw: The Afterlife of the Revolt* (Detroit: Wayne State University Press, 2021); see Dina Porat, 'First Testimonies on the Holocaust', in *Holocaust Historiography in Context*, eds. Dan Michman and David Bankier (Jerusalem: Yad Vashem, 2008), p. 437. See also Sharon Geva, '"With and Despite the Burden of the Past": 1946 in the Life Story of Zivia Lubetkin', *Moreshet: Journal for the Study of the Holocaust and Anti-Semitism*, vol. 14 (2017), p. 220. See also Bella Gutterman, *Fighting for Her People: Zivia Lubetkin, 1914–1978* (Jerusalem: Yad Vashem, 2015) on the life story of Zivia Lubetkin.

2 See Porat, 'First Testimonies on the Holocaust', p. 437.

3 Aharon Megged, 'Yad Vashem', in *Facing the Holocaust: Selected Israel Fiction*, eds. Gila Ramras-Rauch and Joseph Michman-Melkman (Philadelphia: Jewish Publication Society, 1985), p. 33.

4 Haim Hazaz, 'The Sermon', in *Modern Hebrew Literature*, ed. Robert Alter (New York: Behrman House, 1975).

5 See, for example, Orna Kenan, *Between Memory and History: The Evolution of Israeli Historiography of the Holocaust, 1945–1961* (New York: Peter Lang, 2003) and Roni Stauber, *The Holocaust in Israeli Public Debate in the 1950s: Ideology and Memory* (London: Vallentine Mitchell, 2007). Despite widespread belief in the 'soap myth' after the war, most scholars agree there is no evidence to support the allegation that the Nazis used Jewish corpses in the manufacture of soap.

6 See Gil, 'The Shoah in Israeli Collective Memory' and Porat, *The Blue and the Yellow Stars of David*.

7 Hanna Yablonka, *Survivors of the Holocaust: Israel after the War* (New York: New York University Press, 1999). English translation of *Foreign Brethren: Holocaust Survivors in the State of Israel, 1948–1952*, 1994 (Hebrew).

8 Yablonka, *Survivors of the Holocaust*, p. 82.

9 Idit Zertal and Josef Grodzinsky, for example, argue that the Zionist leadership exploited survivors in the drive for statehood. According to the research of Emmanuel Sivan, 'The Life of the Dead: Sabras and Immigrants', *Studies in Contemporary Jewry*, vol. XI (1994), the oft-repeated myth that Holocaust survivors were thrown into battle as 'cannon-fodder' is not completely supported by research. Through a statistical analysis of the actual numbers of war dead Sivan helps to explain some of the bias that developed within the national myth. Some 45 per cent of those recruits killed between December 1947 and January 1948 were sabras, as were 37 per cent of those killed before May 15. Sivan notes that it was the immigrants who arrived since 1940 who constituted a significant forgotten contingent of the war (169). See Anita Shapira, 'Historiography and Memory: Latrun, 1948', *Jewish Social Studies*, vol. 3, no. 1 (1996), pp. 20–61 and Yablonka's discussion of the battle, *Survivors of the Holocaust*, pp. 146–7. Both Shapira and Yablonka note the discrepancies in versions of the battle which differ on the total number of casualties and the number of immigrants among those killed. Yablonka concludes that of the forty-three soldiers lost in the battle for Latrun, fifteen were immigrants.

10 Yehudit Hendel depicts this experience in her short story '*Anashim Acherim Hem*' (They are Different People), which chronicles the experience of one lonely survivor flung into battle immediately after his arrival in Israel. The protagonist's 'different people' are in fact the Sabras, not the new immigrants.

11 Michal Arbell, 'Abba Kovner: The Ritual Function of His Battle Missives', *Jewish Social Studies*, vol. 18, no. 3 (2012), pp. 99–119.

12 See Yael Feldman, Alan Mintz on the literature of 1948 Generation: coupled with the seeming passivity of European Jewry and the failure of the Yishuv to do anything in its defence, the intense shame of the Yishuv and the conflicted emotions towards their diaspora brethren also led to this silence. To the extent that the Holocaust was addressed, however, according to Sidra DeKoven Ezrahi the ideological consistency with which the destruction of European Jewry could be explained within Zionist ideology did not precipitate 'a fundamental crisis in prevailing Israeli perceptions of Jewish destiny'. Hence, the Holocaust could be assimilated into the Zionist 'logic of Jewish regeneration so that it would not shake the foundations of the new state'. Sidra DeKoven Ezrahi, 'Considering the Apocalypse: Is the Writing

on the Wall Only Graffiti?' in *Writing and the Holocaust*, ed. Berel Lang (New York: Holmes and Meier, 1988), p. 145.

13 Sivan, 'The Life of the Dead: Sabras and Immigrants', p. 166.

14 Sivan, 'The Life of the Dead', pp. 166, 170.

15 A statistical analysis of the actual numbers of war dead by Sivan helps to explain some of the bias that developed within the national myth. Some 45 per cent of those recruits killed between December 1947 and January 1948 were sabras, as were 37 per cent of those killed before May 15. Sivan notes that rather than the *gahalezim* of 1948, it is the immigrants who arrived since 1940 who constitute a significant forgotten contingent of the war (169).

16 The Declaration of the Establishment of Israel, in N. Greenwood, *Israel Yearbook and Almanac*, pp. 298–9.

17 Gali Druker Bar-Am, "May the "Makom" Comfort You': Place, Holocaust Remembrance and the Creation of National Identity in the Israeli Yiddish Press, 1948–1961', *Yad Vashem Studies*, vol. 42, no. 2 (2014), p. 2; Bar-Am cites David Shaari, 'Uniqueness of She'erit Hapleta', *Massuah* 28, 2000, 'Barricades of Silence: the She'erit Hapleta and the Land of Israel (Hebrew)', p. 30. Hanna Yablonka, 'Holocaust Survivor Artists in Israel: Another Aspect of a Silence that Never Was', in *The Holocaust – History and Remembrance: Collection Presented to Yisrael Gutman* (Hebrew), ed. Shmuel Almog (Jerusalem: Yad Vashem, 2002), p. 207 and Yablonka, *Survivors of the Holocaust*, p. 9. Israel Gutman, 'The Holocaust and Its Imprint in Jewish History', *Issues in Holocaust Scholarship: Research and Reassessment* (Hebrew) (Jerusalem: Zalman Shazar Center for Jewish History, 2008), p. 21. It is worth noting that while the definition of 'survivors' as noted earlier could be loaded with debates over who was a survivor, how one had survived and hierarchies of 'suffering and survival' for statistical purposes, the state of Israel did not distinguish between one's wartime experiences and their statues as a 'survivor'. See, for example, the discussion in Eliyana Adler, *Survival on the Margins: Polish Jewish Refugees in the Wartime Soviet Union* (Cambridge: Harvard University Press, 2020) of Jews who survived the war in the far reaches of the USSR and may not have been deemed 'survivors' in the DP camps, but were labelled 'survivors' for immigration purposes by the state of Israel.

18 See 'Search Bureau for Missing Relatives', http://www.zionistarchives.org.il/AttheCZA/AdditionalArticles/Pages/ChipushKrovim.aspx (accessed 11 August 2023).

19 Passed by the Knesset on the 20th Tammuz, 5710 (5 July 1950) and published in Sefer Ha-Chukkim No. 51 of the 21st Tammuz, 5710 (5 July 1950), p. 159; the Bill and an Explanatory Note were published in Hatza'ot Chok No. 48 of the 12th Tammuz, 5710 (27 June 1950), p. 189.

20 The boundaries of this law would be challenged over time, perhaps most famously in the case of Brother Daniel, aka Oswald Rufeisen, a Polish-born Jew from Mir active in the Jewish underground there, who converted to Christianity while hiding in a convent during the war, where he was baptized and eventually became a member of the Carmelite Order and a priest. In 1959, Brother Daniel moved to Israel where he was reunited with his brother Aryeh who made it to Palestine in 1941. Forced to renounce his Polish citizenship before moving to Israel, Brother Daniel applied for Israeli citizenship under

the Law of Return, explaining that although his religion was Catholicism, he was still a Jew: 'My ethnic origin is and always will be Jewish. I have no other nationality. If I am not a Jew, what am I? I did not accept Christianity to leave my people. I added it to my Judaism. I feel as a Jew.' (*Time Magazine*, 7 December 1962, p. 54). The Israeli government rejected his application on the grounds that he had abandoned his Judaism by converting to Catholicism, a decision which was upheld by Israel's Supreme Court. Brother Daniel nonetheless spent the rest of his life at a monastery in Haifa and was eventually naturalized as a citizen.

21 See Hanna Yablonka and Moshe Tlamim, 'The Development of Holocaust Consciousness in Israel: The Nuremberg, Kapos, Kastner, and Eichmann Trials', *Israel Studies*, vol. 8, no. 3 (Fall 2003), p. 11.

22 See James Young, 'When a Day Remembers: A Performative History of 'Yom ha-Shoah', *History and Memory*, vol. 2, no. 2 (Winter 1990), pp. 54–75.

23 See Eliezer Don-Yehiyeh, 'Memory and Political Culture: The Holocaust and Israeli Society', in *Studies in Contemporary Jewry*, vol. 9 (Institute for Contemporary Jewry in the Hebrew University of Jerusalem), ed. Ezra Mendelsohn (Oxford: Oxford University Press, 1993), p. 139.

24 For more details on the present location of the forest, see Keren Kayemeth LeIsrael, Jewish National Fund, http://www.kkl-jnf.org/tourism-and-recreat ion/forests-and-parks/martyrs-forest.aspx (accessed 11 August 2023). The forest would also become the site of the monument 'Scroll of Fire', created by Nathan Rapoport and dedicated in 1968. The forest is off the main highway connecting Tel Aviv and Jerusalem, located near Moshav Kisalon, close to Beit Shemesh.

25 See discussion in James Young, *The Texture of Memory: Holocaust Memorials and Meaning* (New Haven, CT: Yale University Press, 1994), p. 234. Batia Donner, *Natan Rapoport: A Jewish Artist* (in Hebrew) (Jerusalem: Yad Ben Tzvi and Yad Ya'ari, 2014) discusses the creation of the monument at Yad Mordecai in even greater detail, pp. 182–214. See also Micha Balf, *Unsilenced Voices: Memory and Commemoration of the Holocaust in the Kibbutz Movement* (Tel Aviv: Hakibbutz HaMeuchad, 2008) (Hebrew).

26 A report about the Warsaw ghetto uprising, GFH Archives 8964.

27 See Brog, 'In Blessed Memory of a Dream', pp. 297–336. See extended discussion in Stauber, *The Holocaust in Israeli Public Debate in the 1950s*.

28 'Martyrs' and Heroes Remembrance (Yad Vashem) Law 5713-1953', Yad Vashem, https://www.yadvashem.org/about/yad-vashem-law.html (accessed 11 August 2023).

29 18 May 1953 debate on Yad Vashem Law in Eliezer Don-Yehiyeh, 'Memory and Political Culture', p. 142.

30 For a vanguard study in this field, see Hanna Yablonka, 'What to Remember and How? Holocaust Survivors and the Shaping of Holocaust Knowledge' (Hebrew), in *The Age of Zionism* (Hebrew), eds. Anita Shapira, Jehuda Reinharz and Jay Harris (Jerusalem: Zalman Shazar Center, 2000), pp. 297–316. On the tension between 'grassroots' Holocaust researchers and the 'professionals' at Yad Vashem, see Boaz Cohen, *The Next Generations: How Will They Know? The Birth and Evolution of Israeli Holocaust Research* (Hebrew) (Jerusalem: Yad Vashem, 2010). See also Mark Smith, *The Yiddish*

Historians and the Struggle to Write a Jewish History of the Holocaust (Detroit: Wayne State University Press, 2019).

31 See as quoted in Tom Segev, *The Seventh Million*, pp. 195–6.

32 For an excellent discussion of the complex historical context of negotiations between Israel and Germany (including dramatic recreations), see the documentary film *Reckonings: The First Reparations* (dir. Roberta Grossman, 2022), https://reckoningsfilm.org/.

33 MK Mordecai Nurock, Knesset Debate, 8 January 1952; see as quoted in Yaakov Sharett, ed., *The Reparations Controversy* (Tel Aviv: Moshe Sharett Heritage Society, 2011).

34 *Herut*, 7 January 1952, see https://www.nli.org.il/en/newspapers/ hrt/1952/01/07/01/article/5/?e=-------en-20--1--img-txIN%7ctxTI-------------1 (accessed 11 August 2023).

35 See *The Jerusalem Post*, 8 January 1952; see reference also here: https://www. degruyter.com/document/doi/10.1515/9783110255386.385/html?lang=en (accessed 11 August 2023).

36 See Jacob Tovy, *Destruction and Accounting: The State of Israel and the Reparations from Germany 1949–1953* (Tel Aviv: Tel Aviv University, 2015).

37 See Liber Losh, ed., *Landsmanshafn in Yisroel* (Yiddish) (Tel Aviv: Association of Immigrants from Poland in Israel, 1961), pp. 33–206.

38 Michlean Amir and Rosemary Horowitz, 'Yizkor Books in the Twenty-First Century: A History and Guide to the Genre', *Judaica Librarianship*, vol. 14, no. 1 (2008), pp. 39–56, here 46.

39 Gali Drucker Bar-Am, '''May the "Makom" Comfort You': Place, Holocaust Remembrance and the Creation of National Identity in the Israeli Yiddish Press, 1948–1961', *Yad Vashem Studies*, vol. 42, no. 2 (2014), pp. 155–95, here 162–3.

40 Ibid., p. 2.

41 Ibid., p. 21.

42 Ibid., pp. 8–9. For more on Yiddish in Israel, see also Rachel Rojanksi, *Yiddish in Israel: A History* (Bloomington: Indiana University Press, 2020).

43 On the founding of Di Goldene Keyt and Sutzkever in Israel, see Rojanksi, *Yiddish in Israel*, pp. 162–76.

44 See David Fishman, *The Book Smugglers: Partisans, Poets, and the Race to Save Jewish Treasures from the Nazis* (Lebanon, NH: ForeEdge, University Press of New England, 2017). On Sutzkever's wartime testimony, see Hannah Pollin-Galay, 'Avrom Sutzkever's Art of Testimony: Witnessing with the Poet in the Wartime Soviet Union', *Jewish Social Studies*, vol. 21, no. 2 (Winter 2016), pp. 1–34.

45 See Avraham Novershtern, 'Avraham Sutzkever z'l', https://www.yadvashem. org/research/about/studies/back-issues/38-1/novershtern.html (accessed 11 August 2023). For a video excerpt of Sutzkever's Nuremberg Trial testimony (in Russian), see https://perspectives.ushmm.org/item/nuremberg-trial-testim ony-of-avrom-sutzkever

46 Sutzkever, 'Poetishe verk,' volume 2 (Yiddish) (Tel Aviv: Yoyvl Komitet, 1963), p. 96; Avraham Sutzkever, *Selected Poetry and Prose*, trans. and ed. Barbara and Benjamin Harshav (Berkeley: University of California Press, 1991), p. 232.

47 Sutzkever, 'Poetishe verk', volume 2, p. 227; English version in Sutzkever, *Selected Poetry and Prose*, p. 357.

48 *Davar*, 19 April 1949, p. 1.

49 See Balf, *Unsilenced Voices*, p. 29 and Gutterman, *Fighting for Her People*, p. 418.

50 Doron Bar, 'Holocaust Commemoration in Israel during the 1950s: The Holocaust Cellar on Mount Zion', *Jewish Social Studies*, New Series, vol. 12, no. 1 (Autumn 2005), p. 17.

51 Ibid., p. 32.

52 E. Vizel (Elie Wiesel), in *Forverts* (New York) (6 November 1960, 23 April 1967).

53 Omer Bartov, 'Kitsch and Sadism in Ka-Tzetnik's Other Planet: Israeli Youth Imagine the Holocaust Author(s)', *Jewish Social Studies*, New Series, vol. 3, no. 2 (Winter 1997), pp. 42–76.

54 David Mikics, 'Holocaust Pulp Fiction', *Tablet Magazine*, 19 April 2012, https://www.tabletmag.com/sections/arts-letters/articles/ka-tzetnik (accessed 9 October 2022).

55 Yael S. Feldman, 'Whose Story Is It, Anyway? Ideology and Psychology in the Representation of the Shoah in Israeli Literature', in *Probing the Limits of Representation: Nazism and the 'Final Solution'*, ed. Saul Friedlander (Cambridge, MA: Harvard University Press, 1992), pp. 223–39.

56 Ibid., pp. 223–4.

57 Ibid., p. 224.

58 Gershon Shaked, 'Facing the Nightmare: Israeli Literature on the Holocaust', in *Facing the Holocaust: Selected Israeli Fiction*, eds. Gila Ramras-Rauch and Joseph Michman-Melkman (Philadelphia: Jewish Publication Society, 1985), p. 276. Thus, Shaked reads Judith Hendel's *Anashim Acherim Hem* as identifying the characters who came from over there as 'another kind of people', even crediting her with feeling the right of 'the other people' to be different. Shaked hence reads the survivor in Hendel's tale as the other, even though this may not be the intent of her usage in the story.

59 See Dan Porat, *Bitter Reckoning: Israel Tries Holocaust Survivors as Nazi Collaborators* (Cambridge, MA: Harvard University Press, 2019), p. 75; Porat cites Knesset Archives, Jerusalem, Knesset Plenary Records, *Divrei Ha-Knesset*, 27 March 1950, pp. 1147–8, 1161.

60 Dan Porat's *Bitter Reckoning* traces the changing views of Israelis towards survivors as collaborators through four main phases in the 1950s–1960s, moving from a perception of complete guilt as collaborators equivalent to Nazi perpetrators to a final perception of them as victims with acknowledgement of the complexity and recognition as victims (and at times even heroes).

61 See Avinoam Patt, 'Rudolf (Rezso) Kasztner', USHMM Holocaust Encyclopedia, https://encyclopedia.ushmm.org/content/en/article/rudolf-rezsoe-kasztner (accessed 11 August 2023).

62 See Stauber, *The Holocaust in Israeli Public Debate in the 1950s*, pp. 78–96.

63 See discussion in Hever, *Suddenly the Sight of War*, pp. 110–11, poem trans. Bella Gutterman, 459–60.

64 See discussion in Boaz Cohen, *Israeli Holocaust Research: Birth and Evolution* (London: Routledge, 2013), p. 21. The poem appears in *Davar*, 30 April 1954.

65 Yechiam Weitz, 'The Holocaust on Trial: The Impact of the Kasztner and Eichmann Trials on Israeli Society', *Israel Studies*, vol. 1, no. 2 (Fall 1996),

p. 7; Moshe Shamir, 'A People that Does Not Know', *Al ha'Mishmar*, 22 March 1957.

66   See also the documentary *Killing Kasztner: The Jew Who Dealt with the Nazis* (dir. Gaylen Ross, 2014).

67   See discussion in Yechiam Weitz, 'The Holocaust on Trial', p. 24.

3 From Eichmann to Begin, 1961–77

1   'The Eichmann Case as Seen by Ben-Gurion', *The New York Times Magazine*, 18 December 1960.

2   See Yehiam Weitz, 'The Founding Father and the War Criminals' Trial: Ben Gurion and the Eichmann Trial', *Yad Vashem Studies*, vol. 36, no. 1 (2018), pp. 211–52.

3   See as discussed in Hanna Yablonka, *The State of Israel vs. Adolf Eichmann* (New York: Schocken Books, 2004), pp. 123–30, 236–7.

4   Boaz Cohen, 'Rachel Auerbach, Yad Vashem, and Israeli Holocaust Memory', *Polin: Studies in Polish Jewry*, vol. 20 (2008), p. 214 and Hanna Yablonka, 'Preparing the Eichmann Trial: Who Really Did the Job?', *Theoretical Inquiries in Law*, vol. 1, no. 2 (2000), pp. 369–92.

5   See Cohen, 'Rachel Auerbach, Yad Vashem, and Israeli Holocaust Memory', p. 214 and R. Auerbach, 'Edim ve'eduyot bemishpat eichmann (terumat 'hamahlekah ligviyat eduyot' shel yad vashem)', *Yediot yad vashem*, 28 December 1961, pp. 35–41.

6   Gali Drucker Bar-Am, 'The Holy Tongue and the Tongue of the Martyrs: The Eichmann Trial as Reflected in Letste Nayes', *Dapim: Studies on the Holocaust*, vol. 28, no. 1 (2014), pp. 17–37.

7   Deborah Lipstadt, *The Eichmann Trial* (New York: Nextbook/Schocken, 2011), pp. 54–5.

8   See, for example, Yad Vashem, 'The Eichmann Trial', https://www.yadvashem.org/yv/en/exhibitions/eichmann/index.asp (accessed 11 August 2023).

9   See Weitz, 'The Holocaust on Trial', p. 19. Haim Gouri, *Mul ta ha'Zekhukhit: Mishpat be'Yerushalayim* [Facing the Glass Booth: The Jerusalem Trial] (n.p., 1962) (Hebrew).

10   State of Israel Ministry of Justice, *The Trial of Adolf Eichmann, Record of Proceedings in the District Court of Jerusalem* (Jerusalem 1992), vol. 3, p. 1237.

11   See Sharon Geva, 'And Now You Are Married and You Have Two Children' Female Witnesses at the Eichmann Trial', *Yad Vashem Studies*, vol. 47, no. 2 (2019), pp. 131–64.

12   Ibid., p. 145; 'Tiurim Mahridim al Hashmadatam Shel Yehude Rusia HaLevana VeUkraine' (Hebrew), *Hatsofe*, 9 May 1961, p. 2.

13   Translation from Geva, 'And Now You Are Married', p. 146; see Gouri, 'Marta's Sabbath Dress', Facing the Glass Booth, pp. 50–1.

14   See Geva, 'And Now You Are Married', p. 146; Testimony of Rivka Yoselevska, The Trial of Adolf Eichmann, Vol. 1, Session 30. See also http://www.nizkor.com/hweb/people/e/eichmann-adolf/transcripts/Sessions/Session-030-03.html (accessed 12 August 2023).

15 See in Geva, 'And Now You Are Married', pp. 143–50. For 'Death Pit to a New Life', see Schnitzer, 'MiBor HaMetim KeHayyim Hadashim', *Ma'ariv*, 9 May 1961, p. 2.

16 State of Israel Ministry of Justice, *The Trial of Adolf Eichmann*.

17 The Trial of Adolf Eichmann, Session 71, 8 June 1961, Testimony of Vera Alexander, http://nizkor.com/hweb/people/e/eichmann-adolf/transcripts/Sessions/Session-071-01.html (accessed 12 August 2023).

18 Gouri, 'Why Fear Death', *Facing the Glass Booth: The Jerusalem Trial of Adolf Eichmann*, p. 43.

19 Testimony of Zivia Lubetkin-Zuckerman, The Trial of Adolf Eichmann, Vol. 1, Session 25; See also at US Holocaust Memorial Museum, RG 60.2100*037, Accession 1999.A.0087, available at https://perspectives.ushmm.org/item/eichmann-trial-testimony-of-zivia-lubetkin (accessed 12 August 2023).

20 Yablonka, *The State of Israel vs. Adolf Eichmann*, p. 72.

21 See in Cohen, 'Auerbach, Yad Vashem and Holocaust Memory', p. 217.

22 In Cohen, 'Auerbach, Yad Vashem and Holocaust Memory', p. 218; cites Rachel Auerbach to Arieh Kubovi, no date; Yad Vashem Archives, AM11/1760.

23 See David Perlov's movie *Memories of the Eichmann Trial*, 1979.

24 See Yechiam Weitz, 'In the Name of Six Million Accusers: Gideon Hausner as Attorney-General and His Place in the Eichmann Trial', *Israel Studies*, vol. 14, no. 2 (Summer 2009), p. 42.

25 Yablonka cites Gouri in *LaMerhav*, 10 September 1961 and 2 May 1961. Analysis of Yablonka in *The State of Israel vs. Adolf Eichmann*, pp. 222–5.

26 In Yablonka, *The State of Israel vs. Adolf Eichmann*, p. 225. Quoted in a pamphlet by Keshev Shabtai, *As Lambs to the Slaughter*, March 1962.

27 Yablonka, *The State of Israel vs. Adolf Eichmann*, p. 226.

28 Ibid., p. 249.

29 See the Criminal Procedure (Trial Upon Information) Ordinance Section 30(2), last part, and Crim. App. 132/57, 11 *Piskei Din*, 1544,1552.

30 See Weitz, 'The Holocaust on Trial', p. 19. Haim Gouri, *Mul ta ha'Zekhukhit: Mishpat be'Yerushalayim* [Facing the Glass Booth: The Jerusalem Trial] (n.p., 1962) (Hebrew), p. 271.

31 Havi Dreifuss, 'Jewish Historiography of the Holocaust in Eastern Europe', in *Polin: Studies in Polish Jewry, Writing Jewish History in Eastern Europe*, vol. 29, eds. Natalia Aleksiun, Brian Horowitz, and Antony Polonsky (Oxford: Littman Library of Jewish Civilization, 2017), p. 228.

32 Dreifuss, 'Jewish Historiography of the Holocaust in Eastern Europe', pp. 232–3.

33 For the gradual entrance of Gutman into Holocaust research, see H. Dreifuss, '"They Are So Alive Inside Me": Israel Gutman (1923–2013): Holocaust Survivor, Ghetto Fighter, and Jewish Historian', *Yad Vashem Studies*, vol. 41 (2014), pp. 23–53.

34 D. Aharon, "Testimonium," *Ma'ariv*, 10 September 1974, p. 31.

35 See 'Ben Gurion in Knesset Denounces Nasser as Would-be Hitler', 30 October 1958, JTA, https://www.jta.org/archive/ben-gurion-in-knesset-denounces-nasser-as-would-be-hitler (accessed 14 August 2023).

36 See Eliezer Livneh, 'The Danger of Hitler', *Haaretz*, 31 May 1967.

37 Quoted after Avraham Shapira, *The Seventh Day: Soldiers' Talk About the Six-Day War* (London: Deutsch, 1970), p. 181.

38 Interview with Abba Eban, 'Die Sackgasse ist arabisch', *Der Spiegel 5*, 26 January 1969, 80–93, here 86.

39 Eliezer Don-Yehiya, 'Review Article: Jewish Messianism, Religious Zionism and Israeli Politics: The Impact and Origins of Gush Emunim', *Middle Eastern Studies*, vol. 23, no. 2 (April 1987), p. 227.

40 See Doron Bar, *Yad Vashem: The Challenge of Shaping a Holocaust Remembrance Site, 1942–1976* (Munich: DeGruyter Oldenbourg, 2021).

41 See Batya Donner, *Natan Rapoport: A Jewish Artist*, pp. 291–320.

42 See Meeting of the Knesset Foreign Affairs and Defence Committee; Jerusalem, 9 October 1972, ISA/A/7056/10, https://www.archives.gov.il/prod uct-page/1695673 (accessed 14 August 2023).

43 See discussion in Ronen Bergman, *Rise and Kill First: The Secret History of Israel's Targeted Assassinations* (New York: Random House, 2019).

44 Daniel Byman, '1967 War and the Birth of International Terrorism', https:// www.brookings.edu/blog/markaz/2017/05/30/the-1967-war-and-the-birth-of-international-terrorism/ (accessed 14 August 2023).

45 Charles Liebman 'The Myth of Defeat: The Memory of the Yom Kippur War in Israeli Society', *Middle Eastern Studies*, vol. 29 (July 1993), p. 412.

46 Irit Keynan, 'The Memory of the Holocaust and Israel's Attitude Toward War Trauma, 1948–1973: The Collective vs. the Individual', *Israel Studies*, vol. 23, no. 2 (Summer 2018), pp. 95–117.

47 Yehuda Amital, 'The Meaning of the Yom Kippur War', in Ehud Sprinzak, 'The Politics, Institutions, and Culture of Gush Emunim', in *Jewish Fundamentalism in Comparative Perspective*, ed. Laurence Silberstein (New York: New York University Press, 1993), p. 119.

48 Segev, *The Seventh Million*, pp. 397–8; see also Shapira, *Israel*, pp. 361–2.

49 See 'Remarks of President Carter, President Anwar al-Sadat and Prime Minister Menachem Begin', 26 March 1979, https://www.presidency.ucsb. edu/documents/remarks-president-carter-president-anwar-al-sadat-egypt-an d-prime-minister-menahem-begin (accessed 30 September 2022).

50 'Begin Says Nobody Should Preach to us on Attacks or Siege', *New York Times*, 5 August 1982.

51 See Dvir Abramovich, *Fragments of Hell: Israeli Holocaust Literature* (Brookline, MA: Academic Studies Press, 2018), pp. 1–30.

52 See Adam Kirsch, 'Aharon Appelfeld's Legends of Home', https://www.newyor ker.com/magazine/2020/03/09/aharon-appelfelds-legends-of-home (accessed 14 August 2023.

53 Philip Roth, 'Walking the Way of a Survivor; A Talk with Aharon Appelfeld', *New York Times*, 28 February 1988, https://www.nytimes.com/1988/02/28/ books/walking-the-way-of-the-survivor-a-talk-with-aharon-appelfeld.html?pag ewanted=all (accessed 14 August 2023).

54 David Samuels, 'A Last Conversation with Aharon Appelfeld', *Tablet Magazine*, 5 January 2018, https://www.tabletmag.com/sections/artsletters/ articles/lastconversation-aharon-appelfeld.') See Aharon Appelfeld, 'Bertha (1965)', in *Facing the Holocaust: Selected Israeli Fiction*, eds. Gila Ramras Rauch and Joseph Michman (Philadelphia: Jewish Publication Society, 1985), pp. 143–60.

55 Abramovich, *Fragments of Hell: Israeli Holocaust Literature*; see also
    Gila Ramras-Rauch, *Aharon Appelfeld: The Holocaust and Beyond*
    (Bloomington: Indiana University Press, 1994).
56 Hanoch Bartov, 'Enemy Territory', in *Facing the Holocaust: Selected Israeli
    Fiction*, eds. Gila Ramras Rauch and Joseph Michman (Philadelphia: Jewish
    Publication Society, 1985).
57 John Felstiner, 'The *Gilgul* of Dan Pagis: Myth, History,
    Silence', *Translation Review*, vol. 32–33, no. 1 (1990), pp. 8–11,
    DOI: 10.1080/07374836.1990.10523474.
58 Dvir Abramovich, "Fragments of Hell: Israeli Holocaust Literature,"
    Introduction.

4 The centrality of the Shoah: 1979–2000

1   See Judith Shribman-Ron, 'Israelis Relive the Holocaust's Horror',
    Washington Post, 13 September 1978, https://www.washingtonpost.com/
    archive/politics/1978/09/13/israelis-relive-the-holocausts-horror/503f6
    f96-2e5e-489b-996a-fb2926aae179/ (accessed 16 September 2022).
2   Dan A. Porat, 'From the Scandal to the Holocaust in Israeli Education',
    Journal of Contemporary History, vol. 39, no. 4, p. 621.
3   Ibid., p. 632. Based on Israeli Ministry of Education, Khozer ha-Mankal
    (Director General's Newsletter) (Jerusalem), 39/8, 1 April 1979).
4   See Porat, 'From the Scandal to the Holocaust in Israeli Education', p. 632.
    Based on 'Va'adat ha-Hinukh ve-Hatarbut – Yom Iyun be-Nosei Hora'at
    ha-Shoah' (Knesset Committee of Education and Culture – A Study Day on
    Holocaust Education), 23 March 1981, Yad Vashem Pedagogical Centre,
    KA-I-68, 3.
5   Yitzhak Shamir, Yom HaShoah Speech, 28 April 1984; in Porat, *Bitter
    Reckoning*, p. 215.
6   Harold Fisch, *The Zionist Revolution: A New Perspective* (New York: St.
    Martin's Press, 1978). The book was published in Hebrew under the title
    *HaTzionut shel Tzion (*The Zionism of Zion) (Tel Aviv: Zmora, Bitan
    Publishers, 1982).
7   Fisch, *The Zionist Revolution*, p. 165.
8   Joseph Ber Soleveitchik, 'Listen! My Beloved Knocks!', in *The Zionist Ideas*,
    ed. Gil Troy, pp. 238–41.
9   Kimmy Caplan, 'Have "Many Lies Accumulated in History Books"? – The
    Holocaust in Ashkenazi Haredi Historical Consciousness in Israel', *Yad
    Vashem Studies*, vol. 29 (2001), pp. 321–76.
10 Ibid.
11 Erin McGlothlin, Leslie Swift, Lindsay Zarwell, and Leah Wolfson, eds., *The
    Construction of Testimony: Claude Lanzmann's Shoah and Its Outtakes*
    (Detroit: Wayne State University Press, 2020); see also Jonathan Freedland,
    'The Day Israel Saw Shoah', https://www.theguardian.com/world/2015/dec/10/
    the-day-israel-saw-shoah (accessed 30 September 2022).
12 Michael Renov, *The Subject of Documentary* (Minneapolis: University of
    Minnesota Press, 2004), p. 127.

13 See Sven Kramer, *Auschwitz im Widerstreit: zur Darstellung der Shoah in Film, Philosophie und Literatur* (Wiesbaden: Deutscher Universitäts-Verlag, 1999), p. 39.

14 See Jonathan Freedland, 'The Day Israel Saw Shoah', *The Guardian*, https://www.theguardian.com/world/2015/dec/10/the-day-israel-saw-shoah (accessed 6 October 2023).

15 See Lawrence Douglas, *The Right Wrong Man: John Demjanjuk and the Last Great Nazi War Crimes Trial* (Princeton: Princeton University Press, 2016). On the place of the Demjanjuk Trial in Israeli collective memory, see Tamir Hod, *Why Did We Remember to Forget? The Demjanjuk Trial in Israel* (Tel Aviv: Resling, 2020) (Hebrew). Hod argues that in many ways, the Demjanjuk trial has actually been largely forgotten in Israel collective memory, perhaps as a result of what was perceived to be a very unsuccessful unsatisfactory outcome.

16 Thomas Friedman, 'Treblinka Trial Becomes an Israeli Obsession', 13 March 1987, https://www.nytimes.com/1987/03/13/world/treblinka-trial-becomes-an-israeli-obsession.html (accessed 14 August 2023).

17 Ibid.

18 See Douglas, *The Right Wrong Man*, pp. 106–7, for example, on survivor memory.

19 Ibid., p. 104.

20 See Porat, *Bitter Reckoning*, p. 217.

21 David Hartman, 'Auschwitz or Sinai', in *The Zionist Ideas*, ed. Gil Troy (Lincoln: University of Nebraska Press/Jewish Publication Society, 2018), p. 256.

22 Adi Ophir, 'On Sanctifying the Holocaust: an Anti-Theological Treatise', *Tikkun*, vol. 2, no. 1 (1987), pp. 61–7.

23 Ibid., pp. 62–3.

24 See Jackie Feldman, 'Marking the Boundaries of the Enclave: Defining the Israeli Collective through the Poland "Experience"', *Israel Studies*, vol. 7, no. 2 (Summer 2002), pp. 84–114.

25 Ibid., p. 105.

26 Limor Livnat, 'Of Holocaust and Heroism', *Ha'aretz*, 19 April 2001; cited in Feldman, 'Marking the Boundaries of the Enclave', p. 1.

27 'Yehoshua Sobol', https://www.jewishvirtuallibrary.org/sobol-yehoshua (accessed 18 June 2023); Frank Rich, 'Sobol's "Ghetto," a Holocaust Drama with Music', *New York Times*, 1 May 1989, https://www.nytimes.com/1989/05/01/theater/review-theater-sobol-s-ghetto-a-holocaust-drama-with-music.html (accessed 14 August 2023).

28 See Ephraim Sicher, 'Holocaust Trauma in the Second Generation: The Hebrew Fiction of David Grossman and Savyon Liebrecht', in *Breaking Crystal*, ed. Sicher, pp. 170–6. Works discussed in Dalia Ofer's text. See also Iris Milner, *Past Present: Biography, Identity and Memory in Second Generation Literature* (Tel Aviv: Am Oved, 2003) (Hebrew).

29 Ephraim Sicher, 'The Return of the Past: The Intergenerational Transmission of Holocaust Memory in Israeli Fiction', *Shofar Winter*, vol. 19, no. 2 (Winter 2001), p. 30.

30 Danieli, Y., 'The Treatment and Prevention of Long-Term Effects and Intergenerational Transmission of Victimization: A Lesson from Holocaust

Survivors and Their Children', in *Trauma and Its Wake*, ed. C. R. Figley (New York: Brunner/Mazel, 1985). See also Natan Kellermann, 'Diagnosis of Holocaust Survivors and Their Children', *Israel Journal of Psychiatry and Related Sciences*, vol. 36 (1999), pp. 55–64 and N. P. Kellermann, 'The Long-Term Psychological Effects and Treatment of Holocaust Trauma', *Journal of Loss and Trauma*, vol. 6 (2001), pp. 197, 218.

31 Dina Wardi, *Memorial Candles: Children of the Holocaust* (London: Taylor & Francis, 1992), pp. 108, 194. On postmemory, see Marianne Hirsch, *The Generation of Postmemory: Writing and Visual Culture after the Holocaust* (New York: Columbia University Press, 2012).

32 Liebrecht, 'Morning in the Park with Nannies', in *The Oxford Book of Hebrew Short Stories*, ed. Glenda Abramson (New York: Oxford University Press, 1996), p. 392.

33 Ibid., p. 183; see Leon Yudkin, 'Holocaust Trauma in the Second Generation: The Hebrew Fiction of D. Grossman and S. Liebrecht', in *Breaking Crystal*, ed. E. Sicher (1998), pp. 170–81; Leon Yudkin, 'Second Generation and the Active Presence: Savyon Liebrecht', in *Literature in the Wake of the Holocaust* (London: European Jewish Publication Society, 2003), pp. 85–104.

34 Savyon Liebrecht, 'Excision', in *Apples from the Desert* (New York: Feminist Press, 1998), pp. 94–8.

35 See https://www.navasemel.com/ and https://forward.com/culture/117704/the-holocaust-novel-from-israel-that-america-can/. For an analysis of 'And the Rat Laughed', see Ranen Omer-Sherman, '"To Extract from It Some Sort of Beautiful Thing": The Holocaust in the Families and Fiction of Nava Semel and Etgar Keret', *Humanities*, vol. 9 (2020), p. 137.

36 Omer-Sherman, 'The Holocaust in the Families and Fiction of Nava Semel and Etgar Keret', pp. 5, 16–17.

37 Dalia Ofer, 'The Past that Does Not Pass: Israelis and Holocaust Memory', *Israel Studies*, vol. 14, no. 1, Israelis and the Holocaust: Scars Cry Out for Healing (Spring 2009), p. 13.

38 Yosefa Loshitzky, '"Post-Memory Cinema" Second Generation Israelis Screen the Holocaust', in *Identity Politics on the Israeli Screen* (Austin: University of Texas Press, 2001), pp. 32–6.

39 See Oren Meyers and Eyal Zandberg, 'The Sound-Track of Memory: Ashes and Dust and the Commemoration of the Holocaust in Israeli Popular Culture', *Media, Culture & Society*, vol. 24, no. 3 (2002), p. 240.

40 See Stephen Franklin, 'Holocaust's Second Generation Sings Out', https://www.chicagotribune.com/news/ct-xpm-1989-08-11-8901030829-story.html (accessed 14 August 2023).

41 Ibid.

42 See Meyers and Zandberg, 'The Sound-Track of Memory', p. 242: the newborn children were supposed to substitute for the families that the survivors had lost, and so the children were confronted from a very early age with impossible expectations. Most of them, including Ya'akov Gilad and Yehuda Poliker, were named after relatives who died in the war, and some of the firstborns were given double and even triple names, so they could commemorate several murdered relatives (Wardi, *Memorial Candles*). See

also https://tlv1.fm/promised-podcast/2021/08/19/the-ash-dust-compassion-edition/.

43 'Chava Alberstein', *Polin Virtual Shtetl*, https://sztetl.org.pl/en/biographies/5763-alberstein-chava.

44 See Hanna Yablonka, 'Oriental Jewry and the Holocaust: A Tri-Generational Perspective', *Israel Studies*, vol. 14, no. 1, Israelis and the Holocaust: Scars Cry Out for Healing (Spring 2009), pp. 94–122.

45 Ethan Bronner, 'In Search of the Soldier in His Past', *New York Times*, 12 December 2008, https://www.nytimes.com/2008/12/14/movies/14bron.html.

46 Segev, *The Seventh Million*; Hebrew original 1991. See also Zertal, *Israel's Holocaust and the Politics of Nationhood*. Dan Michman, ed., *Post-Zionism and the Holocaust: The Public Controversy in Israel on Post-Zionism in 1993–1996 and the Place of the Holocaust in It* (Ramat Gan: Bar Ilan University, 1997) (Hebrew).

47 Segev, *The Seventh Million*, introduction.

48 Ofer, 'The Yishuv, Zionism, and the Holocaust'. A number of experts in the field have attempted to analyse the changing nature of Israel's relationship to the Holocaust since 1948. See, for example, Friling, 'Remember? Forget?', pp. 51–69; Gil, 'The Shoah in Israeli Collective Memory', pp. 76–101; Ofer, 'We Israelis Remember, But How?', pp. 70–85; Porat, *Israeli Society, the Holocaust*; see also Friling and Yablonka, 'Special Issue: Israel and the Holocaust'.

49 See *Ha'aretz*, 'Speech by Yitzhak Rabin at the White House', https://www.haaretz.com/2002-05-13/ty-article/speech-by-yitzhak-rabin-at-the-white-house/0000017f-defb-d856-a37f-fffba4410000 (accessed 14 August 2023).

50 See Arye Naor, 'Lessons of the Holocaust versus Territories for Peace, 1967–2001', *Israel Studies*, Lessons of the Holocaust versus vol. 8, no. 1 (Spring 2003), p. 144; for Feiglin, see KolHair, ii.io. 1995 (Hebrew); Sharon's incitement preceded the assassination of Rabin, *Ha'aretz*, 1 April 1994.

51 See Liat Steir-Livny, 'Is It OK to Laugh about It Yet? Hitler Rants YouTube Parodies in Hebrew', *European Journal of Humour Research*, vol. 4, no. 4 (2017) and Liat Steir-Livny, 'Holocaust Humor, Satire, and Parody on Israeli Television', *Jewish Film & New Media*, vol. 3, no. 1 (2015), pp. 193–219.

52 'Feldermaus at the Olympics', *HaHamishia HaKamerit*, 3 July 2013, https://www.youtube.com/watch?v=1FPRYXbIxDc (accessed 1 August 2022).

53 In the sketch 'Feldermaus at the White House', the two bumbling diplomats attempt to surprise Bill Clinton at the White House with a request to play saxophone at a small party at the Israeli embassy. Rebuffed by a secretary who insists the president is a 'very busy man', Feldermaus loses his patience, insisting he will wait no more: 'We will not be taken like lambs to the slaughter!,' https://www.youtube.com/watch?v=lLIWCW4ewb8 (accessed 1 August 2022). It should also be noted that the name of the diplomat 'Feldermaus' is itself an ironic inversion. In Hebrew the name of the opera by Strauss, *Die Fledermaus*, can also be mistakenly read as Feldermaus. In so doing, the 'bat' from Strauss's humorous farce is transformed into a common 'field mouse'.

54 *HaHamishia HaKamerit*, 'Ghetto', https://www.youtube.com/watch?v=nRTI yI7-Oc&feature=youtu.be (accessed 1 August 2022).

55 *HaHamishia HaKamerit, 'Schindler'*, https://www.youtube.com/watch?v=liYG
   NXMtIhw (accessed 1 August 2017). Steir-Livny points out that, in this case
   in a postmodern sense, 'the satirists remove themselves and their audiences
   even more from the historical event. This skit turns the Holocaust from an
   historical event to a representation of the representation, a situation in which
   the creators do not refer to actual historical events from the Holocaust, but
   rather respond to other texts representing the Holocaust as acts of homage to
   them' (Steir-Livny, 'Is It OK', pp. 103–4).

5 'We are all survivors': Israel and the Holocaust in the twenty-first century

1 According to Pew, 65 per cent of Israeli Jews say 'Remembering the Holocaust'
   is an essential part of what being Jewish means to them (vs 35 per cent
   observing Jewish Law) (https://www.pewresearch.org/religion/2016/03/08/
   identity/ and https://www.pewresearch.org/fact-tank/2016/03/16/a-clo
   ser-look-at-jewish-identity-in-israel-and-the-u-s/).
2 Eitan Haber, 'We Soldiers of the Israel Defense Forces Reached This Place 50
   Years Too Late', *Yediot Ahronot*, 8 April 1992, p. 5.
3 Address of Pope John Paul at Yad Vashem, 23 March 2000, https://www.
   yadvashem.org/pope-visits/john-paul/speech.html (accessed 15 August 2023).
4 'Visit in Israel', 29 May 2000, Website of President of the Republic of Poland,
   https://www.president.pl/archive/news-archive-2000-2010/news-2000/visit-in-
   israel,38243.
5 Yuval Avivi, 'Why Some Israeli High Schools Stopped Trips to Poland', 26
   February 2016, https://www.al-monitor.com/originals/2016/02/poland-high-sch
   ool-holocaust-survivors-israel-flag.html (accessed 19 November 2022). In the
   summer of 2022, as trips to Poland resumed after the Covid-19 pandemic (and
   before fraying Polish-Israeli relations stopped such trips) other prominent voices
   in Israel also advocated for stopping such trips, which in the opinion of Israel
   Holocaust historian, Hanna Yablonka, offered 'no educational value' (https://
   www.haaretz.com/opinion/2022-06-12/ty-article-opinion/teach-about-the-
   holocaust-in-israel-not-poland/00000181-58df-dcf6-a9d7-fbff26710000).
6 See 'Flying Over Auschwitz', *Israeli Air Force*, 27 January 2019, https://www.
   iaf.org.il/9072-50902-en/IAF.aspx (accessed 4 November 2022).
7 See Jack Katzanell, 'Rabbi Says Holocaust Victims Were Sinners', 6 August
   2000, https://abcnews.go.com/US/story?id=96252&page=1 (accessed 17
   October 2022).
8 See Jose Brunner, 'The Never-Ending Story: Trauma and Ideology in the
   Shadow of the Al-Aqsa Intifada', *Theory and Criticism*, vol. 28 (2006),
   pp. 231–39 (all in Hebrew).
9 See as quoted in John Ward Anderson and Molly Moore, 'Israeli Lifted
   Spirits of War Weary Country', *Washington Post*, 2 February 2003, https://
   www.washingtonpost.com/archive/politics/2003/02/02/israeli-lifted-spir
   its-of-war-weary-country/033ac04b-1467-48b2-acaa-fbc72bf4d2e3/ (accessed
   15 August 2023).

10 Arieh Tzur, 'Settlers Compare Gaza Pullout to Holocaust', 21 December 2004, https://www.nbcnews.com/id/wbna6741231 (accessed 15 August 2023).
11 'Tearfully but Forcefully, Israel Removes Gaza Settlers', 18 August 2005, *New York Times*, https://www.nytimes.com/2005/08/18/world/middlee ast/tearfully-but-forcefully-israel-removes-gaza-settlers.html (accessed 15 August 2023).
12 Akiva Eldar, 'US Told Us to Ignore Israeli Map Reservations', *Ha'aretz*, 28 May 2003, https://www.haaretz.com/2003-05-28/ty-article/u-s-told-us-to-ignore-israeli-map-reservations/0000017f-f65b-d044-adff-f7fb839a0000 (accessed 15 August 2023).
13 USHMM website, *Holocaust Denial: Iran Holocaust Cartoon Exhibition*, https://www.ushmm.org/antisemitism/holocaust-denial-and-distortion/holoca ust-denial-antisemitism-iran/2016-holocaust-cartoon-contests-in-iran/timeline.
14 'Yad Vashem Holocaust History Museum', Safdie Architects, https://www.safdi earchitects.com/projects/yad-vashem-holocaust-history-museum.
15 Ibid.
16 See Amos Goldberg, 'The Jewish Narrative in the Yad Vashem Global Holocaust Museum', *Journal of Genocide Research*, vol. 14, no. 2 (June 2012), pp. 191–2.
17 Ibid.
18 See https://www.un.org/en/holocaustremembrance/observance.
19 'Our Living Legacy: The Survivors Declaration', 11 April 2022, read aloud by Zvil Gil in the Valley of the Communities, Yad Vashem, https://www.yadvas hem.org/yv/en/exhibitions/through-the-lens/images/liberation/minshar.pdf (accessed 15 August 2023).
20 Goldberg, p. 201.
21 See Ofer Aderet, 'Yad Vashem at Risk Due to Reliance on Donations, Israel's State Watchdog Says', 19 October 2021, https://www.haaretz.com/isr ael-news/2021-10-19/ty-article/.premium/israels-state-watchdog-says-yad-vas hem-at-risk-due-to-reliance-on-donations/0000017f-e75b-d62c-a1ff-ff7bb 8520000 (accessed 15 August 2023).
22 'Yad Vashem suspends ties with Russian-Israeli oligarch Roman Abramovich', *Times of Israel*, 10 March 2022, https://www.timesofisrael.com/yad-vashem-suspends-ties-with-russian-israeli-oligarch-roman-abramovich/.
23 See Speech by President of Ukraine Volodymyr Zelenskyy in the Knesset, President of Ukraine Official website, 20 March 2022, https://www.president. gov.ua/en/news/promova-prezidenta-ukrayini-volodimira-zelenskogo-v-knes eti-73701.
24 'Bennett empathizes with Zelensky, rejects Holocaust parallel, says mediation ongoing', *Times of Israel*, 21 March 2022, https://www.timesofisrael.com/benn ett-pummeled-by-zelensky-insists-israel-doing-more-than-others-to-aid-ukra ine/ (accessed 15 August 2023).
25 Text of Netanyahu's Holocaust Remembrance Day speech, 18 April 2012, *Times of Israel*, https://www.timesofisrael.com/text-of-netanyahus-holocaust-remembrance-day-speech/, 18 April 2012 (accessed 15 August 2023).
26 https://www.washingtonpost.com/world/middle_east/netanyahu-says-a-palestinian-gave-hitler-the-idea-for-the-holocaust/2015/10/21/0a36d 7da-ee8b-4135-9726-968eceda4cc9_story.html (accessed 15 August 2023).

27 Bashir Bashir and Amos Goldberg, 'Introduction: The Holocaust and the Nakba: A New Syntax of History, Memory, and Political Thought' (New York: Columbia University Press, 2019), pp. 2–3.

28 Ibid., p. 5.

29 Friling, 'Remember? Forget?', pp. 51–69.

30 Avraham Burg, *The Holocaust is Over, Let Us Rise from Its Ashes* (New York: St. Martin's Press, 2008), pp. 16–17. First published in Hebrew in 2007 with the title *Victory Over Hitler* (Le-natseah et Hitler).

31 See Yishai Sarid, *The Memory Monster*, https://restlessbooks.org/bookstore/the-memory-monster.

32 The Memory Monster, Habima National Theatre of Israel, https://www.hab ima.co.il/en/shows/the-memory-monster/.

33 Etan Nechin, 'Dani Dayan's Appointment is the Final Step toward Politicizing Yad Vashem', *Ha'aretz*, 26 August 2021, https://www.haaretz.com/isr ael-news/2021-08-26/ty-article-opinion/.premium/dani-dayans-appointm ent-is-final-step-toward-politicizing-yad-vashem/0000017f-ef5f-d497-a1ff-efdf35f30000 (accessed 18 June 2023).

34 David Silberklang, Dan Michman and Havi Dreifuss, 'Yad Vashem Historians Respond to the Joint Statement of the Governments of Poland and Israel Concerning the Revision of the January 26, 2018, Amendment to Poland's Act on the Institute of National Remembrance', *Yad Vashem*, https://www.yadvas hem.org/research/historians-reaction.html (accessed 18 June 2023).

35 Ibid.

36 See https://www.haaretz.com/opinion/2018-07-04/ty-article/.premium/okay-so-the-poles-didnt-murder-jews/0000017f-da7b-d718-a5ff-faff185d0000 and https://www.nytimes.com/2018/07/05/world/middleeast/israel-poland-holocaust.html (accessed 15 August 2023).

37 Lazar Berman, 'Controversial "Shoah, Nakba" Event at German Institute in Tel Aviv Cancelled', *Times of Israel*, 11 November 2022, https://www.timeso fisrael.com/controversial-shoah-nakba-event-at-german-institute-in-tel-aviv-cancelled/ (accessed 18 June 2023).

38 Liat Steir Livny, *Remaking Holocaust Memory: Documentary Cinema by Third-Generation Survivors in Israel* (Syracuse: Syracuse University Press, 2019), p. 16.

39 Ibid., p. 24.

40 Eva Heyman Instagram account: https://www.instagram.com/eva.stories/.

41 Yuval Mendelsohn, quoted in https://www.nytimes.com/2019/04/30/world/middleeast/eva-heyman-instagram-holocaust.html. See also https://www.haar etz.com/israel-news/2019-04-29/ty-article/.premium/new-memory-genre-holocaust-victims-instagram-draws-fire-for-dumbing-down-history/00000 17f-e912-d62c-a1ff-fd7b44c80000 (accessed 15 August 2023).

42 Isabel Kershner, "A Holocaust Story for the Social Media Generation," *The New York Times*, 30 April 2019, https://www.nytimes.com/2019/04/30/world/middleeast/eva-heyman-instagram-holocaust.html (accessed 15 August 2023).

43 See Zikaron Ba-Salon, https://www.zikaronbasalon.org/about-1.

44 Ibid.

45 In Israel, for example, groups like *Dorot Hemshech* (future generations) and Shem Olam have organized programmes to train children and grandchildren of survivors; likewise, in New York, the Museum of Jewish Heritage has

partnered with descendants of Holocaust survivors for the same purpose. At the Los Angeles Holocaust Museum, 3G@HMLA describes itself as 'a community for grandchildren of Holocaust survivors who are helping to shape the future of Holocaust remembrance and education'.

46 Judy Maltz, 'These Children of Survivors Have Found an Innovative Way of Sharing Their Parents' Holocaust Stories', 30 January 2022, *Ha'aretz*, https:// www.haaretz.com/israel-news/2022-01-23/ty-article-magazine/.highlight/ survivors-children-find-innovative-way-to-tell-their-parents-stories/00000 17f-f667-d5bd-a17f-f67f16420000 (accessed 15 August 2023).

47 About the Moshe Mirilashvili Center, Yad Vashem, https://www.yadvashem. org/research/about/mirilashvili-center/about.html (accessed 15 August 2023).

48 See Isaac Jack Levy, *Sephardim in the Holocaust: A Forgotten People* (Tuscaloosa: University of Alabama Press, 2020) and Haim Asitz, Yitzchak Kerem, Menachem Persof and Steve Israel, eds, *The Shoa in the Sephardic Communities* (Jerusalem: Sephardic Educational Center, 2006).

49 For more on the work of Moreshet, see https://www.moreshet.org/.

50 Steir-Livny, 'Is It OK to Laugh about It', p. 40.

51 In 2014 Israel's Ministry of Education released a Holocaust education curriculum for kindergartners, in conjunction with Yom HaShoah. See http:// www.tabletmag.com/scroll/170448/israel-to-teach-about-holocaust-in-kinde rgarten (accessed 30 November 2017). See also http://cms.education.gov.il/ EducationCMS/UNITS/Moe/Shoa/ganeyeldim (accessed 30 November 2017).

52 *Eretz Nehederet*, https://vimeo.com/35660324 (accessed 1 August 2017).

53 See Wendy Zierler, '"The Jews Are Coming" Offers Hebrew Satire of Jewish History', 28 March 2016, http://jewishstudies.washington.edu/hebrew-hum anities/the-jews-are-coming/ (accessed 14 January 2018).

54 E-mail correspondence with Natalie Marcus and Asaf Beiser, 4 March 2020.

> Natalie: 'My grandparents are Holocaust survivors from both sides, we have some crazy stories from my father's side but basically everybody died in the war and my grandparents are pretty much the only survivors. Asaf's father was himself a survivor. A big part of his mother's side died in the war. If it matters? Well, we have more sketches about Rabin's assassination, which is the big trauma of our generation'.

55 'Final Solution 2.0', *The Jews Are Coming*, 20 May 2016, https://www.yout ube.com/watch?v=Pp3Qi07nJK4 (accessed 14 January 2018). 'Dschinghis Khan' became the basis for several popular covers of the song, including the Hasidic hit song 'Yidn, Yidn Kumt a Heym', by Mordecai Ben-David. A seemingly farcical addition to the end of the sketch, this song is by itself meaningful on multiple levels: The 1979 Eurovision contest in Jerusalem marked the first time Israel hosted the contest as well as the first time Eurovision was held outside the European continent. The performance by the West German group was groundbreaking, as they performed in German, in Israel, for the first time.

Conclusion: Israel and the Holocaust, the future of the past

1 See Michael Lipka, 'A Closer Look at Jewish Identity in Israel and the U.S.', *Pew Research Center*, 16 March 2016, https://www.pewresearch.org/fact-tank/2016/03/16/a-closer-look-at-jewish-identity-in-israel-and-the-u-s/ (accessed 15 August 2023).

2 For the notion of Holocaust as 'proof-text', see Ian Lustick, 'The Holocaust in Israeli Political Culture: Four Constructions and Their Consequences', *Contemporary Jewry*, vol. 37, no. 1 (April 2017), pp. 125–70. For my response to this article, see Avinoam Patt, 'On "Holocaustia" and the Place of the Shoah in Contemporary Jewish Life', *Contemporary Jewry*, vol. 37, no. 1 (April 2017), pp. 187–91. Also available at https://www.polisci.upenn.edu/sites/default/files/Lustick_Patt_%20response%20to%20Lustick_Four%20Constructions%20of%20the%20Holocaust.pdf.

3 Michal Govrin, 'How to Remember the Shoah', https://www.sourcesjournal.org/articles/how-to-remember-the-shoah; for the text of the Hitkansut Haggadah, see https://static.hartman.org.il/dev/uploads/2023/01/Hartman-Hitkansut-Haggadah_Final_Jan-27-2023.pdf?_gl=1*145z2em*_ga*NDAwNTQwMjAyLjE2NzUyNjQ4Njk.*_ga_LHTRZSV7GN*MTY3NjAzNDc4NS4zLjAuMTY3NjAzNDc4NS42MC4wLjA. For Dara Horn's observations, see https://www.tabletmag.com/sections/community/articles/more-meaningful-holocaust-remembrance-hitkansut (accessed 15 August 2023).

INDEX

Note: Figures are indicated by page number followed by 'f'. Endnotes are indicated by the page number followed by 'n' and the endnote number e.g., 20 n.1 refers to endnote 1 on page 20.